Christian Natural Law and Religious Freedom

Deagon addresses the need for a robust theoretical foundation for religious freedom that accounts for its transcendent nature.

What is the idea of religious freedom? Where does it come from? Why should it be protected? These important questions for understanding religious freedom are usually addressed through secular and immanent foundations which are unable to sufficiently grapple with the religious nature of religious freedom – its connection with the divine. Deagon proposes an alternative approach rooted in Christian Natural Law. In Part I of the book, Deagon defines and develops Christian Natural Law, identifying three consistent themes: Love, the True and the Good. In Part II, Deagon deploys Christian Natural Law to articulate a theological framework for religious freedom which shows that religious freedom is an individual and social good, is oriented to the true and is grounded in love. In doing so, Deagon offers a new foundation for religious freedom which properly considers it as a matter of both human and divine action.

This book will be of interest to those engaged in law and religion studies, in particular scholars of religious freedom, theology and jurisprudence and human rights.

Alex Deagon is Associate Professor in the School of Law, Queensland University of Technology. He is an international expert in religious freedom and the author of *From Violence to Peace* (2017) and *Reconciling Freedom and Discrimination* (2023).

Christian Natural Law and Religious Freedom

A Foundation Based on Love, the True, and the Good

Alex Deagon

Routledge
Taylor & Francis Group
LONDON AND NEW YORK

First published 2025
by Routledge
4 Park Square, Milton Park, Abingdon, Oxon OX14 4RN

and by Routledge
605 Third Avenue, New York, NY 10158

Routledge is an imprint of the Taylor & Francis Group, an informa business

British Library Cataloguing-in-Publication Data
A catalogue record for this book is available from the British Library

Library of Congress Cataloging-in-Publication Data
Names: Deagon, Alex author
Title: Christian natural law and religious freedom : a foundation based on love, the true, and the good / Alex Deagon.
Description: Abingdon, Oxon [UK] ; New York, NY : Routledge, 2025. | Includes bibliographical references and index.
Identifiers: LCCN 2025005347 | ISBN 9781032619989 hardback | ISBN 9781032620008 paperback | ISBN 9781032620015 ebook
Subjects: LCSH: Natural law—Religious aspects—Christianity | Freedom of religion | Religious tolerance—Christianity
Classification: LCC KB280 .D43 2025 | DDC 241/.2—dc23/eng/20250207
LC record available at https://lccn.loc.gov/2025005347

ISBN: 978-1-032-61998-9 (hbk)
ISBN: 978-1-032-62000-8 (pbk)
ISBN: 978-1-032-62001-5 (ebk)

DOI: 10.4324/9781032620015

Typeset in Galliard
by Apex CoVantage, LLC

Contents

Foreword

Jacques Maritain, a leading advocate of the 1948 Universal Declaration of Human Rights, was asked how such a sharply divided world holding such radically divergent viewpoints could agree to such a long and definitive list of fundamental rights. He replied: "Yes, we agree about the rights, but on condition no one asks us why."

Since then, scores of religious and philosophical traditions around the world have sought to answer this question "why." Indeed, the Universal Declaration has become something of a mirror for each tradition to reflect anew on its own teachings and practices, and a matrix for each to determine whether and how to support, ground, qualify, critique, or reject various rights. Maritain himself, a distinguished philosopher, led the way for Roman Catholics by defining, defending, and delimiting human rights with a sturdy natural law framework constructed from biblical, classical, and Christian sources, and animated with the Catholic social teachings and personalist theories of his day. His natural law defense of human rights became formative as the Catholic world eventually embraced and advocated human rights at the Second Vatican Council (1962–65) and in subsequent papal encyclicals. Other faith traditions – Protestants, Orthodox Christians, Jews, Muslims, Buddhists, Hindus, Confucians, and Indigenous communities especially – have all since weighed in heavily on human rights, too, producing major rights declarations and defenses and whole libraries of scholarship. So have various philosophical traditions – liberals and libertarians, Marxists and materialists, pragmatists and utilitarians, critics and constructivists of all kinds. Most traditions have affirmed the need for some basic rights and some kind of local if not global human rights framework, even though they have grounded, limited, and criticised specific human rights in radically different ways.

One right in particular, the right to religious freedom, has come under increasing attack today in Western liberal lands. This is new. In 1948, the Universal Declaration robustly

> guaranteed everyone the right to freedom of thought, conscience, and religion, including the freedom to change their religion or belief, and to manifest it in teaching, practice, worship, and observance, either alone or in community with others, and in public or private.

This international provision distilled centuries of constitutional religious freedom guarantees forged by liberals and conservatives alike as cornerstones of constitutional democracy. Indeed, it was a commonplace in Western liberal lands to treat religious freedom as the "first freedom" or "foundational right" on which many other individual and associational rights depend.

Today, however, a growing number of Western liberal scholars have argued that religious rights and freedoms have become obsolete and dangerous in our "secular age." And several apex courts in Western lands have dramatically softened their protections of religious freedom in favor of equality, neutrality, and secularism. Freedom of conscience claims, these critics contend, unfairly assert a person's right to be a law unto himself or herself, at the cost of other people's fundamental rights and the public's legitimate interests. Freedom for religious groups, they charge, too often results in abuses of power, discriminatory policies, or countercultural agendas, some of them violent. Religion, these critics thus conclude, should be viewed as just another category of liberty or association, with no more preference or privilege than its secular counterparts. Religion should be treated as just another form of expression, subject to the rules of rational democratic deliberation just like other ideas and values. To accord religion any special protection or exemption discriminates against the nonreligious. To afford religion a seat at the table of public deliberation or government policy-making invites sectarian self-dealing contrary to the common good. We can no longer afford these traditional legal luxuries.

Enter Alex Deagon, one of a group of distinguished scholars who are leading a renaissance of law and religion study in Australia. Deagon, a constitutional jurist and religious philosopher, is a staunch supporter of human rights in general and religious freedom in particular. He has already published several definitive studies of theology, jurisprudence, and comparative constitutional law on these subjects.

Deagon's bold aim in this learned new volume is to defend religious freedom with an overtly Christian natural law theory predicated on the ideas of love, truth, and the good, and animated by the powerful logic of radical Christian orthodoxy. This effort is bold because religious freedom is highly unfashionable in his Australian academy today and largely absent from the nation's constitutional law, which (in)famously lacks a national bill of rights. It is bold because natural law theory is rejected by many philosophers today as too old-fashioned and self-serving, and by many Christians today as too Catholic and rationalistic. And it is bold because the radical Christian orthodoxy logic at work in this book is criticised by many as too abstract, nostalgic, or sectarian to be of much use for real-world problems of law, politics, and society.

But Deagon, like Jacques Maritain 80 years ago, is convinced that religious freedom and other fundamental rights must be defended by each tradition in its own authentic voice rather than grounded in a bland common denominator logic or dependent on a thin, overlapping consensus. And Deagon, like Maritain, sees natural law theory as a powerful language and logic that Christians since biblical times have used to build fundamental ideas and institutions of law and politics, including those of human rights. Deagon goes his own way, however, in distilling traditional Christian natural law teachings under the enduring tropes of the good, the true, and the loving. He is even more innovative in arguing that authentic religious freedom serves to protect the basic goods that humans need to flourish; to promote the divine truth that humans need to pursue; and to model the love of God, neighbor, and self that humans need to exercise. This is a striking new answer to the question "why" have religious freedom today. And it provides Deagon with a powerful foundation on which to build an expansive new theology and jurisprudence of human rights and religious freedom.

John Witte, Jr.
Distinguished Professor of Law and Religion
Center for the Study of Law and Religion, Emory University

1 Introduction

I. The Need for a Robust Theoretical Foundation for Religious Freedom

Despite universal acknowledgement of religious freedom as an important and fundamental human right, the idea of religious freedom has simultaneously faced limitations and objections as far as it may impact on other important rights such as equality. My previous book uses a theological critique to develop a principled framework for resolving these tensions.[1] The process of considering the scope and limits of religious freedom generally, and specifically with respect to other rights, begs the question of whether religious freedom has a sound theoretical foundation. What actually is religious freedom? Where does it come from? Why should it be protected? And how can such protection be balanced when religious freedom clashes with other rights? These questions are theoretically important but also have a practical urgency as governments around the world seek to balance religious freedom with other rights. The few treatments which attempt to address these kinds of questions primarily take a 'secular' approach, grounding religious freedom in concepts such as ethical autonomy.[2] However, emerging scholarship is starting to recognise the limits of secular foundations, particularly a failure (and arguably an inability) to grapple with the transcendent dimension of religious freedom.[3] This book

1 See Alex Deagon, *A Principled Framework for the Autonomy of Religious Communities: Reconciling Freedom and Discrimination* (Hart Publishing, 2023).

2 See eg Carolyn Evans, *Freedom of Religion Under the European Convention on Human Rights* (Oxford University Press, 2001); Ronald Dworkin, *Religion without God* (Harvard University Press, 2013); Jane Calderwood Norton, *Freedom of Religious Organizations* (Oxford University Press, 2016); Lucy Vickers, *Religious Freedom, Religious Discrimination and the Workplace* (Hart Publishing, 2nd ed, 2016); Ilias Trispiotis, 'Religious Freedom and Religious Antidiscrimination' (2019) 82(5) *Modern Law Review* 864; Tarunabh Khaitan and Jane Calderwood Norton, 'The Right to Freedom of Religion and the Right Against Religious Discrimination: Theoretical Distinctions' (2019) 17(4) *International Journal of Constitutional Law* 1125; Farrah Ahmed, 'The Autonomy Rationale for Religious Freedom' (2017) 80(2) *Modern Law Review* 238.

3 See eg Karen Taliaferro, *The Possibility of Religious Freedom: Early Natural Law and the Abrahamic Faiths* (Cambridge University Press, 2019). For a spirited defense of the need for both

DOI: 10.4324/9781032620015-1

draws on unique theological resources to address the transcendent aspect of religious freedom. In particular, the book develops what I term a 'Christian Natural Law' to identify that religious freedom is grounded in the pursuit of Love, the True and the Good, and explains how religious freedom enhances these virtues both for individuals and communities. It follows that religious freedom should receive substantive legal protection.

Jean Porter has argued that the usual approaches to natural law, and particularly to Aquinas, are too focused on philosophy to the neglect of theology, the scholastics and Scripture. To redress this balance, she seeks to articulate 'a theological account of the natural law' through the accounts of the scholastics (and especially Aquinas), in order to properly incorporate Scripture, as well as provide a bridge to other perspectives.[4] Imbert also notes that a fully developed theory of natural law must take reason into account, including 'dealing with the impact of the noetic effect of sin on . . . the accessibility of the natural law'; this can only occur 'by grounding our metaphysical investigation in the self-contained God of Christian revelation'.[5] My book takes up this challenge by articulating a 'Christian Natural Law' which is intrinsically and necessarily theological. I acknowledge a theological natural law foundation for religious freedom may be difficult to accept in modern society. To an extent this is beside the point: any radical ontology, theological or not, is difficult to accept for many. This does not mean it is wrong – or at least, it does not mean it fails to provide a plausible theoretical foundation. Addressing those who do not share Christian metaphysical premises cannot result in simply denying the existence or relevance of the divine. This would undercut the ontology of Christian Natural Law itself. Rather, there can be some shared agreement on first principles, such as everything has been created by a rational being with a good purpose – in essence, that there is an eternal law. As we shall see in Chapter 3, failure to acknowledge even this basic precept means it is difficult to mount an ontological defense of the good. Providing a robust theoretical foundation for religious freedom entails certain plausible metaphysical commitments many will share. Even for those who do not share them, such commitments remain persuasive or at least understandable because they are grounded in a natural law that is rationally accessible to all.[6]

---

a theological natural law and a transcendent foundation for religious freedom, see Rafael Domingo, *Law and Religion in a Secular Age* (Catholic University of America Press, 2023).

4 Jean Porter, *Nature as Reason: A Thomistic Theory of the Natural Law* (Eerdmans, 2005) 1–2, 4–5, 45.

5 Yannick Imbert, 'Natural Law and Imagination' in Jonathan Crowe and Constance Lee (eds), *Research Handbook on Natural Law Theory* (Edward Elgar, 2019) 295.

6 See Bryan McCall, *The Architecture of Law: Rebuilding Law in the Classical Tradition* (University of Notre Dame Press, 2018) 77–79, 429. Levering also argues that acknowledging Christian Natural Law's metaphysical and theological presuppositions will not necessarily 'incapacitate it for application in a pluralist society', since these presuppositions are based in reason which all people share and can contribute to a just political order. See Matthew Levering, *Biblical Natural Law: A Theocentric and Teleological Approach* (Oxford University Press, 2008) 5–6, 18–19.

Porter notes that a distinctively theological approach to natural law appears to 'fit awkwardly' with more modern accounts which emphasise universality and accessibility, and even claims that one is unlikely to be able to defend such an approach in a way that is 'universally compelling' and 'practically useable'.[7] However, a theological approach offers a different way of thinking about the natural law which 'should be of interest in its own right' and provides 'something more valuable' than secular approaches: theological reflection about human nature.[8] For this book, a theological approach gives us a transcendent, metaphysical grounding for religious freedom which can also be understood as part of a reasoned conception of the good, intelligible to all and 'practically useable', if not 'universally compelling' (though I wonder whether the latter condition sets too high an epistemological bar for any sophisticated theory worth its salt). In any case, a theological natural law basis for religious freedom certainly meets Porter's more modest request for a theological natural law 'responsive to the challenges of our own situation'.[9] As such, and as we shall see particularly in Chapter 5, a Christian Natural Law is entirely consistent with and indeed undergirds the liberal virtues of freedom, equality and democracy. This implies all people may be guided to the True and the Good of religious freedom which can be universally accessed and known, including by those who are not part of the Christian or any other religious tradition. A natural law basis for religious freedom has the 'objectivity' of being 'true . . . shared, common, and universal'.[10] Natural law reason is by definition a 'truly' and 'genuinely' public reason which is 'open at every point to rational questioning, discussion and judgement'.[11]

The fact that a Christian Natural Law is both universal and theological is not incoherent. Rather, it indicates a relational distinction between the universal and particular elements of the natural law. The universal natural law is generally available to human reason but particular elements only become apparent through the aid of grace, including divine revelation. Just as Aquinas saw no inconsistency in developing a universal and supremely authoritative natural law through a theological account, my Christian Natural Law provides a framework of 'immediate practical interest' for understanding why religious freedom is important as a fundamental human right for all, yet with a necessary foundation in and connection to the transcendent.[12] The natural law cannot be fully or rightly understood without Scripture, which places the natural law at the centre of Christian ethical reflection. Since Christians are in the world, such ethical reflection necessarily occurs in conversation with secular

7 Porter (n 4) 5, 32.
8 Ibid 5–6.
9 Ibid 32.
10 Gerard Bradley, 'Natural Law Theory and Constitutionalism' in George Duke and Robert George (eds), *The Cambridge Companion to Natural Law Jurisprudence* (Cambridge University Press, 2017) 398.
11 Ibid 422, 424.
12 See Porter (n 4) 326–327.

and plural moralities, which means natural law should and can speak to these moralities.[13] Christianity is theologically committed to 'respecting and promoting human well-being and happiness', but the force of such arguments and outcomes can be equally appreciated by one who does not share the theological and practical commitments.[14] If this is so, then a Christian Natural Law has much to meaningfully say to the world. Moral dialogue and reasoned consensus, at least on some matters, is possible.[15] They who have ears, let them hear.

Though this book develops theological arguments for religious freedom, the fact that religious freedom is broadly accepted by all suggests it expresses basic aspects of human nature, even if the theological grounds and articulation of those aspects rely on presuppositions which may not be shared.[16] There are other arguments for religious freedom which do not rely on theology.[17] Yet at the very least, a Christian Natural Law provides an additional contribution to these arguments, and I would say a more robust and universal contribution because it accounts for the transcendent dimension of religious freedom in a way that existing arguments do not.[18] Christian Natural Law is a theological construct, but it can consider commonalities shared by all and therefore fruitfully interact with diverse claims in a pluralistic society.[19] Natural law 'permit[s] a robust religious freedom in a pluralized society better than secular approaches' because it facilitates universal access through human reason without degenerating into destructive secularism; natural law acknowledges the theological foundation and guidance of human reason without 'simply duplicating revelation'.[20] A theological natural law approach thus enriches the foundation for religious freedom by providing an ontology which draws on nature, reason, grace and revelation.

A theological natural law foundation is then of course not neutral, but neither is a secular foundation. Both are equally ideological.[21] Religious freedom is 'impossible', or 'at least highly unlikely' by means of secular positivist protection alone.[22] Theological natural law relies on reason, even enhancing that reason through grace and revelation, and draws on divine law to account for the transcendent dimension of religious freedom. The universality of natural law also means it grounds religious freedom in a pluralist society without

13 Ibid 332.
14 Ibid 341.
15 Ibid 342.
16 Ibid 371.
17 For a catalogue see (n 2) and eg Ysabel Andrea Abordo and Alex Deagon, 'Religious Freedom and Freedom from Religious Discrimination: Implications for the Religious Discrimination Bill' (2023) 3 *Australian Journal of Law and Religion* 1.
18 See Porter (n 4) 374.
19 Ibid 395–396.
20 Taliaferro (n 3) 27.
21 See eg my arguments in Alex Deagon, *From Violence to Peace: Theology, Law and Community* (Hart Publishing, 2017) and Alex Deagon, 'Liberal Secularism and Religious Freedom in the Public Space: Reforming Political Discourse' (2018) 41(3) *Harvard Journal of Law and Public Policy* 901.
22 Taliaferro (n 3) 30.

neglecting its transcendent aspects. Theological natural law has all the advantages of secularism (to an even greater extent) with none of the limitations. It is therefore the 'best option' for a just political order with respect to religious freedom for both the religious and non-religious.[23] Just as Porter's 'Thomistic theory of the natural law provides a starting point for developing a theologically informed natural law ethic', so my articulation of a Christian Natural Law provides the basis for the idea of religious freedom.[24]

Consequently, this book addresses the urgent need for a theoretical foundation for religious freedom which uniquely accounts for its transcendent nature through a theological approach. Drawing on the resources of natural law to construct a Christian Natural Law also ensures the foundation is accessible and understandable to people of all faith traditions and none. This satisfies an enduring and deeply foundational issue: articulating a robust theoretical ground for the fundamental human right of religious freedom which takes into account its transcendent dimension without alienating those who may not share particular theological presuppositions. This will be of real value in a range of disciplines. It will be of value for theologians of all different traditions who see the limits of secular foundations for religious freedom and are interested in transcendent theological foundations for freedom of religion. It will be of value to legal philosophers who are interested in the development and application of natural law (a central strand of thought in legal philosophy) to religious freedom. It will also be of value to human rights scholars who require theoretical frameworks for how to reconcile fundamental human rights. Most importantly, it will be of value for religious freedom scholars specifically who are engaging with the vexed problem of where religious freedom comes from and why it should be supported. The featured analysis of natural law and religious freedom will benefit scholars attempting to articulate the nature and scope of religious freedom, consider robust foundations for religious freedom and balance religious freedom with other rights.

II. Natural Law, Theology and Religious Freedom

The significant increase in scholarly literature on religious freedom underscores the need for a robust theological and ontological foundation. In this respect there is some emerging work which separately explores natural law and religious freedom,[25] theology and religious freedom,[26] and a Christian

23 Ibid 28–29.

24 See Porter (n 4) 339.

25 See eg J Daryl Charles, *Natural Law and Religious Freedom: The Role of Moral First Things in Grounding and Protecting the First Freedom* (Routledge, 2018); Karen Taliaferro, *The Possibility of Religious Freedom: Early Natural Law and the Abrahamic Faiths* (Cambridge University Press, 2019); Cory Higdon, 'Roger Williams, Natural Law, and Religious Liberty' (2021) 63(1) *Journal of Church and State* 85.

26 See eg Alex Deagon, 'Reconciling John Milbank and Religious Freedom: Liberalism Through Love' (2019) 34(2) *Journal of Law and Religion* 183; Edward David, *A Christian Approach to Corporate Religious Liberty* (Palgrave Macmillan, 2020); Xavier Menard and Anna Su,

conceptual foundation for religious freedom.[27] In terms of natural law and theology, works by Porter, VanDrunen and McCall draw on theological resources to develop comprehensive theories of natural law, and to varying degrees articulate a theological natural law.[28] In this book I draw on these important resources in the development of my 'Christian Natural Law' but go beyond them in two important ways. First, my book considers Christian theology more broadly than these accounts and reconciles Catholic and Reformed perspectives through Radical Orthodoxy. Second, my book applies my Christian Natural Law to articulate a theological foundation for religious freedom, which these other authors do not attempt.

There are also some emerging accounts which implicitly or explicitly link Christian theology and religious freedom. As a representative sample, and beginning chronologically by publication date, Calderwood Norton's book provides a systematic, normatively grounded analysis of English law and religious organisations.[29] However, Calderwood Norton's normative framework is based on autonomy and therefore fails to properly take into account the transcendent nature of religion. Furthermore, Calderwood Norton's book is intrinsically limited by its jurisdictional focus. My book addresses both these issues by providing a theological foundation for religious freedom which takes account of the transcendent and is not jurisdictionally or temporally limited. Wilken's excellent historical analysis demonstrates that the origins of liberty of conscience and religious freedom are Christian rather than secular.[30] His extensive references to historical Christian writings are an important resource for this book. However, Wilken's book is a historical analysis. My book goes beyond this by articulating conceptual and textual arguments which provide a normative foundation for religious freedom. My book also articulates Christian Natural Law as this foundation, which Wilken's book does not attempt to do. David's book argues that disputes over whether religious freedom rights

'Liberalism, Catholic Integralism, and the Question of Religious Freedom' (2021) 47 *Brigham Young University Law Review* 1171; Andrew Walker, *Liberty for All: Defending Everyone's Religious Freedom in a Pluralistic Age* (Brazos Press, 2021).

27 See eg Robert Wilken, *Liberty in the Things of God: The Christian Origins of Religious Freedom* (Yale University Press, 2019); Joel Harrison, *Post-liberal Religious Liberty: Creating Communities of Charity* (Cambridge University Press, 2020); Alex Deagon, *A Principled Framework for the Autonomy of Religious Communities: Reconciling Freedom and Discrimination* (Hart Publishing, 2023).

28 See eg Porter (n 4); David VanDrunen, *Divine Covenants and Moral Order: A Biblical Theology of Natural Law* (Eerdmans, 2014); McCall (n 6). Crowe also provides a sophisticated defense of natural law ideas which challenges the common perception of natural law as timeless and imposed from above, but it is not an explicitly theological approach. This book draws on Crowe's argument, but extends it and consistently incorporates it into a 'Christian Natural Law'. My book also uses Christian Natural Law as a foundation for religious freedom, which Crowe's book does not attempt to do. See Jonathan Crowe, *Natural Law and the Nature of Law* (Cambridge University Press, 2019).

29 Calderwood Norton (n 2).

30 Robert Louis Wilken, *Liberty in the Things of God: The Christian Origins of Religious Freedom* (Yale University Press, 2019).

should be extended to corporate entities can be resolved by attending to the moral quality of group actions.[31] If groups are viewed as occasions of coordinated activity in accordance with Aquinas, then it follows that limited corporate religious liberty rights should apply to group actions. Though David's book provides an important conceptual contribution to a particular aspect of religious freedom, it does not attempt to provide a broader conceptual foundation for the idea of religious freedom itself. My book provides a deeper theological justification for religious freedom more broadly, articulating a Christian Natural Law for this purpose in a way that David's book does not attempt to do.

Harrison's book provides a theologically informed conceptual foundation for religious liberty.[32] Partially addressing Calderwood Norton's deficient focus on autonomy, Harrison argues for a religious liberty which takes into account the transcendent dimension and develops a post-liberal focus on associational community. My book draws on Harrison's important book, but goes beyond it by articulating a Christian Natural Law which supplements and strengthens Harrison's arguments. For example, where Harrison mentions the pursuit of truth and the common good as aspects of religious freedom, my book delivers a robust and comprehensive account of the True and the Good as principles of a Christian Natural Law foundation for religious freedom, providing a detailed justification that Harrison does not. Walker's book also provides an explicitly Christian ethic for defending religious freedom for all people in a pluralistic age.[33] It provides important theological resources which I draw on to provide theological arguments for religious freedom. However, since the book is targeted directly towards Christians and does not engage with natural law, it does not appeal to those who do not share Christian assumptions. Conversely, my book articulates a Christian Natural Law which relies on universal reason. My book also draws on a broader range of resources under the rubric of Christian Natural Law to provide a more robust and comprehensive conceptual foundation for religious freedom compared to Walker's book.

Thus, there is no literature which combines a specific strand of contemporary Christian theology (Radical Orthodoxy) and natural law to create a robust theoretical foundation for religious freedom.[34] To address this gap, I draw on natural law in the Christian tradition informed by Radical Orthodoxy, or what I call 'Christian Natural Law', to articulate a conceptual and ontological foundation for religious freedom. The closest attempts to do something similar are those by Charles and Taliaferro. Charles attempts to demonstrate the importance of natural law ethics in establishing and preserving basic human rights

31 Edward A David, *A Christian Approach to Corporate Religious Liberty* (Palgrave Macmillan, 2020).

32 Joel Harrison, *Post-Liberal Religious Liberty: Forming Communities of Charity* (Cambridge University Press, 2020).

33 Andrew T Walker, *Liberty for All: Defending Everyone's Religious Freedom in a Pluralistic Age* (Brazos Press, 2021).

34 I define and explain Radical Orthodoxy in Chapter 4.

such as religious freedom. Charles therefore provides an important conceptual foundation for religious freedom, grounded in natural law.[35] Charles does aim to provide an ontological foundation for religious freedom in his work, which I draw on in this book.[36] However, my book will also extend and go beyond Charles to articulate an explicitly theological foundation for religious freedom, a 'Christian Natural Law' which better accounts for the transcendent dimension of religious freedom.

Taliaferro re-examines the traditions of natural law for the purposes of defending an idea of religious freedom that has appeal in our contemporary secular society.[37] She explores a new way to examine the idea of religious freedom through mediation between competing conceptions of human and divine law. Taliaferro correctly acknowledges the importance of a theological foundation for religious freedom which takes into account its transcendent dimension, and my book draws on Taliaferro's argument. However, as Taliaferro acknowledges through the title of her book, she focuses on early (pre-modern) forms of natural law across a variety of religious traditions. Her articulation of natural law therefore lacks the precision entailed through engagement with modern natural law scholarship. Conversely, this book provides specificity by identifying and articulating clearly defined principles of Christian Natural Law through analysis of contemporary natural law scholarship (in Chapters 2 and 3), which I then draw upon to construct a detailed conceptual foundation for religious freedom. These principles, which are shared and universally applicable, simultaneously achieve Taliaferro's aim of a conceptual foundation for natural law which may appeal to all.

Though it is not my primary purpose in this book to explain how a theological natural law foundation for religious freedom may be acceptable to modern society, I have addressed this elsewhere through the application of Christian virtues which are shared and universally applicable.[38] In any case, as already noted, in this book I also implicitly address the problem by relying on a Christian Natural Law which is post-(secular) liberal but still supports and undergirds the liberal virtues of freedom, equality and democracy, guiding the community to the true and the good which can be universally accessed and known.[39] As Taliaferro correctly notes, a 'purely secular defense of religious

35 Charles (n 25).
36 Ibid viii, 14, 33.
37 Taliaferro (n 3) 7–8, 15–16, 20–21.
38 See eg Alex Deagon, 'Reconciling John Milbank and Religious Freedom: "Liberalism" through Love' (2019) 34(2) *Journal of Law and Religion* 183; Deagon (n 1) Introduction.
39 See eg Harrison (n 27); Taliaferro (n 3) 23–31. In effect, since religious freedom is the pursuit of true religion for the common good (see Chapter 5) through natural law, the idea has a broad appeal which can be rationally engaged by all. My use of liberal and non-liberal language to explain this phenomenon is the outworking of a theological approach which simultaneously transcends and fulfils liberalism. This means I can consistently appeal to truth from a Christian perspective in a way that is accessible to those who do not share Christian presuppositions. See eg Deagon, *Liberalism Through Love* (n 38); Deagon (n 1) Introduction.

freedom' 'simply won't do', because in order to be legitimate for religion and religious people such a defense must 'recognize the authority of the divine law'.[40] My proposal therefore provides a robust, transcendent foundation for religious freedom through Christian Natural Law, yet I also rely on universal virtues and ideas that have appeal for those who are not part of the Christian or any other religious tradition. Taliaferro rather vaguely discusses natural law as pursuing 'natural ends' or the 'good life' through the application of reason, but I provide more specificity through a Christian Natural Law foundation of religious freedom which pursues the Good, the True and Love, explaining in detail what these concepts entail.[41] In this book I will be focusing on the theological ontology of natural law (its source and grounding), not the epistemological question (how we know the natural law through reason), though there will necessarily be some discussion of the epistemological aspect when I consider the relationship between nature, grace, revelation and reason. It should also be noted that I do not attempt to consider every aspect of every metaphysical theory of natural law. Rather, I draw on particular aspects of some prominent theories to build a specifically 'Christian Natural Law'.[42]

III. Two Threshold Issues

There is an initial need for conceptual clarity with respect to two important issues in contemporary articulations of natural law: not deriving normative premises from descriptive ones (known as the fact-value distinction), and ensuring that the idea of the good is not reducible to utilitarianism. On the first point, my explicit metaphysical grounding of the good in a Christian framework is a grounding in 'non-natural facts' (facts about God). This grounding is therefore not susceptible to the fact-value distinction, which relies on deriving normative values from natural facts only. In addition, to the extent that my work draws on Finnis and the new natural lawyers, their theory is that the good is 'ontologically basic' (not grounded in anything). It is also, consequently, not susceptible to the fact-value distinction.[43] In any case, as Porter outlines, there are good reasons to think that the fact-value distinction is either fallacious or limited in its application. Specifically, the argument presupposes a strict distinction between facts and values, or between the factual and the normative. It is likely such a strict distinction does not exist.[44] In the case of a Christian Natural Law, an orthodox theological approach would see God's normative morality as grounded in facts about his nature. For example,

40 Taliaferro (n 3) 124–126, 129.

41 Cf ibid 26, 28, 132–133.

42 For a volume which explores these various ontological and epistemological questions in detail, see George Duke and Robert George (eds), *The Cambridge Companion to Natural Law Jurisprudence* (Cambridge University Press, 2017).

43 See Jonathan Crowe, *Natural Law and the Nature of Law* (Cambridge University Press, 2019) 15–16 for further discussion.

44 See Porter (n 4) 123–124.

when we say 'God is good', God both defines and obliges good according to his nature. This eternal law resolves the is/ought problem by collapsing the distinction:

> The 'is' of being is established by a law ruling that being: the eternal law as a rational plan for the universe. Things do not just exist, but exist according to a rational plan that is a law obligating conformity to that plan of being.[45]

In other words, the 'is' entails the 'ought'. This is further explained in Chapter 3.

On the second point, religion (or religious freedom) as a basic good has intrinsic value, and is not instrumental to the achievement of other ends such as freedom more broadly. The argument for religious freedom as upholding the basic good of religion and the common good is not utilitarian, though there may of course be ancillary social benefits. The existence of these benefits is not what makes religious freedom good. It merely adds to the proposition that it is an intrinsic good. Finnis notes that the 'limited relevance of consequences' is an (anti-utilitarian) requirement of practical reasonableness; this does not mean consequences have no relevance where consequences support the efficient upholding of a good.[46] I will explain this further in Chapter 5.

IV. Argument and Structure of the Book

This book aims to articulate a theological foundation for religious freedom. For this purpose I consider natural law in the Christian tradition. Part I of the book, comprising Chapters 2 through 4, articulates what I mean by 'Christian Natural Law'. Chapter 2 outlines what is meant by natural law in the Christian tradition, starting with Aquinas, and surveys the diversity of denominational positions with respect to natural law. It considers Catholic, Protestant and Anglican approaches and nuances within these. In particular, the chapter notes the distinct Catholic emphasis on nature, tradition and reason in contrast with the Protestant emphasis on sin, Scripture and grace. However, it argues the Protestant emphasis on sin and grace complements the Catholic emphasis on nature and reason. Our natural reason is indeed limited by sin, but through grace it is sufficiently enhanced to grasp the natural law. There is consequently a consistent theological theme of grace enabling nature, and revelation illuminating reason, across the Christian traditions of natural law.

Chapter 3 argues that even ostensibly secular accounts of natural law have theological presumptions and theological content. For example, though Finnis claimed to articulate a natural law separate from questions of God's existence

45 See McCall (n 6) 88.

46 See eg John Finnis, *Natural Law and Natural Rights* (Oxford University Press, 2nd ed, 2011) 100–126. See also McCall (n 6) 169–170.

and nature, his account of basic goods and practical reason actually relies on the idea of nature enhanced by grace. Indeed, any natural law which has a conception of the good is necessarily making a theological claim with respect to what is good for humans as such. To make sense of human nature, the natural law is also theological in a particularly Christian way. It is also worth noting that since Chapter 3 demonstrates that all natural law is properly speaking theological, the fact that a Christian Natural Law is theological is no intrinsic disadvantage compared to other theories of natural law. This means a Christian Natural Law cannot be rejected purely on the basis that is theological, unless one rejects all natural law. It also follows that if a Christian Natural Law is acceptable as natural law, it has the potential to be universally acceptable under the assumptions of natural law as a rational standard which all people can engage with. Finally, the fact that Christian Natural Law is theological satisfies the requirement for a transcendent dimension to the theoretical foundation for religious freedom.

Chapter 4 argues that exploring the symbiotic operation of grace, nature, revelation and reason in natural law reveals three foundational theological principles which hold across Christian tradition: Love, the True and the Good. These principles constitute a Christian Natural Law. Radical Orthodoxy reconciles these Christian principles regarding natural law as applied to religious freedom because it brings all these ideas under the rubric of a Christian theology with a focus on the Incarnation. Drawing on Aquinas, the chapter shows that the Incarnation is the ultimate revelation of God, an act of divine grace which enables comprehension of the divine through divinely guided and illuminated nature; this reconciles the Protestant and Catholic traditions of natural law. Moreover, the person who has more charity (Love) will see God the more perfectly (True) and will increase one's desire to see God, enhancing participation in the beatific vision (Good). The Incarnation is the theological foundation for natural law and thus entails Love, the True and the Good.

Part II of the book, comprising Chapters 5 through 7, suggests how this 'Christian Natural Law' provides a robust ontological and theological foundation for religious freedom. Chapter 5 argues that the Good, which is composed of the basic goods and the common good, provides a foundation for religious freedom by encouraging people to pursue the good of religion which contributes to a flourishing human community. For Aquinas, the ultimate human end is participation in the beatific vision, intellectual union with God. The good of religion has to do with pursuing this end, and entails freedom to facilitate the efforts of persons and communities to establish a harmonious relationship with the transcendent source of meaning and value known as God. Religious freedom also enhances the common good in numerous ways in accordance with the principles of practical reasonableness. Chapter 6 argues that the True is an aspect of a Christian Natural Law foundation for religious freedom in two interconnected senses. First, religious freedom aims for the pursuit of truth. Second, the truth religious freedom pursues is theological – in the biblical text, 'truth' is translated as *aletheia*, which means the revelation of God through

Christ. Specific divine revelation in Scripture and general divine revelation in nature provide a theological foundation for religious freedom both textually and conceptually. The chapter then considers this textual evidence supporting religious freedom, in conjunction with conceptual evidence such as the law of love and intrinsic dignity of humans as created in the image of God.

Chapter 7 concludes the book by arguing that Love, the True and the Good are symbiotic and mutually reinforcing aspects of a theological foundation for religious freedom. Love is the culmination of the True and the Good, and religious freedom is an expression of Love, because it brings people to the ultimate Good and Truth – God Himself – which is paradigmatically expressed through the Incarnation of Christ and is only possible through the loving sacrifice of Christ on the cross. In particular, the law of love, to love your neighbour as yourself, as ultimately displayed through Christ, is most significantly expressed in the Parable of the Good Samaritan and underpins religious freedom. Proclaiming the parable in response to the question of what 'love my neighbour' really entails, Jesus' Good Samaritan is good because he embodies the truth of the moral law. The law of love compels us to protect those who have their most basic freedoms threatened. The first principle of the natural law – to do good and avoid evil – therefore will not be satisfied unless we advocate for religious freedom.

Part I

Articulating Christian Natural Law

2 The Different Traditions of Christian Natural Law

I. Introduction

This chapter outlines what is meant by natural law in the Christian tradition, starting with Aquinas, and surveys the diversity of denominational positions with respect to natural law. It considers Catholic, Protestant and Anglican approaches and nuances within these. In particular, the chapter notes the distinct Catholic emphasis on nature, tradition and reason in contrast with the Protestant emphasis on sin, Scripture and grace. However, it argues the Protestant emphasis on sin and grace complements the Catholic emphasis on nature and reason. Our natural reason is indeed limited by sin, but through grace it is sufficiently enhanced to grasp the natural law. There is consequently a consistent theological theme of grace enabling nature, and revelation illuminating reason, across the Christian traditions of natural law.

Section II of the chapter briefly outlines Aquinas' system of natural law articulated in the context of his Christian theology. Aquinas forms the foundation for all subsequent Christian treatments of natural law, including varying perspectives on the powers of natural reason and the necessity of guidance through Scripture. Section III explains the Roman Catholic approach, which largely follows Aquinas and emphasises the importance of reason and tradition alongside Scripture in knowing and applying the natural law. Section IV considers various Protestant approaches to natural law including Reformed, Lutheran and Anglican. Focusing on Luther and Calvin as broadly representative, it argues that the alleged Protestant resistance to natural law is more apparent than actual, and more a distinction of emphasis than a distinction in substance. In particular, Protestant approaches continue the Catholic heritage of natural law but emphasise the effect of sin on natural reason and the importance of grace in the form of divine guidance toward moral knowledge through Scripture and the illumination of natural reason. The Anglican compromise, which acknowledges the importance of both natural reason and Scripture, implies the Catholic and Protestant approaches to natural law can be reconciled. As Section V summarises, our natural reason is limited by sin, but it is enhanced by divine grace to know and apply the natural law. Both Catholics and Protestants agree on this. Section VI concludes and transitions to the next chapter.

DOI: 10.4324/9781032620015-3

Natural law, broadly speaking, promises the 'possibility of arriving at moral truths by reference to truths of ontology and a metaphysics that is comprehensible to human reason'; natural law therefore offers a 'secure foundation' for understanding what is required for individual and common good.[1] Drawing from Thomas Aquinas, a thirteenth-century scholastic theologian and the classical proponent of natural law, George notes that the first principle of natural law is that good is to be done and evil is to be avoided. This means the first principle of morality, as apprehended through practical reason, is to will and act in such a way that the good is brought about, which produces 'integral human fulfilment'.[2] This is specified by considering and identifying the various requirements of human flourishing, such as friendship, knowledge and religion.[3] These are elsewhere called the 'basic goods'.[4] The basic goods are the essential, irreducible forms by which humans understand what is good for them to think, do and be.

John Finnis, a twentieth-century legal theorist who articulates a modern formulation and revivification of Thomist natural law, argues the basic goods are life, knowledge, play, aesthetic experience, sociability (friendship), practical reasonableness and religion. These goods are exhaustive, all equally fundamental, and are self-evident and basic in the sense that they are arrived at through practical reflection rather than derived by logic from some higher authority.[5] As will be discussed further in Chapter 3, Finnis claims this implies a theory of natural law can be articulated without reference to God.[6] However, a 'Christian' natural law must necessarily contain theological presumptions and theological content.[7] These include that there is a special revelation of God's nature and the moral law through Scripture (divine law), which also assumes a

1 Jaqueline Lang, 'Natural Law Reasoning in Applied Ethics' in George Duke and Robert George (eds), *The Cambridge Companion to Natural Law Jurisprudence* (Cambridge University Press, 2017) 216.

2 Robert George, 'Natural Law, God and Human Dignity' in George Duke and Robert George (eds), *The Cambridge Companion to Natural Law Jurisprudence* (Cambridge University Press, 2017) 59.

3 Ibid 59.

4 See eg John Finnis, *Natural Law and Natural Rights* (Oxford University Press, 2nd ed, 2011); See also John Finnis, 'Aquinas and Natural Law Jurisprudence' in George Duke and Robert George (eds), *The Cambridge Companion to Natural Law Jurisprudence* (Cambridge University Press, 2017) 18–19.

5 See generally Finnis, *Natural Law and Natural Rights* (n 4) 59–97. Of course, there are other views and articulations of these basic goods. See eg Jonathan Crowe, *Natural Law and the Nature of Law* (Cambridge University Press, 2019) 35–36, who notes that there is significant overlap between different categorisations of the good, different theories might reasonably articulate the good differently, and there is probably no 'uniquely best' account. Finnis himself adds the good of 'marriage' in later work. For my purposes in this book I use Finnis' initial list as the classically accepted version.

6 Finnis, *Natural Law and Natural Rights* (n 4) 48–49.

7 See generally Jennifer Herdt, 'Christianity and Natural Law and Natural Rights' in John Witte Jr and Rafael Domingo (eds), *The Oxford Handbook of Christianity and Law* (Oxford University Press, 2023).

general revelation of God's nature and the moral law through creation (natural law); that the reality of sin has affected human ability to know and live in accordance with the natural law, and hence the need for redemption; and that there is a spiritual life, and redemption is the restoration of that spiritual life through communion with God in Christ, which is the ultimate good revealed in divine law and indicated by natural law.[8]

II. Aquinas and Christian Natural Law

Natural law has a prominent place in Christian legal thought. Many see the beginning of the doctrine in Romans 2:14–15,[9] where the Apostle Paul states that despite the Gentiles not possessing a written or revealed moral law (divine law), by nature they do what the law requires as it is written in their hearts and conscience (natural law). Early church fathers, most prominently Augustine, also identified a natural law which is part of the supreme reason, the eternal law. However, it was Aquinas who first articulated a systematic doctrine of natural law.[10]

Natural law from the Christian perspective therefore typically begins with Aquinas, and has traditionally found the source of the civil law in a higher law based in the existence and nature of the Christian God.[11] As Jacobs emphasises:

> It is clear that, in natural law theorizing from antiquity to early modern times, the role of theistic considerations is a crucial matter. Medieval Christian thinkers' beliefs concerning creation, revelation, and providence shaped their conceptions of the scope and power of unaided human reason, the relation of natural law to divine wisdom and divine will, and how 'right reason' is to be understood.[12]

In the Christian tradition of monotheism, questions regarding rationality and its relationship with revelation in the context of natural law theory are of distinct importance.[13] Aquinas viewed right reason as intrinsically connected with faith, and the rationale for having such emphasis on right reason is the fact that

8 Owen Anderson, 'Natural Law and Philosophical Presuppositions' in Norman Doe (ed), *Christianity and Natural Law* (Cambridge University Press, 2017) 205–206.

9 All Scripture references are to the English Standard Version unless otherwise specified.

10 Norman Doe, 'Natural Law in an Interfaith Context: The Abrahamic Religions' in Norman Doe (ed), *Christianity and Natural Law* (Cambridge University Press, 2017) 198.

11 For more detail see Alex Deagon, 'Rendering to Caesar and God: St Paul, the Natural Law Tradition and the Authority of Law' (2014) 13(3) *Law, Culture, and the Humanities* 469–492; Alex Deagon, *From Violence to Peace: Theology, Law and Community* (Hart Publishing, 2017) 85–90, which some material in this section draws upon.

12 J Jacobs, 'Introduction' in J Jacobs (ed), *Reason, Religion, and Natural Law: From Plato to Spinoza* (Oxford University Press, 2012) 8.

13 Ibid.

'reason enables human beings to be responsive to the normative authority of law, and to pursue the good on the basis of an understanding of it'.[14]

Aquinas thus defines law as 'a dictate of practical reason emanating from the ruler who governs a perfect community', and so there is an eternal law or *lex eterna*, which is God's law and which fulfils these criteria.[15] Since the eternal law of God is a subset of the content of the divine intellect and is therefore truth, and to some extent people by grace know God and know truth, to this extent they know the eternal law.[16] The 'divine law' or *lex divina* allows people to participate 'more perfectly in the eternal law' through clarifying the eternal law against the limitations of pure human reason, and consists of the true revelation contained in Holy Scripture, the Old and New Testaments of the Bible.[17] Those who do not have this law of revelation nevertheless do by nature (illuminated by grace) those things which are of the law, and so know what is good and what is evil by conscience.[18] This is the 'natural law' or *lex natura*, which humans apprehend through their possessing a 'share of the Eternal Reason', and so they are able to 'participate in the eternal law through reason'; hence, the natural law is 'the rational creature's participation of the eternal law'.[19] In this sense the natural law provides the framework which is in turn built upon the foundation of the eternal law. The natural law is the participation of rational creatures in the eternal law through the determination of means to achieve the ends set by the eternal law. The natural law is therefore 'deeply connected' to the eternal law.[20]

Through human reason (enlightened by grace as a subset of the divine reason or *logos*), the precepts of the natural law 'proceed to the more particular determinations', which are called positive or 'human laws'.[21] All human law or *lex humana*, as it accords with right reason, ultimately derives from the eternal law. Hence, if a law deviates from right reason (implying it does not accord with the eternal law of God or immutable truth), it is unjust, and therefore lacks the necessary quality of law.[22] It is also worth noting that Aquinas' articulation of the natural law illustrates the discussion expanded in later chapters of his relationship between reason and grace – namely, that divinely illuminated human reason participates in the eternal law of God by grace, and if human law does not accord with this eternal law, it is necessarily against reason.

In short, Aquinas accepted that humans are able to discern what is right and good through natural reason imprinted on the human heart, the divine

14 Ibid 9.
15 Thomas Aquinas, *Summa Theologica* II Q91 Art 1.
16 Ibid Q93 Arts 1–2.
17 Ibid Q91 Arts 4–5.
18 Ibid Q91 Art 2.
19 Ibid.
20 Bryan McCall, *The Architecture of Law: Rebuilding Law in the Classical Tradition* (University of Notre Dame Press, 2018) 41.
21 Thomas Aquinas, *Summa Theologica* II Q91 Art 3.
22 Ibid Q93 Art 3.

light. The impact of sin means natural reason still requires guidance through revelation. 'The natural law mirrors the order and structure of creation . . . this order and structure remained self evident through revelation and reason'.[23] The general Christian tradition of natural law concerns, then, 'the existence of God-given universal principles' which God 'revealed' to humanity; natural law 'is a form of divine law' implanted in all humans to know what is right and good, and is discoverable through the exercise of reason and conscience.[24] According to Jean Porter, the natural law in the traditional scholastic context is sanctioned in God's authority as the supreme law-giver, and it combines nature, reason and Scripture.[25] The natural law is pre-conventional in the sense that it is not subject to the mores of society, and is a law in the sense that it consists of fixed moral principles. Ultimately, nature is reasonable and reason natural; they are grounded in and reflective of a transcendent reality, the will of a divine legislator.[26]

The account of law provided by Aquinas has been the most influential and the measure of subsequent natural law theories.[27] The prevailing scholarship thus links natural law theory with the tradition of Aquinas, and 'if Aquinas was indeed the leading light in formulating the tenets of natural law . . . its essentially religious character follows almost as a matter of course'.[28] A close tie between Christianity and natural law is therefore 'axiomatic'.[29] Of course, since all persons are governed by natural law, not just Christians, and the natural law is discoverable through reason and conscience which is not exclusive to Christians, it does not automatically follow that one must be a Christian or accept all Christian doctrine to affirm natural law.[30]

The fact that all natural law theory is ultimately linked to Aquinas implies that subsequent natural law theories necessarily share some common features, even across different denominational approaches and traditions. For example, Scripture is universally important for any Christian approach to natural law. The Ten Commandments are often provided as an illustration or exemplification of the natural law in the sense that they are part of the divine law and part of the law written on people's hearts.[31] Sandberg notes that 'support for natural law approaches is not divided by denominational lines', and includes many

23 J Daryl Charles, *Natural Law and Religious Freedom: The Role of Moral First Things in Grounding and Protecting the First Freedom* (Routledge, 2018) 57.

24 Norman Doe, 'Preface' in Norman Doe (ed), *Christianity and Natural Law* (Cambridge University Press, 2017) xiv.

25 Jean Porter, *Natural and Divine Law: Reclaiming the Tradition for Christian Ethics* (Novalis, 1999) 30.

26 Ibid 69.

27 Patrick Brennan and William Brewbaker, *Christian Legal Thought: Materials and Cases* (Foundation Press, 2017) 404.

28 RH Helmholz, 'Natural Law and Christianity' in Norman Doe (ed), *Christianity and Natural Law* (Cambridge University Press, 2017) 1.

29 Ibid 2.

30 Ibid 3. I explore and address this tension further in Chapter 3.

31 Ibid 5–7.

scholars from various traditions including Catholic, Anglican and Protestant.[32] Catholic, Protestant and Anglican approaches all endorse the general natural law idea that there are 'universal standards found in nature that are normative', and these standards have been 'implanted' in human nature through the exercise of reason.[33] Sections III and IV of this chapter consider Catholic, Protestant and Anglican approaches to natural law, identifying some distinctions between them. More importantly, in Section V the chapter articulates the common themes between these distinct approaches, explaining that in a Christian Natural Law, grace enhances nature and revelation illuminates reason to enable knowledge of natural law.

III. The Roman Catholic Approach

The Roman Catholic approach largely follows Thomas Aquinas, as articulated earlier.[34] It affirms that God rules his rational creatures through a natural law.[35] In addition to God's special divine revelation in Scripture, the Roman Catholic approach has a high regard for the traditional teaching of the Church as authoritative, and on the power of human reason to discern moral standards.[36] The Roman Catholic account assumes persons are made in the image of God and have genuine powers of agency. Reason is constitutive of moral goodness and relied upon to discern between good and evil.[37] Pope John Paul II emphasises the importance of Aquinas and his synthesis of faith and reason, with the implication that 'any study of natural must be conversant with Aquinas'.[38]

The natural law is also an essential component of Roman Catholic canon law.[39] In particular, Roman Catholic natural lawyers typically appeal to four sources of authority: Scripture, tradition, reason and experience. Tradition includes the patristic writings and the doctors/scholastics of the church, as well as the magisterium (official teaching office of the Roman Catholic Church). Reason includes reflection on the natural law and the human sciences.[40] The Catholic Catechism refers to the natural law as the original moral sense which enables all persons to discern between good and evil, and it is universal in its precepts and authority.[41] The natural law consists of objective moral values,

32 Russell Sandberg, 'Towards a Jurisprudence of Christian Law' in Norman Doe (ed), *Christianity and Natural Law* (Cambridge University Press, 2017) 231.

33 Ibid 232. Charles provides a detailed catalogue of perspectives on natural law from across different Christian traditions. See Charles (n 23) xiv, 55–58, 64–76, 260–261, some of which are already cited or engaged in this chapter.

34 Helen Costigane, 'Natural Law in the Roman Catholic Tradition' in Norman Doe (ed), *Christianity and Natural Law* (Cambridge University Press, 2017) 18–20.

35 Brennan and Brewbaker (n 27) 404.

36 Costigane (n 34) 22–24.

37 Ibid 18.

38 Charles (n 23) 56–57.

39 See Helmholz (n 28) 8–12.

40 Costigane (n 34) 22.

41 Ibid 23.

an ethical language common to all persons through reason which produces social flourishing.[42] Contemporary natural law theorists in the Catholic tradition, such as John Finnis, proceed from such grounds to identify a natural law which apparently exists apart from the divine.[43] Yet, the natural law 'acquires its full meaning in the history of salvation', for the Gospel 'includes, assumes and fulfils the requirements of the natural law'.[44] Canon law sees natural law as the ability and right of the Church to exist independently of the state and retain exclusive jurisdiction in the governance of ecclesial life, implementing natural law principles such as freedom, justice, truth and solidarity to ensure human flourishing.[45] Canonists often connect natural law and divine law, arguing that since God is the author of natural law, natural law is another kind of divine law which is established and revealed. The canons in turn are derived from the divine law.[46]

The Roman Catholic Church has therefore also conceived of natural law as intrinsically connected to the divine. Pope John Paul II has referred to the 'dependence of human reason on Divine Wisdom' and thus the natural law 'has God as its author'.[47] The Church fundamentally rejects the rationalist notion of a fully autonomous human reason capable of perceiving the natural law without divine assistance.[48] Similarly, the Catholic scholastics argued that Scripture (divine law) reflects the deliverances of reason, yet Scripture also serves to 'correct and extend rational deliverances, and given the constraining effects of sin, they are to some extent necessary if we are to arrive at anything like an adequate moral knowledge'.[49] As Costigane summarises, Aquinas' position on natural law 'continues to shape Roman Catholic thought' and the concept of natural law 'has an important place in the teaching of the Roman Catholic Church'.[50] It is a universal ethic discovered through reasoned reflection on human nature and moral experience, and is expressed through the teaching of the Church.[51]

42 Ibid 26. See also Russell Hittinger, *On the Dignity of Society: Catholic Social Teaching and Natural Law* (Catholic University of America Press, 2024).

43 See Chapter 3 for a more detailed articulation of this natural law, which nevertheless remains intrinsically theological and dependent on the divine for reasons alluded to here and explained more fully in that chapter.

44 Costigane (n 34) 28.

45 Ibid 29.

46 Ibid 30.

47 Pope John Paul II, *Veritatis Splendor* ss 36–37, cited in McCall (n 20) 432.

48 McCall (n 20) 432.

49 Jean Porter, *Nature as Reason: A Thomistic Theory of the Natural Law* (Eerdmans, 2005) 247.

50 Costigane (n 34) 35.

51 Ibid. The Orthodox tradition of natural law largely follows the Catholic approach with an emphasis on nature, and that divine law includes both Scripture and Tradition. There are some differences. For example, there is not the detailed and systematic treatment of natural law that exists in the Roman Catholic tradition, but rather a series of open disputes. As a result, natural law in the Orthodox tradition is not codified and prescriptive like canon law, but emergent and corrective. In addition, the idea of nature is focused on the human heart as a facility of the soul able to discover natural law, rather than the use of reason. For more detailed analysis see

IV. Protestant Approaches

A. Protestantism Broadly

Catholics are not alone in affirming the idea of a natural law. The Protestant Reformation carried over (with important modifications) the intellectual heritage of Roman Catholicism, including the idea that, to assist people in distinguishing between good and evil,

> God promulgated a natural law that directs and binds human creatures; that this law of nature has been written on every human heart; that conscience and reason serve as natural lights leading people to act in accord with natural law . . . [and] that while human cognition of the natural moral order was obscured by sin, the natural law still yields sufficient data.[52]

However, Protestants have typically been more wary regarding the human ability to apprehend the eternal law by nature, and have questioned whether the natural law debt to Roman Catholicism means the idea of natural law does not take the noetic effects of sin seriously enough.[53] Charles explains that the Protestant reformers 'presuppose the notion of the natural law and maintain continuity with their Catholic counterparts therein'.[54] Both Luther and Calvin, while emphasising the deep and pervasive effect of sin, acknowledge the existence of a law written on the human heart (following, for example, Romans 2:14–15). This law written on the human heart reflects the divine law expressed through the Decalogue (the Ten Commandments) and is also called the natural law.[55]

Paul Babie, 'Natural Law in the Orthodox Tradition' in Norman Doe (ed), *Christianity and Natural Law* (Cambridge University Press, 2017) 36–57.

52 Stephen Grabill, *Rediscovering the Natural Law in Reformed Theological Ethics* (Eerdmans, 2006) 2. See also Porter (n 49) 40–44.

53 Brennan and Brewbaker (n 27) 404; Grabill (n 52) 2–4. For a brief overview of this issue also see David VanDrunen, 'Natural Law and Reformed Theology' in Jonathan Crowe and Constance Youngwon Lee (eds), *Research Handbook on Natural Law Theory* (Edward Elgar, 2019) 216–218. See also the general account in Johnathan Stonebraker and Sarah Irving, 'Natural Law and Protestantism: A Historical Reassessment, and Its Contemporary Significance' (2015) 4(3) *Oxford Journal of Law and Religion* 421. Stonebraker and Irving survey many of the same sources as this chapter does in arguing that there is a consistent strand of Protestant engagement with and use of the natural law which provides a foundation for Protestant reliance on natural law in engagement with the moral arguments of the modern world. See also VanDrunen (n 53) 218–222; Charles (n 23) 64–76; and Mary Anne Plaatjies van Huffel, 'Natural Law in the Reformed Tradition' in Norman Doe (ed), *Christianity and Natural Law* (Cambridge University Press, 2017) 128–131 for overviews of the Protestant critique of natural law, responses, and implications for natural law arguments in the contemporary context.

54 Charles (n 23) 58.

55 Ibid.

In this way, typical Protestant accounts of natural law (broadly encompassing Reformed, Presbyterian, Baptist, Puritan, Evangelical, Lutheran and Methodist traditions) focus on Scripture as their central and authoritative text, both for grounding the natural law and informing human interpretation of it. Protestant approaches also emphasise the core authority of Scripture as the source of all divine law.[56] The Decalogue is often characterised as the prototypical statement of the natural law. The importance of incorporating and relying on divine revelation in conjunction with reason for apprehension of the natural law in the Protestant tradition is due to the noetic effects of sin:

> For Protestants . . . natural law likely must be, and perhaps ought to be, informed by and based upon their religious beliefs and revelation, as opposed to unaided human reason alone . . . a Protestant natural law would not, and – given the Protestant assumptions about human nature – possibly could not, be based upon reason alone. Rather, Protestants would utilize reason together with reliance on Scripture to show a clearer natural law.[57]

Protestants have also more recently recognised that the natural law tradition provides a vernacular to meaningfully and substantively discuss moral issues in a religiously pluralistic world, because it assumes the existence of a universal moral knowledge applicable to all persons and the ability of all persons to apprehend this universal moral knowledge through their reason.[58]

B. *Reformed, Lutheran and Presbyterian Approaches: Luther and Calvin*

The Reformed/Presbyterian branch of the Protestant Reformation promulgates the doctrines of God's sovereignty over the world and people, including in salvation, the dire effects of sin, the sufficiency and efficacy of Christ's atonement for salvation, and justification by faith alone.[59] Most other Protestant traditions, including the Baptist and Anglican traditions, also have strongly reformed roots (although differing on some matters of doctrine). Anglican and Baptist theologians also developed theologies of law along Thomist lines,

56 Porter (n 49) 10. See also Russell Hittinger, *The First Grace: Rediscovering the Natural Law in a Post-Christian World* (ISI, 2003) 3–37.

57 Stonebraker and Irving (n 53) 433–434. For example, prominent Reformed theologian David VanDrunen has provided a substantive and detailed theological account of natural law grounded in the biblical text and narrative, especially covenantal development. See David VanDrunen, *Divine Covenants and Moral Order: A Biblical Theology of Natural Law* (Eerdmans, 2014).

58 Grabill (n 52) 7. For comprehensive lists of recent research in natural law, including from Protestant perspectives, see Charles (n 23) xiv FN 17, 260–261 FN 6.

59 VanDrunen (n 53) 204. This broadly encompasses Puritan and Evangelical perspectives as well, so this chapter does not consider them separately.

including the existence of a natural law in postlapsarian humanity which can distinguish between good and evil.[60]

The wariness of the Reformed approach to natural law stems from the assumption that natural law cannot be reconciled with the Reformed doctrine of total depravity. As Grabill helpfully articulates,

> The confusion here stems from an improper demarcation of the scope of total inability [depravity]. The Reformed doctrine of total inability teaches that, in matters pertaining to justification, people are unable to perform any saving good; however, in nonsalvific matters, some vestiges of natural light remain such that good and evil are distinguishable and virtue and good works are preferred forms of human behaviour.[61]

In other words, total depravity does not completely extinguish nature, which includes human ability to know the good (even if the ability to act on that knowledge and perform the good has been extinguished).[62] Instead, Protestant thinkers affirm the existence of common grace (grace given by God in varying degrees to all) which enables persons to apprehend and perform the good beyond their pure nature, and despite the noetic effects of sin.[63] Furthermore, as noted by Aquinas, the provision of the divine law or Scripture (which is also a kind of grace) helps to ameliorate the limited and damaged human capacity for moral knowledge. 'Aquinas' appreciation of why it was necessary for God to promulgate the divine positive law [therefore] enjoys remarkably much in common with much Protestant skepticism about the natural law or the human capacity to know it'.[64]

In other words, access to the natural law is limited and defective due to the pervasive effects of sin on our noetic faculties. Our reason and conscience are corrupted, as is our ability to discern what is good and right. Yet, humans retain

60 Ibid 213. This chapter does not consider the Anabaptists, which were an early Protestant group who were eventually splintered into other groups including what became the Baptists. Goodliff argues that the Baptists do not have their own explicit theology of natural law but have rather adopted a Calvinistic form of it, and for that reason with respect to the Baptists there is no need to add to the analysis of Calvin already present in this chapter. For more information on the Anabaptists and the Baptists see John Witte Jr, *The Blessings of Liberty: Human Rights and Religious Freedom in the Western Legal Tradition* (Cambridge University Press, 2021) 89–91 and Paul Goodliff, 'Natural Law in the Baptist Tradition' in Norman Doe (ed), *Christianity and Natural Law* (Cambridge University Press, 2018). This chapter also does not consider the Methodists, who have not really produced a systematically distinctive approach to natural law. See John Harrod, 'Natural Law in the Methodist Tradition' in Norman Doe (ed), *Christianity and Natural Law* (Cambridge University Press, 2018) 118 and the chapter generally for further information.

61 Grabill (n 52) 8.

62 Ibid 12.

63 Brennan and Brewbaker (n 27) 411–412.

64 Ibid 412.

a limited moral capacity which is enhanced by common grace.[65] As VanDrunen puts it, 'common grace preserves nature', and the human capacity for natural law (attaining moral knowledge through universal reason and conscience) is not possible without the common grace God provides to all people.[66] So VanDrunen concludes that natural law is, 'according to traditional Reformed and broader Christian doctrine, a universal standard revealed to all people and binding on all people through the testimony of conscience'.[67] Stonebraker and Irving also explain that a Christian Natural Law informed by Reformed thought bolsters traditional or secular natural law approaches by exposing the limits and dangers of pure human reason, and providing clear guidance as to the content of the natural law through reference to divine revelation.[68]

Leigh considers that Witte 'successfully refutes the . . . ahistorical . . . idea that the Protestant reformers of the sixteenth century were somehow uninterested in natural law'; rather,

> Early Protestants not only regularly referred to these terms in their writings, but they also used them to develop distinctive approaches that contributed to the development of human rights, religious freedom, and democratic revolution based on their teachings on Scripture, human nature, divine sovereignty, and the Decalogue.[69]

As Witte summarises:

> Many Protestants have viewed natural law and natural rights with suspicion, if not derision. Some view natural law and natural rights as inextricably tied to Catholic moral theories that Protestants have always purportedly rejected . . . A number of critics view the occasional references to natural law and natural rights among some early Protestant reformers as a scholastic hangover that later Protestants happily

65 See eg Van Huffel (n 53) 122, 131; Goodliff (n 60) 146. See generally Constance Youngwon Lee, 'The Spark That Still Shines: John Calvin on Conscience and Natural Law' (2019) 8(3) *Oxford Journal of Law and Religion* 615; Porter (n 49) 43.

66 VanDrunen (n 57) 34–35.

67 David VanDrunen, *Natural Law and the Two Kingdoms: A Study in the Development of Reformed Social Thought* (Eerdmans, 2009) 432–433. Nevertheless, VanDrunen cautions that contemporary appeals to natural law exist in a religiously pluralistic and even relativistic society, and that begs the question of how Christians can make natural law arguments with theological integrity and at least some persuasiveness. This book provides a model which addresses VanDrunen's concerns by articulating a natural law argument for religious freedom which is theologically faithful and even embedded in Christianity while simultaneously proceeding without a pure reliance on theological arguments (see eg Ch 5, which commends religious freedom as a basic and common good).

68 Stonebraker and Irving (n 53) 435.

69 Ian Leigh, 'Religious Liberty and Human Rights: Their Origin, Their Development in the Anglo-American Legal Tradition, and Why They Are Still Needed' (2023) 38(1) *Journal of Law and Religion* 118, 120–121.

> expunged from the tradition by a clearer reading of scripture . . . such skepticism . . . is not good history. The reality is that early modern Protestant theologians and jurists . . . expounded complex theories of natural law and natural rights with considerable alacrity, and these proved to be important to the development of human rights and religious freedom in the Western legal tradition.[70]

For example, Martin Luther argued that the Decalogue expressed the duties owed under natural law and knowledge of the natural law comes through both Scripture and natural reason. John Calvin also drew on concepts of natural law and natural rights in the context of duties owed to God and neighbour.[71] This section therefore focuses on Luther and Calvin as broadly representative of the Lutheran/Reformed perspective.[72]

A key aspect of the Protestant movement characterised by Luther, Calvin and others was the 'freedom of the church', or specifically the freedom of the individual conscience to dissent from Roman Catholicism.[73] A major contribution was the grounding of rights in the biblical duties and moral teachings of Scripture:

> The reformers cast duties toward God as a set of rights that others could not obstruct – the right to religious exercise, to honoring God and God's name, to rest and worship on the Sabbath, and to be free from false gods and false oaths. They cast duties toward neighbors, in turn, as the neighbors' right to have that duty discharged. One person's duties to honor parents and not to kill, commit adultery, steal, bear false witness, or covet thus gives rise to another person's rights to the marital household, life, property, fidelity, and reputation.[74]

The reformers also gave new emphasis to the religious rights and liberties of individuals in both religious and civil law.[75] The Protestant teachings of Luther and Calvin discussed the natural rights of persons and the liberty to live and worship according to their conscience as a function of their created dignity. Simultaneously, all persons are sinful and therefore require the constraint of the law to deter them from evil and point them towards good.[76]

In particular, Luther grounded his natural law in his 'two kingdoms' framework. Luther argued that God has ordained two kingdoms in which people

70 John Witte Jr, *The Blessings of Liberty: Human Rights and Religious Freedom in the Western Legal Tradition* (Cambridge University Press, 2021) 76.

71 Leigh (n 69) 120–121.

72 For a detailed analysis of other contributors see Witte (n 70) Ch 3 and Grabill (n 52).

73 Witte (n 70) 30. See also John Witte Jr, *The Reformation of Rights: Law, Religion and Human Rights in Early Modern Calvinism* (Cambridge University Press, 2007), which Witte draws upon in this work.

74 Witte (n 70) 31.

75 Ibid 32.

76 Ibid 33.

are destined to live. The earthly kingdom is the 'realm of creation, of natural and civil life, where a person operates primarily by reason and law'; the heavenly kingdom is the 'realm of redemption, of spiritual and eternal life, where a person operates primarily by faith and love'.[77] The kingdoms are parallel and interact but ultimately are distinct. Christians are citizens of both kingdoms. As citizens of heaven, Christians are free in conscience (subject to God) but are still required to obey the authorities of the earthly kingdom which are established by God.[78] In *The Freedom of a Christian*, Luther wrote that 'A Christian is a perfectly free lord of all, subject to none. A Christian is a perfectly dutiful servant of all, subject to all'.[79] As I have explained elsewhere:

> The first of these statements expresses the truth that salvation is only possible by faith alone, which comes through the Word of God, unmediated by any human authority or institution. By faith, the Christian is completely free, and has confidence of acceptance with God . . . Having experienced this freedom, Christians willingly subject themselves, serving their neighbours and acting for the common good rather than in their own interests . . . Luther's two statements correspond to the twofold nature of man and the twofold government instituted to rule those natures. For Luther, the spiritual realm pertains to the inner person – the conscience – which is ruled exclusively by the Holy Spirit, without law. This spiritual government is a voluntary rule which cannot be imposed by force. By contrast, the 'outer realm' pertains to temporal matters, which for Luther had a broad compass, referring to everything outside of a Christian's relationship with God. In contrast to the government of the word, the temporal government of the sword is a coercive power that exists to maintain order and peace.[80]

In general terms, the Lutheran Reformation therefore did not depart significantly from traditional ideas with respect to natural law. Luther held that there is a natural law discoverable by reason which forms the basis for moral life and just laws.[81] The natural law is exemplified in Scripture through the law of love and the Decalogue, but it can only be fulfilled through divine love, a continuous giving by God which means the natural law cannot be apprehended or

77 Ibid 81.
78 Ibid.
79 Martin Luther, 'The Freedom of a Christian, 1520' in Theodore G Tappert (ed), *Selected Writings of Martin Luther: 1520–1523*, tr WA Lambert (Fortress Press, vol 2, 2007) 3, 20.
80 See Alex Deagon and Benjamin Saunders, 'Principles, Pragmatism and Power: Another Look at the Historical Context of Section 116' (2020) 43(3) *Melbourne University Law Review* 1033, 1047–1050; David VanDrunen, *Natural Law and the Two Kingdoms: A Study in the Development of Reformed Social Thought* (William B Eerdmans Publishing, 2010); Matthew J Tuininga, *Calvin's Political Theology and the Public Engagement of the Church: Christ's Two Kingdoms* (Cambridge University Press, 2017).
81 Antti Raunio, 'Natural Law in the Lutheran Tradition' in Norman Doe (ed), *Christianity and Natural Law* (Cambridge University Press, 2018) 77–78.

implemented 'on the basis of human capacity alone'.[82] The earthly authorities operate by this law of nature, which is ordained by God and written in Scripture. Knowledge of the natural law also comes through natural reason as rational persons perceive the law of God written on their heart. Since sinful persons sometimes choose not to obey this law, the earthly authorities should promulgate and enforce it. 'The basis of natural law is God, who has created this light, but the basis of positive law is the earthly authority'.[83] Hence the Lutherans agreed that the natural law could not be independent of theology. Rather, the natural law was an 'earthly reflection of the divine law', and pure rationality could not access the mind of God.[84]

As for Calvin, he frequently mentioned concepts associated with natural law, but it cannot be said that he offered a systematic treatment of natural law in a way comparable to Aquinas.[85] 'Calvin, at least in principle, leaves open the formal possibility of developing a systematic doctrine of natural law founded on natural knowledge of God the Creator, even though that possibility remains materially unfulfilled in his mature statement of doctrine'.[86] Calvin believed that the natural light of reason still shone brightly enough to illuminate the distinction between good and evil and what is required for right conduct. This light of reason is a 'universally imprinted nonsalvific knowledge of God' and is a 'constitutive aspect of the [postlapsarian] human mind' which, taken with the 'general grace of God', is sufficient for humans to apprehend moral truth.[87] Importantly, again, this light of reason is ineffective with respect to salvation and has a 'distinct epistemological status from God's supernatural revelation in Christ and the Scriptures'.[88] So for Calvin, human reason enlightened by grace can know natural law.

Calvin takes a particularly dim view of pure human nature, underscoring the 'indispensability of divine grace'.[89] According to Calvin, without grace, human nature 'is so vitiated and almost blotted out that nothing remains after the ruin except what is confused'.[90] Yet limited human understanding and ability remains, though it is necessary for the deficiency to be supplemented by divine grace and the revelation contained in the Scripture.[91] As Calvin puts it,

> Yet the fact remains that some seed of political order has been implanted in all men. And this is ample proof that in the arrangement of this life

82 Ibid 80.
83 Luther, cited in Witte (n 70) 83.
84 Knud Haakonssen, 'Early Modern Natural Law Theories' in George Duke and Robert George (eds), *The Cambridge Companion to Natural Law Jurisprudence* (Cambridge University Press, 2017) 84–85.
85 Grabill (n 52) 15.
86 Ibid 71.
87 Ibid 71–72.
88 Ibid 77.
89 David Little, 'Calvin and Natural Rights' (2009) 10(3) *Political Theology* 411, 422.
90 John Calvin, *Institutes of the Christian Religion* (Hendrickson, 2008) bk. I, ch XV, para. 4.
91 Little (n 89) 423, 426–427.

> no man is without the light of reason . . . It is a fact that the law of God which we call the moral law is nothing else than a testimony of natural law and of that conscience which God has engraved on the minds of men.[92]

VanDrunen considers that for Calvin, sin has corrupted the use of reason and obscured the natural law. The divine law is required for guidance. Yet there remains a seed of natural knowledge of God and the good which is implanted in the human heart (see eg Romans 2:14–15). Conscience is the method of obtaining this natural knowledge of the good imprinted on the human heart, which Calvin calls the natural law.[93] Calvin's distinction between earthly and heavenly things is important here. Though sin has corrupted natural knowledge of heavenly or spiritual things absolutely, human reason continues to operate (basically and imperfectly) at the level of earthly things, including legal and political affairs.[94]

Drawing on these themes, Lee persuasively argues that Calvin's account of conscience, damaged and imperfect as it is by sin, retains a partial reflection of the image of God. Conscience is the 'spark that still shines'[95] This means humans can apprehend moral knowledge. Illuminated by divine grace, the possibility of this moral knowledge enables a formal doctrine of natural law.[96] Human reason is perverted but not totally destroyed. Pure reason can never attain a saving or true knowledge of God. However, God's grace has provided human reason with a limited ability or moral knowledge with respect to earthly or civil affairs through conscience.[97] Lee explains:

> Calvin posits his idea of conscience by drawing a distinction between the little insight left in fallen humans and perfect moral knowledge. Regarding the latter, Calvin unequivocally states that perfect knowledge of God encapsulates obedience to love God above all else and our neighbours as ourselves. Calvin notes that part of this knowledge is set out as precepts of the second tablet of the Decalogue. However, another aspect of this knowledge manifests itself in human nature immanently [in the law written on the heart . . .]. Thus, for Calvin, natural law corresponds to the moral law that humans can know innately apart from God's revealed law in the Scripture. Conscience is thus the mechanism for apprehending the natural law. In so claiming, Calvin concludes that natural reason exists universally apart from supernatural reason.[98]

92 Calvin (n 90) bk. II, ch II, para. 13; Calvin, cited in Little (n 89) 423.

93 VanDrunen (n 53) 206–207.

94 Ibid 207. See also Constance Youngwon Lee, 'John Calvin's Natural Law Theory' in Jonathan Crowe and Constance Youngwon Lee (eds), *Research Handbook on Natural Law Theory* (Edward Elgar, 2019) 98–99.

95 Calvin (n 90) bk. I, ch XV, para. 4; bk. II, ch II, para. 12.

96 See Constance Youngwon Lee, 'The Spark That Still Shines: John Calvin on Conscience and Natural Law' (2019) 8(3) *Oxford Journal of Law and Religion* 615.

97 Ibid 632–633.

98 Ibid 633–634.

Yet, this is only 'made possible through common grace', for the conscience itself is 'contingent on common grace for its operationality'.[99] Thus, again, for Calvin human reason enlightened by grace can know the natural law. As Van Huffel summarises, the natural law is grounded in human nature as created by God and allows humans moral knowledge. 'For Calvin, God endowed humankind with a knowledge of the natural law . . . this is one expression of the grace of God and His gift of a moral sense to humankind'.[100]

More broadly, the Calvinists also argued for a basic separation between the church and state. The church should govern its own doctrine, practice and property and has no authority to undertake the functions of state (eg punish crime, collect taxes, make war), while the state should not interfere with or undertake the functions of the church (eg preach the word, administer the sacraments, appoint clergy).[101] Calvin argued that the 'civil' and 'ecclesiastical' realms were substantively different and a distinction should be maintained between them.[102] However, unlike some other Protestants, Calvin thought that the state and the church ought to cooperate as complementary powers established by God to achieve a godly community.[103]

Part of that cooperation was to ensure that persons would have liberty, including in religious matters.[104] Like Luther, Calvin considered that God had written the natural law on the hearts of persons, revealed it in Scripture and summarised it in the Decalogue.[105] This is illustrated through the Calvinists relying on biblical principles and an inversion of the typical biblical passages commanding subjection to civil authorities to argue for a right to civil disobedience, including in matters of religion.[106] As Witte concludes:

> Calvinists also built on the idea of fundamental rights, whose chronic and pervasive breach by a tyrant triggered the most basic right to resist and revolt . . . The most important rights, they reasoned, had to be the religious rights of liberty of conscience and free exercise of religion. After all, persons are created first and foremost as subjects and ambassadors of the Creator God and called to honor God above all else. The Ten

99 Ibid 635. Lee (n 94) 101 explains this move more fully – namely, Calvin's soteriology and choice of words implies that human conscience exists and functions in a 'relational dichotomy' with God.

100 Van Huffel (n 53) 122. For a similar account see Lee (n 94) and Van Huffel (n 53) 121–126.

101 Witte (n 70) 92.

102 See eg Calvin (n 90) bk. IV, ch XI, paras. 3–16.

103 Witte (n 70) 93.

104 This is despite a widely held view that Calvin himself was quite intolerant of diverse beliefs. See eg Christoph Strohm, 'Calvin and Religious Tolerance' in Martin Hirzel and Martin Sallman (eds), *John Calvin's Impact on Church and Society 1509–2009* (Eerdmans, 2009) 175–191. For a nuanced analysis of Calvin's changing views on religious liberty, see John Witte Jr, 'Moderate Religious Liberty in the Theology of John Calvin' (1996) 31 *Calvin Theological Journal* 359.

105 Witte (n 70) 93–95.

106 Ibid 100–102. See also VanDrunen (n 53) 209–210.

Commandments enjoined them to worship God, to observe the Sabbath, and to avoid blasphemy and idolatry. The New Testament ordered the faithful to "obey God rather than men." If the political magistrate – created by God and representing God's authority on earth – breaches a person's rights to discharge these religious duties, then nothing can be sacred and secure any longer.[107]

C. *The Anglican Approach*

Anglicanism arose out of a schism from the Roman Catholic Church, creating a separate Protestant church known as the Church of England. However, the legal thought and practice of the Anglican Church continued to develop out of a Catholic framework. For example, while the teaching of the Church is subject to the divine law contained in Scripture, that which is enacted by the Church is consistent with Scripture.[108] Anglican theologians such as Richard Hooker took a largely Thomist approach to the issue of natural law. A universal law of God is written on the hearts of all, and can be accessed through reason; this is called the natural law. This natural law is further revealed and clarified through the divine law contained in Scripture.[109] The Anglican approach then tends to mediate between the Catholic and other Protestant perspectives, continuing the Catholic way of relying on a combination of Scripture, reason and tradition without an 'over-reliance on . . . revealed divine law'[110] 'Reason is acknowledged as necessary in the interpretation of Scripture' and the 'law of reason' has a central role, but Scripture is still given high value and is seen as the 'dominant normative source'.[111]

V. Reconciling the Approaches and Common Themes

The Anglican compromise suggests that the distinct emphases of the Catholic and Protestant traditions of natural law do not necessarily imply they are irreconcilable. Indeed, Koffeman outlines areas of commonality and interdenominational dialogue, including in natural law. 'The appeal to natural law . . . was a common feature of theology and legal thought . . . the concept itself is very much rooted in the theological history of all major denominations'.[112] There is common ground in a 'shared view of the normative authority of Scripture as well as the significance of natural law and wisdom in the order of creation'.[113]

107 Witte (n 70) 102–103.
108 Will Adam, 'Natural Law in the Anglican Tradition' in Norman Doe (ed), *Christianity and Natural Law* (Cambridge University Press, 2017) 58–60.
109 Ibid 63–65.
110 Ibid 66–67.
111 Ibid 73, 76.
112 Leo Koffeman, 'Natural Law in the Ecumenical Movement' in Norman Doe (ed), *Christianity and Natural Law* (Cambridge University Press, 2018) 182 and generally.
113 Ibid.

As mentioned earlier, and as will be explained in further detail in the following chapters, we can deduce through the common source of Thomas Aquinas that our natural reason is limited by sin, but through grace it is sufficiently enhanced to grasp the natural law. The rational creature can in this sense only participate in the eternal law through grace, or divine illumination of their limited natural faculties. The Catholic approach extols the powers of human nature and reason to discern moral good. Yet, Catholicism also acknowledges natural law reliance on divine law, the importance of Scripture as a guide, and rejects the notion of a fully autonomous natural reason which can apprehend the natural law without divine assistance, or grace. Similarly, the Protestant approaches point out the severe noetic effects of sin without claiming a complete extinguishing of human nature. Humans retain a limited and damaged ability to know the natural law through their nature and reason, which is manifested through their conscience and the law written on the heart. For a proper knowledge of moral and divine truth or a full revelation of the natural law, nature and reason must be enhanced by grace and directed by the divine law articulated in Scripture (which is also a kind of grace).

As such, the Protestant emphasis on sin and grace complements the Catholic emphasis on nature and reason. Both agree that humans can apprehend the natural law through their nature and an exercise of reason which is enhanced by grace and illuminated by divine law. This is affirmed by Beckwith. As he explains, when one 'attends to what Aquinas actually taught (and with which the Catholic Catechism is in full agreement), the distance between' Protestant and Catholic ideas of natural law 'seems almost negligible'.[114] Consistent with the Protestant approaches, the Catholic approach to natural law is not independent of Scripture/the divine law/divine revelation in three senses. First, 'the natural law participates in the eternal law, which is also the source of the divine law'; this means 'God is the source of the natural law', including the rational nature of human beings which also eternally exists in the mind of God.[115] Second, natural law is 'incomplete and inadequate given human nature' and the 'fallen state'; Aquinas acknowledges that God must provide the divine law to guide the apprehension of the natural law.[116] Just like the Protestants, 'the Thomistic and Catholic view of natural law does in fact hold that the Fall has had a deleterious effect on our noetic powers'.[117] Third, the Bible itself teaches both the existence and the content of the natural law, and

114 Francis Beckwith, 'Natural Law, Catholicism and the Protestant Critique: Why We Are Really Not That Far Apart' (2019) 25(2) *Christian Bioethics* 154, 160. See also Francis Beckwith, *Never Doubt Thomas: The Catholic Aquinas as Protestant* (Baylor University Press, 2019); Patrick McKinley Brennan and William Brewbaker III, *Christian Legal Thought: Materials and Cases* (Foundation Press, 2017) 397–426; Stephen Grabill, *Rediscovering the Natural Law in Reformed Theological Ethics* (Eerdmans, 2006).

115 Beckwith, *Natural Law* (n 114) 160–161.

116 Ibid 161.

117 Ibid 162.

therefore deferring to the authority of Scripture requires acknowledging the natural law.[118] There is consequently a consistent theological theme of grace enabling nature, and revelation illuminating reason, across the Christian traditions of natural law. Porter precisely articulates this reconciliation of Christan Natural Law which I adopt for the remainder of this book:

> With the Catholic approach, it shares a confidence in our capacity to arrive at genuine moral knowledge, even though our limitations as creatures and as sinful . . . set constraints on our capacities for moral discernment . . . With the Protestant approach, it shares a commitment to locating the natural law within a specifically theological and scriptural context and drawing on it as a basis for a distinctively 'Christian' natural law.[119]

Therefore, both the Catholics and Protestants have important strengths to draw on in articulating a Christian Natural Law. The Catholics are right that nature and the exercise of reason, illuminated by grace, can yield genuine and true moral knowledge. The Protestants are right that our moral qualities have been pervasively damaged by sin and we require God's grace through Scripture and illumination to yield genuine and true moral knowledge. Combining these, pure nature and pure reason cannot apprehend the natural law without the illumination of grace and the guidance of Scripture.[120]

VI. Conclusion: The Christian Tradition of Natural Law

This chapter has surveyed how various Christian traditions have positioned themselves with respect to the natural law. Thomas Aquinas, the first to systematically articulate a theory of natural law, intrinsically builds his theory within a theological framework of grace enabling nature and revelation illuminating reason. Since all subsequent Christian Natural Law traditions have a common source in Aquinas, they share his theological framework and emphasise the different aspects of it to varying degrees. Catholic approaches tend to emphasise nature and reason while Protestant approaches tend to emphasise sin and grace. Yet, these distinct approaches all agree that human nature is damaged by sin, that a fully autonomous human reason capable of discerning true moral knowledge does not exist, and that nature and reason must be guided by the divine law and assisted by grace to properly apprehend the natural law. Thus, a Christian Natural Law entails the propositions that grace enables nature and revelation illuminates reason. The next chapter brings these

118 Ibid 161–162. See eg Romans 2:14–15; Charles (n 23) 55–56; David VanDrunen, *Divine Covenants and Moral Order: A Biblical Theology of Natural Law* (Eerdmans, 2014).
119 Porter (n 49) 325.
120 Ibid 398–399.

propositions into conversation with contemporary natural law theories, arguing that these ostensibly 'secular' natural law theories are actually theological in a Christian sense. This means the theological categories of sin, grace, nature, reason and revelation are simultaneously natural law concepts which operate together. Chapter 4 explores the ontological and epistemological structure of their operation to complete the construction of a Christian Natural Law which can be deployed to articulate a robust theoretical foundation for the idea of religious freedom.

3 The Theological Nature of Traditional 'Secular' Natural Law

I. Introduction

The previous chapter explained how various Christian theological traditions position themselves with respect to natural law, and identified some common themes between these traditions in terms of the relationship between nature, grace, reason and revelation. This chapter brings these ideas into conversation with contemporary natural law theories to help build a 'Christian Natural Law'. In particular, I argue that ostensibly secular accounts of natural law are actually theological in the Christian sense. As explained in the previous chapter, the idea of natural law itself was first systematically articulated by scholastic theologian Thomas Aquinas as part of his *Summa Theologiae*. Subsequent substantive accounts of natural law have theological presumptions and theological content.[1] For example, though Finnis claims to articulate a natural law separate from questions of God's existence and nature, his account of basic goods and practical reason actually relies on a metaphysical framework and the idea of nature enhanced by grace. Crowe's diachronic approach to natural law is also theological because it can be incorporated into Aquinas' classical natural law as part of an expanded 'divine law' which contains both the Book of Nature (general revelation about human goods and practices from observation), in conjunction with the Book of Scripture (special revelation with specific divine commands). Even the explicitly secular strains of natural law led by scholars such as Michael Moore and Mark Murphy have latent theological elements, for any natural law which has a conception of the good (as all natural law does) is necessarily making a theological claim with respect to what is good

1 It should be noted for the purposes of this claim that I am talking about 'substantive natural law', as opposed to the 'procedural natural law' of Fuller and his ilk. Fuller's perspective does not construct a metaphysical conception of the law's moral foundations and so is not strictly 'natural law' in the sense I mean in this book. See eg David Luban, 'Natural Law as Professional Ethics: A Reading of Fuller' in Ellen Frankel Paul, Fred Miller Jr, and Jeffrey Paul (eds), *Natural Law and Modern Moral Philosophy* (Cambridge University Press, 2001); Kristen Rundle, 'Opening the Doors of Inquiry: Lon Fuller and the Natural Law Tradition' in George Duke and Robert George (eds), *The Cambridge Companion to Natural Law Jurisprudence* (Cambridge University Press, 2017).

DOI: 10.4324/9781032620015-4

for humans as such. Furthermore, I argue the natural law is also theological in a particularly Christian way. The natural law makes sense of Christian claims about sin and redemption, and about the relationship between nature, grace, revelation and reason.

Section II considers Aquinas' conception of natural law and responds to arguments that it is not intrinsically theological. Section III engages with Finnis and the new natural law. It identifies two criticisms: that Finnis' basic goods are not objective, and that Finnis' account of natural law is not theological. I argue that though Finnis' natural law is not explicitly theological, it requires a theological framework to operate; a theological natural law is entirely consistent with Finnis' approach, and Finnis himself at least implicitly recognises this. Mooring the basic goods to a theological framework also resolves the problem of the objectivity of the basic goods by providing a metaphysical ground for them. Section IV turns to natural law post-Finnis, arguing that influential contemporary natural law theories are theological. Michael Moore, Mark Murphy and Jonathan Crowe all articulate conceptions of the good, and so in that sense make implicit theological claims. Moore's explicitly secular approach requires metaphysical (theological) foundations to be successful, while Crowe's diachronic natural law can be made more plausible by incorporating it into a theological framework. Section V explicitly articulates the general principle suggested in the previous parts: that since all natural law theories have a conception of the good, and having a conception of the good entails making a theological claim, it follows that all natural law theories are theological to some extent. Moreover, natural law is theological in a particularly Christian way, putting Christian claims regarding sin and redemption in a coherent theological context. Section VI therefore transitions to the next chapter, which finalises the construction of a Christian Natural Law by using Radical Orthodoxy to explicitly connect the natural law themes of nature, grace, revelation and reason to the Incarnation.

II. Aquinas and the Theological Conception of Natural Law

As indicated in the previous chapter, Aquinas' conception of natural law is theological. I use conception here in two related senses. First, Aquinas is the *originator* of a systematic natural law expressed in theological terms. Second, Aquinas' *idea* of natural law is intrinsically theological. The idea of natural law as theological is therefore grounded in a long tradition stemming back to Aquinas.[2] It is true that Aquinas acknowledges that moral truth can be

2 Yannick Imbert, 'Natural Law and Imagination' in Jonathan Crowe and Constance Lee (eds), *Research Handbook on Natural Law Theory* (Edward Elgar, 2019) 289. See generally Matthew Levering, *Biblical Natural Law* (Oxford University Press, 2008).

grasped by rational reflection apart from revelation,[3] as indicated by the Apostle Paul in Romans 2:14–15:

> For when nations, who do not have the law, by nature do what the law requires, they are a law to themselves, even though they do not have the law. They show that the work of the law is written on their hearts, while their conscience also bears witness, and their conflicting thoughts accuse or even excuse them.

Here Paul is distinguishing between those nations which have a written moral law (specifically Israel who have received the law from God by revelation) and those who do not. Those who do not have a written moral law know by nature or conscience what the moral law requires, and act in a corresponding way. This is the idea of knowing and practicing the moral law 'by nature'. The essence of natural law, then, is that there are objective moral principles which depend upon the nature of the universe and which may be discovered by reason; these principles constitute the natural law. Yet, even this conception of the natural law remains grounded 'in a divine source'.[4] Hittinger in particular has observed that problems arise when the natural law is viewed as detached from a higher or transcendent authority, and theology is intrinsically related to morality in this sense. The ultimate claim is that there is an order prior to the human law, a moral order which should inform the human law, and that this order is in effect the divine mind.[5] Taliaferro also suggests that natural law in Aquinas is theological because it is necessarily guided and informed by the divine law, and human reason is enlightened by grace. It is 'necessary' to reveal a divine law because humans are not 'competent' to judge moral matters unaided; the natural law is therefore necessarily 'related to something higher': the 'creator' who is 'the author of nature'.[6]

Hence, Aquinas identifies the limits of pure reason and argues for reliance on three mutually reinforcing sources: 'nature (eternal law), reason (natural law), and Scripture (divine law)'.[7] In terms of reason or the natural law, the 'formal first principle' of natural law is that 'good is to be pursued and done,

3 Thomas Aquinas, *Summa Theologica* I Q94 Art 2.

4 Robert George, 'Natural Law, God and Human Dignity' in George Duke and Robert George (eds), *The Cambridge Companion to Natural Law Jurisprudence* (Cambridge University Press, 2017) 67. See also Knud Haakonssen, 'Early Modern Natural Law Theories' in George Duke and Robert George (eds), *The Cambridge Companion to Natural Law Jurisprudence* (Cambridge University Press, 2017) 76–77, who acknowledges the theological underpinnings of early natural law theories.

5 See Russell Hittinger, *The First Grace: Rediscovering the Natural Law in a Post-Christian World* (ISI, 2003).

6 Karen Taliaferro, *The Possibility of Religious Freedom: Early Natural Law and the Abrahamic Faiths* (Cambridge University Press, 2019) 26, 28, 30.

7 Bryan McCall, *The Architecture of Law: Rebuilding Law in the Classical Tradition* (University of Notre Dame Press, 2018) 209.

and evil avoided'.[8] The good is reducible to specific kinds of human goods, the 'basic' or 'intrinsic, self-evident forms of human good', including life, knowledge, practical reasonableness and, significantly, 'friendship with the divine transcendent source of all these goods' (religion).[9] Porter argues that even Aquinas' articulation of the first principles of practical reason (such as to pursue good and avoid evil, the Golden Rule, the law of love) rely on metaphysical, and particularly theological, truths: 'these first principles are metaphysical principles . . . as grasped by the rational creature . . . some level of . . . theological understanding is needed to formulate these principles'.[10] This reinforces the view that Aquinas' theory of natural law is 'fundamentally theological'.[11]

In terms of nature or the eternal law, Aquinas' conception of natural law necessarily 'touches the supernatural in that it is a participation in the eternal law'.[12] Natural law theory 'is an entire metaphysical system of law' which 'rests on the foundation of the eternal law'; 'it is impossible to discuss natural law without reference to at least some understanding of the rational divine lawgiver', for natural law is inextricably connected to the rationality and goodness of the divine.[13] Failure to acknowledge the eternal law leaves natural law without a rational and robust foundation.[14] It logically follows that in terms of Scripture or divine law, for Aquinas, 'the supernatural . . . serves as a foundation for the natural. Thus, some level of commitment to supernatural realities is inherent in a comprehensible jurisprudence of natural law', including commitment to that which is revealed in the divine law.[15] Furthermore, 'failure to accept all that God reveals about himself and His law' (divine law as expressed in the revelation of Scripture) 'will lead to an incomplete and fractured account of natural law' and the good.[16] Porter concludes that 'the conception of human nature informing a Thomistic account of the natural law is finally a theological conception, insofar as it considers what it means to be human in the light of theological perspectives epitomised by the motif of the Image of God'.[17]

With this insight we can refine Finnis' claim that Aquinas' position is 'everything that has been divinely revealed about God's will for human conduct . . . is also discoverable by human understanding and reason independently of any

8 John Finnis, 'Aquinas and Natural Law Jurisprudence' in George Duke and Robert George (eds), *The Cambridge Companion to Natural Law Jurisprudence* (Cambridge University Press, 2017) 18.
9 Ibid 18–19.
10 Jean Porter, *Nature as Reason: A Thomistic Theory of the Natural Law* (Eerdmans, 2005) 263–264.
11 Ibid 323.
12 McCall (n 7) 134.
13 Ibid 168, 170.
14 Ibid 170, 172.
15 Ibid 420–421.
16 Ibid 508 (FN 285).
17 Porter (n 10) 395.

knowledge or belief in God's existence, purposes or . . . revelation'.[18] While strictly true in the sense that the atheist can discern the good just as well as the theist, this formulation neglects Aquinas' theological qualifications – namely, that human understanding and reason must be enlightened by God's grace and guided by divine revelation to discern the good.[19] So Finnis' epistemological point neglects the ontological point that God's existence and nature is metaphysically necessary for any natural law which has a conception of human good, especially since a conception of human good includes a position on religion as a good.[20] Moreover, even Finnis acknowledges that Aquinas sees divine revelation (Scripture) as lending 'some clarity and assurance to what is ascertainable by conscientious rational reflection', albeit without explaining that for Aquinas true rational reflection which leads to apprehending the good also requires an act of grace to enable the mind.[21]

Lisska also claims that 'Aquinas' account of natural law does not depend upon the existence or commands of God'; it 'is possible theoretically to develop an account of natural law theory . . . within the texts of Aquinas . . . without an ontological dependence on the existence of God'.[22] Of course, it is worth noting from the outset that these are actually distinct propositions. The first proposition is that Aquinas' account does not ontologically depend on the existence of God. The second proposition is that it is possible to develop an account of natural law theory from Aquinas that does not ontologically depend on the existence of God. Demonstrating the first proposition requires a faithful exposition of Aquinas' ontology with respect to natural law as Aquinas himself would view it, while demonstrating the second merely requires drawing on the resources provided by Aquinas to articulate a theory of natural law which Aquinas himself may not necessarily endorse. In any case, Lisska's apparent move to achieve both involves creating a dichotomy between Aquinas' ontology and his theology by focusing on Aquinas' theory of natural kinds:

> Natural law moral theory depending on a theory of natural kinds is a metaphysical issue resolved in Aquinas' ontology, not his theology. Therefore, a consistent account of Aquinas' natural law is independent conceptually of the proposition that God exists.[23]

18 Finnis (n 8) 22.

19 See eg Aquinas (n 3) I Q12 Arts 4–5. See also Section III of this chapter and Chapter 4 for expanded justifications of this claim.

20 McCall (n 7) 428.

21 Finnis (n 8) 25. See eg Aquinas (n 3) I Q12 Arts 4–5. This enabling and enlightening grace is alluded to throughout this chapter, grounded in the theological survey in the previous chapter. The precise nature and mechanism of this grace is set out in more detail in the next chapter.

22 Anthony Lisska, 'God, Aquinas, and Natural Law Theory' in Jonathan Crowe and Constance Lee (eds), *Research Handbook on Natural Law Theory* (Edward Elgar, 2019) 79.

23 Ibid 80.

The theory of natural kinds appeals to a 'human essence' without 'any appeal to eternal law', and therefore the concept of an essence does not require 'any appeal to God's existence'.[24] Lisska considers that structurally in Aquinas, the natural law is not dependent on the eternal law and argues using a *reductio*:

> If the natural law is dependent on the eternal law, then human knowers must be able to know the eternal law. And if the eternal law were understood as the set of Divine Ideas in the Divine Mind, it would follow that humans must directly know God's nature. Everyone knows Aquinas's response to this proposition.[25]

However, Lisska's account of Aquinas is mistaken both conceptually and structurally. Conceptually, Aquinas' ontology is intrinsically and indissolubly linked to his theology. Aquinas is clear that one cannot understand God's nature and human nature without the exercise of divinely enabled reason, without participating in the divine mind through grace.[26] So Aquinas' account of natural law cannot be conceptually independent of God's existence, for the very apprehension of the natural law requires divinely enabled participation in the eternal law (the divine mind), which necessarily entails God's existence. In addition, turning to the question of structure, Lisska is right that Aquinas rejects the proposition that humans can directly know God's nature. But he fails to properly consider the interplay of grace, nature, reason and revelation in Aquinas' structure of natural law. No, humans cannot directly (naturally) know God's nature by (unaided) reason. But through the exercise of divinely enlightened reason, reason and nature enhanced by grace, humans can participate in the eternal law and apprehend aspects of the divine mind and the divine nature – and this apprehension is further clarified by revelation through the divine law.[27] Lisska himself acknowledges that in Aquinas' structure, 'Grace perfects Nature', but fails to consider that the existence of grace entails the existence of God who provides that grace.[28] Therefore, Aquinas' account of natural law is necessarily theological, requiring grace and revelation to enlighten and clarify nature and reason for humans to know God and the natural law. Porter notes for similar reasons that Lisska's analytical reading of Aquinas is limited, and a truly 'Thomistic' theory of natural law should place

24 Ibid 83.
25 Ibid 87–88.
26 See eg Aquinas (n 3) I Q12 Arts 4–5. See also Chapter 4 for an expanded justification for this claim. As Levering summarises, since Aquinas holds that natural law is participation in the eternal law, it is plain he would not endorse the idea of an autonomous natural law independent of theology. Matthew Levering, *Biblical Natural Law: A Theocentric and Teleological Approach* (Oxford University Press, 2008) 17.
27 McCall (n 7) 428–429.
28 Lisska (n 22) 86.

greater emphasis on Aquinas' theological context.[29] A Thomistic approach entails a 'distinctively theological natural law ethic'.[30]

The preceding discussion also implies that if any natural law tradition has a conception of the good, and the good is theologically grounded, that natural law tradition is necessarily taking a theological position. This is especially so with respect to the good of religion, since considering the good of religion involves considering what is good for humans in terms of engagement with the divine, broadly conceived.[31] The following parts bear out this suggestion through analysis of contemporary natural law theories, starting with Finnis, and Section V articulates this idea in more detail, drawing on the analysis in the rest of the chapter. There are two threshold points to address for the purposes of this argument. First, there is a broader theoretical context for the claim that the secular is really theological, which I assume in this chapter. The theology of Radical Orthodoxy holds that the idea of the secular itself is grounded in theological concepts. I have explained and sustained this claim in more detail elsewhere and I draw upon it further in the next chapter.[32] Second, this also implies that as far as any theory takes a position on the good, it is actually taking a theological position. It is then the task of the author to provide more detail justifying such a position and critiquing others by drawing on particular theological traditions. I do this in the previous and subsequent chapters.

III. John Finnis and the Theology of New Natural Law

John Finnis is properly viewed as the founder of modern natural law jurisprudence and one of its leading proponents, continuing to exert a strong influence on the trajectory of natural law theory.[33] Finnis claims that Aquinas considers the natural law to be self-evident, but the existence of God is not self-evident, and that his will cannot be discovered without revelation. Finnis proceeds to arguably articulate a theory of natural law 'without needing to revert to questions of God's existence and will'.[34] He states that according to Aquinas, 'a positive or human law is derived from the natural law by a deductive process', and 'obtains its force from the natural law', which Finnis defines as 'the set of principles of practical reasonableness which order human life and community'.[35] Finnis discusses the origin of the phrase 'natural law',

29 Porter (n 10) 47 (FN 77).

30 Ibid 51.

31 John Finnis, *Natural Law and Natural Rights* (Oxford University Press, 2nd ed, 2011) 89–90.

32 See Alex Deagon, *From Violence to Peace: Theology, Law and Community* (Hart Publishing, 2017).

33 Jonathan Crowe, 'Natural Law Beyond Finnis' (2011) 2(2) *Jurisprudence* 293, 308.

34 John Finnis, *Natural Law and Natural Rights* (Oxford University Press, 1980) 48–49.

35 Ibid 280–281.

emphasising that a primary use of ***natura*** refers to 'practical reason according to human nature'.[36] Hence for Finnis, according to Aquinas, even though the eternal law is from God, human apprehension of the eternal law by the natural law is 'through human reason'.[37]

Specifically, Finnis proposes a set of basic or self-evident goods or values discovered by practical reason which constitute the natural law, or objectively knowable moral principles directed towards facilitating human flourishing. For Finnis, the basic goods required for authentic human flourishing in a legal community are life, knowledge, play, aesthetic experience, sociability (friendship), practical reasonableness and religion.[38] Finnis claims that these basic goods are basic in the sense that they are 'self-evident, obvious. [They] cannot be demonstrated, but equally [they] require no demonstration'.[39] Finnis clarifies in later work:

> My thesis, then, is this: one's primary understanding of human good, and of what it is worthwhile for human beings to seek to do, to get, to have and to be, is attained when one is considering what it would be good, worthwhile to do, to get, to have and to be – i.e., by definition, when one is thinking practically.[40]

This practical thinking is distinct from theoretical thinking in the sense that theoretical thinking is focused on the metaphysical truth of some object based on its nature, though Finnis notes that this distinction is merely operational in the sense that the different ways of thinking have different objectives; there is really only 'one intelligence', and often the practical and theoretical intersect.[41] So there exists a legitimate theoretical investigation of nature which must incorporate practical considerations if the account is to be considered satisfactory. This method of apprehending the good presupposes that the process involves objective judgements about ethics and morality.[42]

In other words, as George puts it:

> Knowledge that comes as the fruit of practical reflection becomes available to (i.e., provides data for) speculative inquiry (e.g., in metaphysics or theology). On the basis of one's practical grasp of the intelligible ends of human acts, one may derive propositions about the nature of human beings. The point is that in the epistemological mode of inquiry, our (practical) knowledge of human good(s) is methodologically prior to our (speculative) knowledge of human nature.[43]

36 Ibid 374–376.
37 Ibid 400.
38 Ibid 85–89.
39 Ibid 64–65.
40 John Finnis, *Fundamentals of Ethics* (Georgetown University Press, 1983) 12.
41 Ibid 10–11.
42 Ibid 20–23.
43 Robert George, 'Recent Criticism of Natural Law Theory' (1988) 55 *University of Chicago Law Review* 1371, 1416.

In the ontological mode, the basic human goods depend on human nature, ultimately connected to God; this does not imply that our knowledge of the goods depends upon prior speculative inquiry.[44] So in effect, Finnis argues that the basic goods are connected ontologically to God but disconnected epistemologically. They may be known by separate moral experience and practical reasoning which may then inform a speculative theological or metaphysical inquiry.

There are at least two criticisms of Finnis' account. The first is the issue of how we know the basic moral goods. Weinreb argues that Finnis' reliance on simply being reasonable in order to inexorably arrive at the basic goods is a 'merely wilful' attempt at sophistry to reach conclusions assumed on other grounds, and will only convince the already committed.[45] The grandiose assertions for the reasonable, objective, self-evident goods of morality are then not followed by the articulation of concrete moral propositions, indicating a discussion at the level of abstraction rather than reality: 'It is not unfair to characterize the typical argument for natural law as a combination of large claims about the objectivity of morality in general and singular reticence about the truth of any concrete moral propositions in particular'.[46] Furthermore, Finnis is simply replicating his own worldview, characterising traditional Catholic views as universal claims of reason. Finnis' goods exhibit his privileged position and deny the experience of marginalised and excluded members of society.[47] Fundamentally, Finnis is critiqued for putting his natural law theory beyond rational dispute by calling his particular 'selection' of goods self-evident; Thomist natural law theory in general is often critiqued in a similar vein for relying on a particularly Catholic morality.[48] It follows that these kinds of notions of the good should not be accepted as objective or universal, and cannot undergird a full natural law.

Boyle contends that Aquinas too believes the first principles of morality to be self-evident and naturally known. However, this does not mean that knowledge of these principles is beyond dispute. Since the notion of self-evidence is predicated upon understanding the terms of the proposition and the

44 Ibid 1416–1417.

45 Lloyd Weinreb, 'The Moral Point of View' in Robert George (ed), *Natural Law, Liberalism, and Morality* (Clarendon Press, 1996) 198–199. I think this objection as expressed is overstated, but it illustrates the problem that even Finnis admits – the basic goods may appear as contrived.

46 Ibid 199–200. But see George (n 43) 1386–1390, where he provides a defense of Finnis to similar objections in other work by Weinreb.

47 Valerie Kerruish, 'Philosophical Retreat: A Criticism of John Finnis' Theory of Natural Law' (1983) 15 *University of Western Australia Law Review* 224, 244. But see Joseph Boyle, 'Natural Law and the Ethics of Traditions' in Robert George (ed), *Natural Law Theory: Contemporary Essays* (Clarendon Press, 1992), where Boyle argues that natural law theory is dependent on moral traditions (such as Catholicism) in some ways, but tradition-independent in others; he claims this can account for moral diversity and does not undermine moral theorising in the natural law context.

48 See eg Stephen Macedo, 'Against the Old Sexual Morality of the New Natural Law' in Robert George (ed), *Natural Law, Liberalism, and Morality* (Clarendon Press, 1996).

connection between the terms, it is possible for the first moral principle or the first principle of natural law to be self-evident without people assenting to its self-evidence or even its truth (though Aquinas holds that the first principles are so easily grasped that they should be self-evident to all, even if people are not conscious of this knowledge and cannot articulate it). Further discussion and argumentation regarding the principle is possible – debate is not precluded because they are self-evident, since self-evident just means they cannot be deduced from more basic truths.[49] As we have seen, Finnis is fundamentally of the view that people with no knowledge of God can still know the basic moral principles which form the natural law through natural reason, even if that knowledge may be distorted or incomplete.[50] Nevertheless, Finnis admits that 'the limitation of natural reasoning . . . leaves somehow subjective and questionable' the objective moral principles apprehended by practical reason.[51] The solution to this impasse is alluded to by Greenawalt – connecting the morality undergirding natural law with the existence of God as a transcendent moral reality or intellect which can be apprehended universally through the exercise of reason.[52]

This leads into the second criticism, which is particularly relevant for this chapter. Some claim that the 'new natural law theory' stated by Finnis (and his oft-collaborator Germain Grisez) is not truly natural law in the Thomist tradition since Grisez and Finnis say that practical reason operates on its own first principles without dependence on antecedent speculative knowledge drawn from metaphysics or theology.[53] For example, Lloyd Weinreb and Jean Porter reject Finnis' interpretation of Aquinas, for according to them Finnis claims that the Thomist natural law theory is not ontological, and is severable

49 Boyle (n 47) 23–25.

50 John Finnis, *Natural Law and Natural Rights* (Oxford University Press, 2nd ed, 2011) 30, 392.

51 Ibid 405.

52 Kent Greenawalt, 'How Persuasive Is Natural Law Theory?' (2000) 75(5) *Notre Dame Law Review* 1647, 1676.

53 George (n 43) 1408–1409. George's article is a full response to this kind of criticism. See also Robert George, 'Natural Law and Human Nature' in Robert George (ed), *Natural Law Theory: Contemporary Essays* (Clarendon Press, 1992). Finnis contends that a full account of nature can only be understood practically. 'Practical Reasonableness' can be called a theory of natural law because practical reasoning's first principles identify the basic goods. See John Finnis, 'Natural Law and Legal Reasoning' in Robert George (ed), *Natural Law Theory: Contemporary Essays* (Clarendon Press, 1992) 135–136. See Douglas Den Uyl and Douglas Rasmussen, 'Ethical Individualism, Natural Law, and the Primacy of Natural Rights' in Ellen Frankel Paul, Fred Miller Jr, and Jeffrey Paul (eds), *Natural Law and Modern Moral Philosophy* (Cambridge University Press, 2001) 47–51 for a general account of the 'new natural law', which sees ethics as a matter of practical reason rather than metaphysics (eg Finnis, Grisez, George) and 'traditional natural law' which sees metaphysics as necessary for ethics (eg Hittinger, McInerny, Veatch). Yet, as I will show, Finnis and the new natural law also necessarily incorporate metaphysics (and theology more specifically). Furthermore, despite these methodological differences, it remains clear that these approaches have a conception of the good, which means they engage in theology.

from Aquinas' context of the eternal law of God. This is to 'radically distort the Thomist framework', and to 'misconceive' the fact that the 'natural law exists on the basis of the eternal law and eternal reason rationally ordering the universe' – in other words, for Weinreb and Porter, Finnis' account of natural law in Aquinas is not theological enough.[54]

Although I am obviously sympathetic to Porter's broader project, her claim that Finnis' account of Thomist natural law is not theological enough is probably overstated. Holistically considered, and despite Finnis' own claims to the contrary, the account provided by Finnis is manifestly theological. The primary difference is in the priority of theology. In particular, where Finnis claims that practical reason precedes speculative reason (and therefore apprehension of speculative truths is unnecessary for natural law reasoning), I argue that apprehension of speculative (metaphysical, theological) truths is necessary for practical reasoning. This solidifies natural law as properly ontological in character. As one pre-Finnis natural law theorist has noted: 'All genuine natural law philosophy . . . must be unreservedly ontological in character . . . the idea of natural law obtains general acceptance only when metaphysics is dominant'.[55] This simultaneously expresses the principle that all natural law is theological, since the metaphysical and the ontological is also theological.

Attempting a middle ground, George suggests that speculative arguments can be useful, not by 'establish[ing] the self-evidence of a self-evident practical truth', but by removing 'a particular doubt about that truth'.[56] They 'may be employed affirmatively in support of a self-evident practical truth, often with persuasive force'.[57] If we consider the natural law claim that the objective moral principles are based in a transcendent morality, the speculative arguments of theology could be useful. A certain amount of speculative knowledge is required for the exercise of moral reasoning and practical judgement, and this speculative knowledge could be that gained from theological argument.[58] But this approach still seems to underplay the metaphysical reliance of practical reasoning on speculative reasoning. As I shall explain, divine guidance through grace and revelation is needed both for a robust ontology of the good and for a proper apprehension of the good. So in this sense both criticisms are correct, but Finnis and the new natural law theory can be redeemed (if one pardons the theological pun) by incorporating speculative reasoning

54 Lloyd Weinreb, *Natural Law and Justice* (Harvard University Press, 1987) 109. See also Jean Porter, *Nature as Reason: A Thomistic Theory of Natural Law* (Eerdmans, 2005) 38–39.

55 AP d'Entreves, cited in Douglas Den Uyl and Douglas Rasmussen, 'Ethical Individualism, Natural Law, and the Primacy of Natural Rights' in Ellen Frankel Paul, Fred Miller Jr, and Jeffrey Paul (eds), *Natural Law and Modern Moral Philosophy* (Cambridge University Press, 2001) 45.

56 George (n 43) 1411.

57 Ibid 1412.

58 Ibid 1413; cf Germain Grisez, Joseph Boyle, and John Finnis, 'Practical Principles, Moral Truth, and Ultimate Ends' (1987) 32(1) *American Journal of Jurisprudence* 99, 109.

and providing a metaphysical grounding for the goods discerned through divinely assisted practical reason.

Porter questions whether practical reason is itself sufficient to generate a moral theory constituting the natural law. Appeals to speculative and metaphysical considerations appear to be necessary.[59] McCall argues that

> theories of law that fail to fully accept the eternal law as a real law and as indispensable to the entire legal system are forced either to reject the natural law altogether or minimise it to such an extent that natural law becomes irrelevant.

McCall cites Finnis and the new natural law theory as an example of the latter.[60] In particular, Finnis' failure to rely on God opens up the criticism of inconsistency, for Finnis relies on theology to save his ethical theory (which grounds his natural law) from relativism while simultaneously rejecting the proposition that God is necessary for his natural law.[61] A more coherent approach is to acknowledge the intrinsically theological nature of natural law by 'placing God at the foundation'.[62] Finnis' dismissal of God also ignores the fact that Aquinas' natural law is informed by revelation and the unity of practical and speculative reason.[63] Indeed, 'Aquinas places eternal law as a real and ontologically necessary law at the very heart of his jurisprudence'.[64] Natural law is consequently theological, and in this sense we can still usefully rely on Finnis and practical reason to articulate the good, bolstered by a robust speculative and metaphysical foundation through theology. But without that foundation, Finnis' discussion is 'free-floating . . . it involves an attempt to build law in thin air'.[65]

The basic goods only become self-evident when practical reason is combined with speculative reason; that is, when they are viewed in the light of philosophical and theological reflection on human nature.[66] 'Contrary to Finnis' claim that Aquinas does not base his understanding of natural law on metaphysical knowledge, Aquinas does found his understanding of natural law on primary philosophical truths concerning the essence of man'.[67] Aquinas' conception of the goods is also 'rooted in a metaphysics of cosmic order and harmony', which Finnis glibly dismisses.[68] While even an atheist like Michael Moore acknowledges that recourse to the divine law is necessary in any theory

59 Porter (n 54) 244.
60 McCall (n 7) 70–71.
61 Ibid 71–73.
62 Ibid 73.
63 Ibid 75.
64 Ibid 77.
65 Ibid 79.
66 Ibid 136, 178.
67 Ibid 137.
68 Ibid 137, 141.

of natural law which countenances the existence of God, Finnis and his ilk deny this; in doing so, they undercut an essential metaphysical foundation for the natural law and remove a significant source of illumination for comprehending its precepts.[69]

Thus, Porter observes that 'reason, like nature, underdetermines the moral conclusions that are supposed to flow from it'.[70] This implies nature and reason require guidance from grace and revelation (divine law), placing a natural law ethic into a theological framework. This is true even of the new natural lawyers, for Porter demonstrates that even the basic goods must be grounded in a metaphysical framework: 'the difficulties raised by the Grisez/Finnis theory of the natural law at least suggest that "pure reason" is no more promising than "pure nature" as a basis for a theory of morality'.[71] In fact, since Finnis' theory of natural law is theological (as I will show in more detail), it is more precisely Finnis' claim that his theory is secular which is problematic. If we see the theory of basic goods as supported by a metaphysical framework, as Finnis seems to do despite his claims, then the difficulties vanish. We can have a set of basic goods arrived at through practical reason, operating in and supported by theological (speculative) truths. A theological account of the natural law consequently recognises, again, that pure reason must be supplemented by revelation and pure nature must be supplemented by grace.

The necessity of theology is borne out in the work of Finnis, who in effect relies on metaphysical and theological assumptions to ground his natural law. According to Crowe, Finnis 'thinks natural law comes directly from God'; 'it expresses aspects . . . of God's creative intention'.[72] This can be seen through Finnis' response to the classic fact/value dilemma or is/ought dichotomy mentioned in Chapter 1. For Finnis, the is/ought dichotomy is not even a problem – the basic goods are beyond demonstration or inference and therefore there is no deduction or inference of values from facts.[73] Finnis considers the consequent objection that there is something 'fishy about appeal to self-evidence', and responds by noting the numerous instances of reliance on non-demonstrable principles such as the rules of logic.[74] In other words, because the principles of theoretical rationality cannot be meaningfully denied without disqualification from the pursuit of knowledge, nor can these principles be demonstrated without reliance on themselves, it follows that these principles are basic or self-evident. Finnis claims that his basic goods are in a similar category.[75]

69 Ibid 209–210.
70 Porter (n 54) 127.
71 Ibid 130–131; see generally 127–131.
72 Jonathan Crowe, *Natural Law and the Nature of Law* (Cambridge University Press, 2019) 3. See eg Finnis (n 50) 389–390.
73 See Finnis (n 34) 66.
74 Ibid 67–68.
75 Ibid 69.

In this context of refuting the claim that norms are being illicitly derived from facts, Finnis has more recently clarified his self-evidence argument by saying that the statement 'the first principles of natural law are not inferred or derived from anything' translates to the first principles of natural law (norms) are not deduced from any prior, more knowable proposition of fact.[76] The basic human goods 'entails an account of human nature' but does not 'presuppose such an account. They are not an attempt to deduce reasons for action from some pre-existing theoretical conception of human nature'.[77] Such a deduction would 'defy the logical truth' that 'a syllogism's conclusion cannot contain what is not in its premises' – specifically, an ought cannot be derived from an is.[78] So Finnis agrees that oughts are always derived from oughts; it is impossible to derive an ought from an is. Grisez, Boyle and Finnis similarly claim that the moral ought cannot be derived from the theoretical is or some metaphysical truth, since moral reasoning is an intrinsically practical process.[79] Moreover, as 'first principles', the 'principles of practical knowledge . . . cannot be derived from any theoretical knowledge. Thus, they cannot be verified by experience or deduced from any more basic truths through a middle term. They are self-evident'.[80] Though they are self-evident, they are not theoretical intuitions. Rather, natural dispositions provide the data which undergirds the insights through which one knows the first moral principles.[81] In saying this, they also acknowledge that theoretical knowledge enhances the initial insights into the substantive goods.[82] This is a clue that Finnis' new natural law theory is more ontological than he realises.

Ultimately, by attempting to avoid the fact-value dilemma, Finnis ignores the ontological fact that nature has rationality because it is the creation of a rational divine mind. The goods in his expression of his theory, then, 'lack metaphysical and epistemological foundations' and are not persuasive to those who do not already agree; Finnis is therefore also constrained by a lack of guidance from the divine law.[83] It follows that theoretical reflection on the existence and nature of a transcendent moral being is necessary prior to apprehending the basic goods which are (as Grisez, Boyle and Finnis hold) ontologically based in that being. Grisez, Boyle and Finnis admit that morality retains its roots in nature since the normative aspect is just the 'integral directiveness' of the principle arrived at through practical reasoning.[84] This directiveness leads to the inference of God's existence and nature in the

76 Finnis (n 50) 439.

77 John Finnis, 'Natural Law and Legal Reasoning' in Robert George (ed), *Natural Law Theory: Contemporary Essays* (Clarendon Press, 1992) 135.

78 Ibid.

79 Grisez et al (n 58) 102, 127.

80 Ibid 106.

81 Ibid 108.

82 Ibid 109.

83 McCall (n 7) 418–419; Hittinger (n 5) 21.

84 Grisez et al (n 58) 127.

ontological sense, and to the consciousness of being divinely enabled and guided in the epistemological sense. In the final analysis, if morality is normatively based in God's nature, then this provides a plausible reason for accepting the moral values stemming from the fact of God's nature. Rather than merely claiming that moral values exist, they have their basis in the least arbitrary and subjective stopping point – the paradigm of moral goodness, or the transcendent moral nature. In essence, one can conclude the fact is also an ought and so the derivation is legitimate to the extent that the moral ought corresponds to the ontological fact of God's moral nature.

Such an approach is not intrinsically inimical to Finnis. The use of arguments for God's existence in a natural law context also occurs in work by Finnis and Grisez; indeed, Finnis has stated that any attempt to ground morality in God requires as a prerequisite arguments for why anything like God exists at all, and arguments for why God might be an appropriate ground.[85] So Finnis acknowledges that his account of natural law necessarily assumes antecedent speculative truth; it is therefore intrinsically ontological and theological. Finnis has not retreated from this position, and in his 2011 postscript to *Natural Law and Natural Rights*, he also acknowledges that his initial statement regarding the limited utility of pure reasoning about the nature of God was perhaps too hasty, and through reflection on Aquinas' purely natural arguments about the nature of God it can be concluded that pure reason can assist in establishing 'a good deal' (epistemologically) about objective moral principles which have their ontological foundation in God.[86] If it is also true that, as Finnis and Grisez state, 'the ultimate moral principle is beyond human reason', then it can only be fully apprehended through participation in divine reason.[87] On this view it seems that apprehending the good is a function of natural reason, which for Aquinas and Finnis is the same as participation in the divine reason and enlightenment through the divine reason, since the good has its source in the divine. The incorporation of theology (which as a function of natural reason is use of the divine reason) in acknowledging the existence of the divine provides the speculative or metaphysical content necessary to apprehend the good.

Finnis states that one can 'gain access to the transcendent source of being, goodness and knowledge' through the exercise of reason, and that the universal ability to access this source is due to the belief that this exercise of reason is naturally (and therefore universally) and inextricably bound with or participation in the divine reason.[88] Thus, when Finnis refers to 'reason', he actually means reason illuminated by revelation, an exercise of nature enabled by grace. According to Finnis, the term 'natural' law and the consequent distinction

85 Finnis (n 50) 378–388; see also Germain Grisez, 'Natural Law, God, Religion and Human Fulfilment' (2001) 46(1) *American Journal of Jurisprudence* 3, 11–14; Germain Grisez, *God? Philosophical Preface to Faith* (St Augustine's Press, 2004).

86 Finnis (n 50) 424–425, 477.

87 Grisez et al (n 58) 126.

88 Finnis (n 34) 392–393.

between 'natural' reason and revelation drawn by some theologians has given 'credence to the supposition that the term "natural" signifies immanence and secularism at the expense of transcendence or the supernatural'.[89] Finnis rejects such a supposition as 'muddled', arguing that what Plato, Aristotle and others mean by nature actually 'implies participation in the divine intellect and divine reason', entailing 'faith in the existence of God'.[90] The 'assertion of objective norms of human flourishing and principles of human reasonableness' then lead to the 'affirmation' of some transcendent source of these, which the philosophers term God.[91] Reason is therefore something God-given, and 'practical reasonableness entails the imitation of God' where practical reason refers to the human reasoning process which considers what would be good for humans to do, have, get and be.[92] Moreover, the 'basic values grasped by practical reason' gain an 'objectivity', 'constancy', and 'impartiality' reinforced by faith in God.[93]

Regarding Aquinas and natural law as divine participation in the eternal law, Finnis argues that for Aquinas, it is 'necessary to postulate an intellect far superior to the human intellect', which has the 'power of understanding without imperfection', 'allows us to reason', and 'activates our individual intelligences through light or illumination'.[94] Aquinas then 'identifies this separate intellect as God', and God's grace is necessary for proper participation in the eternal law by divinely assisted human reason.[95] Finally, according to Finnis, Aquinas concludes that 'every activity of reasoning derives from nature' – which, bearing in mind Finnis' earlier definition of the term nature as participation in the divine, implies nature is enhanced by grace.[96] This basis is logically, if not chronologically, prior to Finnis' articulation of the basic forms of human good, which form the first principles of natural law. As Finnis and others clarify in later work, 'if one believes that unqualified goodness – goodness itself – is found in God, one will regard him as the source of the goodness of all the basic goods'.[97] Any contingent reality points to a transcendent source, and the

89 Ibid 394–395.
90 Ibid.
91 Ibid.
92 M Rhonheimer, 'Practical Reason, Human Nature, and the Epistemology of Ethics: John Finnis's Contribution to the Rediscovery of Aristotelian Ethical Methodology in Aquinas's Moral Philosophy: A Personal Account' (2012) 57 *Villanova Law Review* 873, 879.
93 Finnis (n 34) 397.
94 Ibid 399–400.
95 Ibid.
96 Ibid 401. See also John Finnis, *Natural Law and Natural Rights* (Oxford University Press, 2nd ed, 2011) 30, 378–388, 392–393, 424–425, 477; Germain Grisez, Joseph Boyle, and John Finnis, 'Practical Principles, Moral Truth, and Ultimate Ends' (1987) 32(1) *American Journal of Jurisprudence* 99; Germain Grisez, 'Natural Law, God, Religion and Human Fulfilment' (2001) 46(1) *American Journal of Jurisprudence* 3, 11–14; Germain Grisez, *God? Philosophical Preface to Faith* (St Augustine's Press, 2004); Robert George, 'Natural Law' (2008) 31(1) *Harvard Journal of Law and Public Policy* 171.
97 Germain Grisez, Joseph Boyle, and John Finnis, 'Practical Principles, Moral Truth, and Ultimate Ends' (1987) 32(1) *American Journal of Jurisprudence* 99, 135.

directiveness of practical knowledge is also a contingent reality which points to a transcendent source.[98]

Therefore Finnis, following Aquinas, accepts that even the exercise of practical reason is itself divinely enabled, so that it is ultimately God's grace rather than purely natural reason which allows apprehension of the good. Reason is fully enabled by grace rather than pure nature, and so even in Finnis' framework the natural law remains theological.[99] Natural law is premised on the existence of a transcendent moral reality known as God, and this moral reality is universally accessible through the exercise of reason as participation in the divine. Furthermore, the apprehension of this morality occurs firstly through the act of speculative reasoning, which infers the existence of and participation in the divine intellect before it proceeds to practically articulate the first principles of morality. Importantly, though this involves the exercise of natural or pure reason, any exercise of natural or pure reason assumes divine enlightenment and participation in the divine reason.

The exercise of practical reason based in the divine also reflexively points to the divine. Grisez argues that

> relevant aspects of human nature can become known only by reflecting upon the principles of practical reason and the basic goods to which the principles direct human action, and those principles and goods can be known reflectively only by considering human acts.[100]

The basic goods are apprehended either through theoretical reflection on the human data (acts), or 'by insights that grasp the self-evident truth of the practical principles', which is 'how everyone first comes to know them'.[101] In particular, as people become aware of being guided towards the intelligible goods by practical reason, they also 'become at least dimly aware of the more-than-human source of that guidance'; Grisez proceeds to contend that knowing this source as intelligent, directive and benevolent leads to the conclusion that the source must be the 'creator': God.[102] God guides all human beings by the principles of practical reason.[103] George also alludes to the fact

98 Ibid 141–142.

99 See John Finnis, *Natural Law and Natural Rights* (Oxford University Press, 2nd ed, 2011) 30, 378–388, 392–393, 401, 424–425, 477; Germain Grisez, Joseph Boyle, and John Finnis, 'Practical Principles, Moral Truth, and Ultimate Ends' (1987) 32(1) *American Journal of Jurisprudence* 99; Germain Grisez, 'Natural Law, God, Religion and Human Fulfilment' (2001) 46(1) *American Journal of Jurisprudence* 3, 11–14; Germain Grisez, *God? Philosophical Preface to Faith* (St Augustine's Press, 2004); Robert George, 'Natural Law' (2008) 31(1) *Harvard Journal of Law and Public Policy* 171.

100 Germain Grisez, 'Natural Law, God, Religion and Human Fulfilment' (2001) 46(1) *American Journal of Jurisprudence* 3, 9.

101 Ibid 9–10.

102 Ibid 13–14.

103 Ibid 17. Hence, McCall can argue that since natural law is participation in the eternal law, it is both meaningless and ontologically questionable to conceive of a natural law apart from the divine. The natural law is necessarily theological and has its intrinsic foundation in

that the human capacity to practically reason is a kind of 'sharing' in 'divine power' which makes sense of the theological claim that humans are made in the image of God.[104] Furthermore, our limited God-like capabilities begs the question of whether 'beings capable of such powers could exist apart from a divine source and ground for their being', producing 'openness to' or 'the roots of an argument for' theism.[105] Therefore, many natural law theorists

> believe that the moral order, like every other order in human experience, is what it is because God creates and sustains it as such. In accounting for the intelligibility of the created order, they infer the existence of a free and creative intelligence – a personal God.[106]

Many of these same theorists also believe these moral truths can be apprehended without specific revelation from God (such as that in the Mosaic Law) through the natural human capacity for reason.[107] It is consequently important to distinguish between the specific revelation of moral content by God, and what may be termed the universal revelation of moral reasoning given by God. All people may grasp moral principles without reading it in Scripture (though their apprehension is limited and requires clarification and guidance by the divine law), but the claim here is that the human capacity itself to engage in practical moral reasoning is specifically created and enabled by God, and so in this sense is by grace rather than nature. As such, the epistemological connection between practical reasoning and the first principles of morality requires a theological *a priori* element.

This means the basic goods may be apprehended by (natural) practical reason. However, the existence of the basic goods and the exercise of practical reason to apprehend these goods presuppose the existence of the divine being (ontology) and participation in this being (epistemology). Theology, then, provides the speculative knowledge required to exercise practical reason which may then apprehend the basic goods – all of which is participation in the divine reason and enabled by the divine reason. Both Aquinas and Finnis articulate their theories in the context of universally accessing nature through reason in connection with a transcendent reality conceived broadly as God. Moral reasoning is universally applicable by the very virtue of its connection with the transcendent moral intellect, and moral reasoning is not necessarily limited to Christian believers since grace-enabled nature is universal.

---

the eternal law. Even when people do not acknowledge this foundation, they nevertheless unconsciously participate in it by virtue of exercising their God-given rationality, and may eventually become aware of the divine nature of the process. See McCall (n 7) 168–172, 429.

104 Robert George, 'Natural Law, God and Human Dignity' in George Duke and Robert George (eds), *The Cambridge Companion to Natural Law Jurisprudence* (Cambridge University Press, 2017) 63. Aquinas calls this 'participation'.

105 Ibid 63–64.

106 George (n 99) 180–181.

107 Ibid 181.

This position also addresses the fragile objectivity of Finnis' basic goods. As already noted, and as Anderson summarises, 'one criticism about these self-evident goods is that Finnis is relying not so much on self-evidence as his own intuition', which leaves his articulation of the basic goods 'open to doubt'.[108] However, the exercise of intuition requires an understanding of the concepts involved (such as the presupposition of the law of non-contradiction), which suggests 'some knowledge of the nature of being is required'.[109] Since the goods in question are human goods, 'the belief about what is good presupposes claims about being and about the nature of the being for which it is good. These in turn presuppose claims about the nature of reality and God'.[110] The basic goods 'presuppose God and human nature when understood correctly'.[111] More broadly, it follows that any conception of the good entails theological assumptions. Finnis' apparently flimsy intuition actually presupposes theological claims. The basic goods may or may not be self-evident, but Finnis relies on the intuition of practical reason to arrive at them, and that intuition is actually grounded in a theological ontology. The basic goods are correspondingly more securely grounded in theological and metaphysical tradition. Not only is the good itself then ontologically based in God, but apprehension of the good through reason is divinely enabled.[112] The ability to exercise natural reason is illumined by grace and revelation, and despite Finnis' desire to articulate a natural law apart from God's existence and nature, his natural law is essentially theological.

IV. The Latent Theological Nature of Contemporary Articulations of Natural Law

Subsequent contemporary articulations of natural law are distinct from the theological natural law of Aquinas and Finnis. In particular, thinkers such as Mark Murphy, Michael Moore and Jonathan Crowe take a specifically non-religious (or in Moore's case, explicitly secular) approach, departing from Aquinas and Finnis in terms of relying on religious sources. However, they all continue to affirm the distinguishing features of natural law jurisprudence such as the necessary role of ethics, the central place of a moral basis for legal

108 Owen Anderson, 'Natural Law and Philosophical Presuppositions' in Norman Doe (ed), *Christianity and Natural Law* (Cambridge University Press, 2017) 208. See eg Russell Hittinger, *Critique of the New Natural Law Theory* (University of Notre Dame Press, 2020).

109 Anderson (n 108) 209.

110 Ibid 210.

111 Ibid 211.

112 See John Finnis, *Natural Law and Natural Rights* (Oxford University Press, 2nd ed, 2011) 30, 378–388, 392–393, 401, 424–425, 477; Germain Grisez, Joseph Boyle, and John Finnis, 'Practical Principles, Moral Truth, and Ultimate Ends' (1987) 32(1) *American Journal of Jurisprudence* 99; Germain Grisez, 'Natural Law, God, Religion and Human Fulfilment' (2001) 46(1) *American Journal of Jurisprudence* 3, 11–14; Germain Grisez, *God? Philosophical Preface to Faith* (St Augustine's Press, 2004); Robert George, 'Natural Law' (2008) 31(1) *Harvard Journal of Law and Public Policy* 171.

obligation, and the existence of objective moral values. In this sense, contemporary natural law remains strongly Thomist in methodology and content and is directed by the related work of Finnis. All these authors have conceptions of the good, and Moore and Crowe take actual theological positions which inform their natural law theories. To this extent I argue contemporary natural law therefore retains latent theological dimensions.[113]

McCall observes that 'modern natural law cannot prevail as a compelling system without the philosophical and theological commitments of classical natural law jurisprudence'.[114] However, Murphy rejects the traditional natural law thesis that law's existence conditions must necessarily be linked to substantive merits such as being good, just or reasonable. He provides what he terms a 'plausible' alternative which is a 'distinctive view about law's nature': 'it is essential to law to be the right kind of thing to exhibit certain positive normative features'.[115] For example, Murphy says, if we suppose that 'being backed by decisive reasons for compliance' is a non-defectiveness condition for law, some laws may fail to exhibit this feature.[116] However, it is plausible that 'being the right sort of thing' to be backed by decisive reasons is essential to law and 'it counts as a merit of law' that it is the right sort of thing to be backed by decisive reasons.[117] This means 'law's existence depends on normative facts' and 'law's existence conditions include some merits'.[118] Though Murphy's argument is analytical rather than substantive, it actually has substantive implications. For if we were to substitute 'being good' or 'being just' or 'being reasonable' as a 'first-order normative feature' (rather than using 'being backed by decisive reasons for compliance' as Murphy does – he himself uses the phrases interchangeably), then it follows from Murphy's formulation that his natural law thesis entails the view that law is the right sort of thing to be good, just or reasonable, and it counts as a merit of law that it is the right sort of thing to be good, just or reasonable.[119] This, in my view, is a conception of the good with respect to law, even if in a second-order way. And if Murphy articulates a substantive conception of the good with respect to law, that is a kind of theological claim (as noted earlier, and as explained in more detail in

113 See eg Mark Murphy, *Natural Law in Jurisprudence and Politics* (Cambridge University Press, 2006); Michael Moore, 'Good without God' in Robert George (ed), *Natural Law, Liberalism, and Morality* (Clarendon Press, 1996); Jonathan Crowe, *Natural Law and the Nature of Law* (Cambridge University Press, 2019). I of course do not claim to provide a comprehensive study of all contemporary natural law theories, but I choose these thinkers as broadly representative. Crowe provides a comprehensive catalogue in Jonathan Crowe, 'Natural Law Beyond Finnis' (2011) 2(2) *Jurisprudence* 293, 294–296.

114 McCall (n 7) 3.

115 Mark Murphy, 'Two Unhappy Dilemmas for Natural Law Jurisprudence' in George Duke and Robert George (eds), *The Cambridge Companion to Natural Law Jurisprudence* (Cambridge University Press, 2017) 365–366.

116 Ibid 366.

117 Ibid.

118 Ibid.

119 Ibid 364–365.

Section V). The conclusion that Murphy articulates a conception of the good is also supported by the fact that Murphy has actually developed substantive conceptions of the good in other work.[120]

Moore has articulated what he terms the 'metaethical thesis of natural law', which is that there are 'objective moral truths' independent of God.[121] He acknowledges that traditional natural law theories, and even the modern natural law theory articulated by Finnis, to various degrees rely on objective morality sustained in the existence of God.[122] Consistent with Aquinas and Finnis, Moore defines morality's objectivity as moral realism, ontologically conceptualised as the propositions that moral qualities like the good exist, and their existence does not depend on what any person or group of persons believe about them.[123] However, contrary to Aquinas and Finnis, Moore argues that the existence of God does not strengthen the case for morality's objectivity, and asserts that God is not necessarily good in terms of an ultimate foundation for objective morality. Instead, there can be conceived an objective morality which exists independently of God.[124] He claims that there does not need to be a source for moral laws, making an analogy with scientific laws which are not laid down by scientists, or anyone else.[125] Moore proceeds to suggest that if there is not an analogy between moral and scientific laws in this sense, the Platonic claim that the good 'just exists' is no more 'queer' than the claim that God (who lays down the moral laws) 'just exists'.[126]

Moore candidly admits his presupposition that God does not exist, yet concedes moral realism is the best, scientific explanation of various facets of our common moral experience.[127] Indeed, Moore even contends that the existence of God may be incompatible with objective morality because it assumes the

120 See eg Mark Murphy, 'The Common Good' (2005) 59 *Review of Metaphysics* 133; Mark Murphy, *Natural Law in Jurisprudence and Politics* (Cambridge University Press, 2006). Crowe's caveat that natural law is primarily concerned with law as a rational standard rather than a moral standard can also be understood in this way. See Crowe, *Natural Law* (n 72) 146–148. Viewing law as requiring a rational standard (as either an existence condition or a non-defectiveness condition) entails having a conception of the good with respect to the law: that a law which does not engage human rationality is not a 'good' law. See also Crowe (n 72) 175. This conclusion is similarly supported by Crowe's substantive conception of the good through basic goods and the common good (see Crowe [n 72] chs 2 and 4), as well as his specific statements on the natural law outlook as centrally concerned with the good, which I have noted in more detail in Section V.

121 Michael Moore, 'Natural Law's Relational Thesis' in Ellen Frankel Paul, Fred Miller Jr, and Jeffrey Paul (eds), *Natural Law and Modern Moral Philosophy* (Cambridge University Press, 2001) 115.

122 Michael Moore, 'Good Without God' in Robert George (ed), *Natural Law, Liberalism, and Morality* (Clarendon Press, 1996) 221.

123 Ibid 222.

124 Ibid 224–225.

125 Ibid 229.

126 Ibid 231.

127 Ibid 259–260.

same person-relative structure of moral relativism.[128] In other words, since God is often viewed as personal, and God has particular views about morality, this implies that morality is person-relative and therefore lacks objectivity. In the context of Moore's argument that objective morality does not require the existence of God, Charles Taliaferro considers that Moore's constraint on the definition of God (that is, God is not necessarily or intrinsically good) is stacking the deck in favour of the skeptic. Provisionally allowing this concept of God begs no question, and is in fact necessary to get the argument off the ground since God as the basis and source of the good is the very concept under discussion.[129] Such a notion of the divine also addresses many of Moore's worries about arbitrariness in the sense that on Moore's view, God could will any action as morally good or evil based on a whim, and this is obviously an undesirable state of affairs. However, if we accept that God is essentially good or good by nature, that He is the paradigm of goodness and the highest good, then God would not (indeed cannot) command an evil action as this is impossible by definition.[130]

What Moore does not address is why we should reasonably accept the paramountcy and postulates of morality when it may disadvantage the moral agent (for example, through a paramount moral principle such as charitable *agape* love, the sacrifice of self for the sake of others). This is a serious challenge to the reasonableness of morality, and the existence of some sort of divine order alleviates that challenge. A divine or transcendent source strengthens the stature of objective morality in the face of criticism that its paramount nature is unreasonable.[131] Furthermore, in Moore's position of a world without God, there is no reason to think that there is any intrinsic goodness or morality in a world of brute facts; morality or value is just another one of these facts, a rose by another name. The distinction between personal intrinsic moral value and ordinary factual value is lost.[132] Garcia also specifically addresses Moore's reservations relating to the compatibility between God and objective morality. In particular, Moore presumably sees a problem with making objective or mind-independent morality dependent on God's mind. However, there are important differences between the human mind and God's mind; human minds are mutable, lack knowledge, are imperfectly rational and wise, and may be swayed by illicit or excessive passions. God's mind is subject to no such limitations, and so there is no danger in having objective morality stem from the mind of God. Indeed, this would mean that morality is fixed and determined,

128 Ibid 261.

129 See Charles Taliaferro, 'God's Natural Laws' in Robert George (ed), *Natural Law, Liberalism, and Morality* (Clarendon Press, 1996) 283–284.

130 Ibid 285–286.

131 JLA Garcia, '*"Deus sive Natura"*: Must Natural Lawyers Choose?' in Robert George (ed), *Natural Law, Liberalism, and Morality* (Clarendon Press, 1996) 272–273.

132 Ibid 275.

and universally accessible through reason; it also provides good reasons for believing that morality is of paramount importance.[133]

The fact is that by rejecting God or assuming God is not intrinsically good, Moore has taken a theological position. He also has a conception of the good by virtue of his moral realism, which also entails a theological position. But it is a theological position which lacks robust metaphysical foundations. As alluded to above by Finnis, Grisez and George, the existence of moral goods and the experience of practical reason are powerful reasons for believing in the existence of a God who is the Good, and raise significant questions which Moore's atheistic moral realism cannot adequately address. Thus, there seems to be good reason to think that the existence of some transcendent moral reality such as God strengthens the natural law appeal to objective morality from an ontological perspective. God's existence as the Good explains why objective morality exists, why it is universal, and why its moral content ought to form the basis for natural law.[134]

Like Finnis, Jonathan Crowe's natural law as expressed in his most recent book is ostensibly non-theological. Essentially Crowe argues that while the fundamental principles of natural law do not change as a function of their manifestation in the human social practices which constitute human flourishing, the details of natural law can and do change as the human social practices which constitute human flourishing change in distinct and dynamic historical environments.[135]

So, unlike Finnis, Crowe's alternative approach to natural law is to reject Finnis' view that natural law is outside history. Rather, the natural law is

133 Ibid 276–277.

134 This kind of speculative reasoning regarding God's existence also involves natural theology. It is important to note here that I am not making a positive argument that natural theology provides the only plausible foundation for a natural law ethic. Rather, like Crowe has concluded in his most recent work, I am saying that given the theological nature of natural law, theology adds plausibility to the natural law ethic, and natural theology helps address some of the objections to God as the foundation for objective morality and natural law raised by Moore and others. See Jonathan Crowe, 'Philosophical Challenges and Prospects for Natural Law Foundations of Human Rights' in Tom Angier, Iain Benson, and Mark Retter (eds), *The Cambridge Handbook of Natural Law and Human Rights* (Cambridge University Press, 2022) 485–500; Jonathan Crowe, 'Natural Law with and without God' (2024) 4 *Australian Journal of Law and Religion* 17–33. As Imbert observes, in a theological context of natural law where divine order is associated with a normative dimension, 'an evaluation of the strength and varieties of moral arguments for God would have its legitimate place'. Yannick Imbert, 'Natural Law and Imagination' in Jonathan Crowe and Constance Lee (eds), *Research Handbook on Natural Law Theory* (Edward Elgar, 2019) 281. For further explanation and examples of natural theology, see eg Charles Taliaferro, 'God's Natural Laws' in Robert George (ed), *Natural Law, Liberalism, and Morality* (Clarendon Press, 1996); Alistair McGrath, *The Open Secret: A New Vision for Natural Theology* (Blackwell, 2008); William Lane Craig and JP Moreland (eds), *The Blackwell Companion to Natural Theology* (Blackwell, 2009).

135 See Jonathan Crowe, *Natural Law and the Nature of Law* (Cambridge University Press, 2019) 22–26, 29–30, 93–95.

'objective and normative, but nonetheless socially embodied, historically extended, and dependent on contingent facts about human nature'.[136] We can examine social practices and contingent environmental factors in different historical times and places to discern 'goods and principles that are common to humans as a whole'.[137] Crowe argues such an approach retains a distinctively natural law outlook by virtue of its explanation of why certain forms of human good ('basic goods') promote 'human flourishing and the common good'.[138]

Davies characterises Crowe's natural law as not relying on the existence of God, a 'secular foundation'.[139] Though Davies intends it as a criticism, she notes that 'faith in God often seems to be in the background, even of "secular" natural law theory'.[140] This expresses the standard view that the new natural law is secular; yet, as I have argued here, natural law is in fact grounded in an ethical tradition that is profoundly theological.[141] Davies' criticism is unconsciously insightful, for the point also applies to Crowe's natural law. Crowe's approach is theological because it can be incorporated into Aquinas' traditional natural law as part of an expanded 'divine law' which contains both general revelation about human goods and practices from observation, in conjunction with special revelation with specific divine commands. This metaphor expresses God's double gift of truth as two books – the book of Scripture (special revelation) and the book of nature (general revelation). Since the same good and truthful God is the author of both books, they cannot disagree with each other, assuming both books are properly understood.[142] Truth is a unity. This implies the divine law, as the revelation of God's Truth, encompasses both Scripture and nature.

Hence, even Aquinas is clear that the content of the natural law can change as God adds to it or as humans learn to flourish differently in different environments across history.[143] Porter also observes that Aquinas allows for variability in the particular specifications of the natural law, and even McCall's strongly theological articulation of natural law incorporates concrete human social processes by acknowledging that the natural law is intentionally underdetermined to promote greater rational participation.[144] Neoh sees the theological aspect of Crowe's natural law as entailing the view that 'God and humans are co-creators of natural law. God needs human cooperation, inasmuch as humans need

136 Ibid 6.
137 Ibid 6–7.
138 Ibid 8–9.
139 Margaret Davies, 'The Time, Nature and Place of Natural Law' (2019) 44 *Australasian Journal of Legal Philosophy* 106, 109.
140 Ibid 108.
141 See eg Tim Murphy, 'Natural Law and Natural Justice: A Thomistic Perspective' in Jonathan Crowe and Constance Lee (eds), *Research Handbook on Natural Law Theory* (Edward Elgar, 2019) 318–319.
142 R Blackwell, 'Introduction' in T Campanella (ed), *A Defense of Galileo* (University of Notre Dame Press, 1994) 24–25.
143 Thomas Aquinas, *Summa Theologica* I Q94 Arts 4–5. Crowe does acknowledge this: see Jonathan Crowe, 'Is Natural Law Timeless?' (2021) 33 *Bond Law Review* 1, 6.
144 See eg Porter (n 10) 321; McCall (n 7) 288–292.

divine providence, for the unfolding of natural law in the world'.[145] This seems roughly equivalent to the idea of nature and grace, each necessary but mutually symbiotic, working together to produce and apprehend the forms of good which constitute the natural law. Crowe's approach is therefore also theological in this sense of having a (diachronic) conception of the good.

Crowe admits theological commitments provide the best explanation of and the most plausible foundation for natural law, which entails an admission that theology adds plausibility to his own natural law theory.[146] Crowe explains that theism, including Christian theology, is entirely consistent with his diachronic approach to natural law. It 'seems at least possible that God intends natural law to be progressively shaped and discovered by humans through . . . social and historical processes', and this view is 'not without biblical foundations' in the sense that God's moral law is progressively revealed through the Adamic, Noahic and Mosaic Covenants, culminating in the revelation of Jesus Christ himself as instituting a new law of love, the fulfilment of the law.[147] Crowe does note that his view of natural law could also 'be accepted by someone who does not believe in God', but as I have explained and as Crowe accepts, his theory of natural law fits best within a theological framework.[148]

A theological natural law also satisfies Crowe's requirements that natural law is ontological and that natural law provides a rational standard for conduct.[149] Natural law is ontological because it is grounded in the eternal law, entailing a theological metaphysics; natural law provides a rational standard for conduct because it is ultimately grounded in the divine, which is paradigmatic rationality.[150] The epitome of law is expressed through God's divine law as revealed in Scripture, but also draws on and completes natural inclinations found in creation.[151] In particular, there is a fundamental unity in God's revelation, creation, providence, wisdom and activities. The basic natural law precept of the Golden Rule is also found in the Old and New Testament. There is a 'unity in God's creative and redemptive work', and a 'congruity between creation and revelation'.[152] This further supports the argument that divine law includes both the book of nature and the book of Scripture, and thus Crowe's approach is theological as part of apprehending the divine law.

145 Joshua Neoh, 'Political Natural Law' (2019) 44 *Australasian Journal of Legal Philosophy* 117, 118.
146 See Jonathan Crowe, 'Philosophical Challenges and Prospects for Natural Law Foundations of Human Rights' in Tom Angier, Iain Benson, and Mark Retter (eds), *The Cambridge Handbook of Natural Law and Human Rights* (Cambridge University Press, 2022) 485–500; Jonathan Crowe, 'Natural Law with and without God' (2024) 4 *Australian Journal of Law and Religion* 17–33.
147 Crowe (n 135) 244–245.
148 Ibid 246.
149 See Jonathan Crowe, 'Clarifying the Natural Law Thesis' (2012) 37 *Australian Journal of Legal Philosophy* 159.
150 McCall (n 7) 352–353.
151 Porter (n 10) 50.
152 Ibid 66–67.

Therefore, a similar fate to Finnis awaits the natural law jurisprudence of those such as Moore who are atheistic moral realists. His defense of moral realism 'ends up on shaky metaphysical and epistemological ground', for he cannot explain how and why morality exists.[153] Moore also is more prone to error because he 'cuts himself off from the aid of the divine law'.[154] He ignores the limitations of human rationality imposed due to sin, and therefore ignores necessary 'additional illumination' and 'invaluable aid' through revealed divine law.[155] As Hittinger acknowledges, the divine law is the 'tutor of divine revelation' which makes apprehension of the natural law 'easier and clearer'.[156]

> To avoid ultimate collapse at the theoretical level, defense and exposition of natural law must rest explicitly on an understanding of the foundational role of eternal law and incorporate to some extent the tutorial and corrective role of divine law.[157]

Divine assistance is necessary for both our natural and supernatural ends.[158] George aptly concludes: 'the absence of a divine source of the natural law would be a puzzling thing, just as the absence of a divine source of any and every other intelligible order in human experience would be a puzzling thing'.[159]

V. A General Principle: Natural Law and the Good in Christian Theology

So far, I have mentioned the general proposition that since all natural law has a conception of the good, at least to this extent all natural law is theological. This general principle is exemplified through Murphy, Moore and Crowe as explained earlier: Moore and Crowe take explicit theological positions (while simultaneously articulating conceptions of the good); Murphy, despite his analytical approach, also articulates a substantive conception of the good. To further support the proposition, I will explain how all natural law has a conception of the good (including with respect to religion), and argue the fact that all natural law has a conception of the good – especially with respect to religion – implies that any natural law necessarily takes a theological position. As Hittinger summarises, 'there are no theological claims completely separate from propositions about what is good for human beings and about the moral norms regulating the choice of these goods'.[160]

153 McCall (n 7) 425.
154 Ibid 425; see eg 426–428.
155 Ibid 427.
156 Hittinger (n 5) xx.
157 McCall (n 7) 432.
158 Ibid.
159 Robert George, 'Natural Law' (2008) 31(1) *Harvard Journal of Law and Public Policy* 171, 181.
160 Hittinger (n 5) xv.

Crowe explains that the role of the good 'is a recurring and central theme of the natural law tradition'.[161] There is also broad agreement that 'religion' or 'spirituality' are one of the basic forms of good.[162] Crowe further acknowledges that the 'central question of political philosophy, from a natural law perspective, is how society can best be ordered to serve both the local and the global common good'.[163] Crowe and Lee consider that the 'most distinctive and radical contribution of natural law' is that discussion about rules, rights and interests 'makes little sense . . . without embedding them in discussions of the good'; natural law theory places an 'emphasis' on the 'foundational role of the good in normative discourse'.[164] Crowe and Lee therefore define the 'natural law outlook' as the view that there are 'certain forms of life that are intrinsically good for humans by virtue of their nature', and 'these forms of life play a fundamental role in explaining the purpose of social, political and legal institutions'.[165] The natural law tradition therefore explores 'what constitutes a flourishing human life' through exploring 'the nature of human goods' and how their pursuit shapes human communities.[166] In other words, any natural law theory must have a conception of the good.

Crowe defines the 'natural law outlook' characteristic of the new natural law as consisting of basic incommensurable forms of good, a duty to promote the common good, and understanding law as a rational standard for conduct. Practical reasoning to discern these goods is grounded in human nature.[167] Natural law theory 'explores the deep structure of morality' through the exercise of reason, which directs us to basic human goods essential to genuine human flourishing; recognising 'this deep normative value in any human person's flourishing corresponds to, and presupposes, an ontological foundation'.[168] Similarly, Crowe suggests that Finnis' emphasis on practical reasoning indicates Finnis may see goods as 'grounded' in 'non-natural facts – such as, perhaps, facts about God'.[169] It is 'at least possible that, on his view, the basic goods correspond to human nature . . . due to their respective roles in God's overall plan for human flourishing'.[170] The ontological foundation of the good in God

161 Jonathan Crowe, 'Intelligibility, Practical Reason and the Common Good' in Jonathan Crowe and Constance Lee (eds), *Research Handbook on Natural Law Theory* (Edward Elgar, 2019) 296.

162 Ibid 296–297.

163 Crowe (n 135) 114–115.

164 Jonathan Crowe and Constance Lee, 'The Natural Law Outlook' in Jonathan Crowe and Constance Lee (eds), *Research Handbook on Natural Law Theory* (Edward Elgar, 2019) 2.

165 Ibid.

166 Ibid.

167 Jonathan Crowe, 'Metaphysical Foundations of Natural Law Theories' in George Duke and Robert George (eds), *The Cambridge Companion to Natural Law Jurisprudence* (Cambridge University Press, 2017) 103–104.

168 Gerard Bradley, 'Natural Law Theory and Constitutionalism' in George Duke and Robert George (eds), *The Cambridge Companion to Natural Law Jurisprudence* (Cambridge University Press, 2017) 398.

169 Crowe (n 167) 105.

170 Ibid 112.

is also present in Aquinas himself, for he actually defines law as 'nothing other than an ordinance of reason for the common good, made by the person who has care of the community, and promulgated'.[171] This means

> law that is not in the service of the common good is defective as law. In contemporary terms, the common good has an indispensable explanatory role to play in an adequate natural law characterization of law's existence and defectiveness conditions . . . it is only by understanding the purpose and function of law – the good that it serves – that we are fully able to understand what law is.[172]

And Aquinas perceives that the good of the law, its purpose or its 'proper effect' according to divine providence, is to 'make [people] good'.[173] On this basis, a conception of the good with respect to law, and any conception of the good more broadly, necessarily takes a theological (effectively on a Thomistic spectrum) position. To have a conception of the good is necessarily to make a theological claim about what is good for humans as such. Specifically, if there are certain forms of life that are inherently good for humans, and religion is one (all strands of natural law agree with these propositions), then natural law necessarily takes a position on religion as a good. This means natural law necessarily makes a theological claim. Natural law necessarily cannot be theologically neutral.[174]

Moreover, the natural law is theological in a particularly Christian sense. There must be a natural law to make sense of the Christian claims about sin and redemption, and this means it must be the highest human good for humans to know God. This is evident in special revelation, which also states there is a general revelation of God's nature and the moral law.[175] McCall explains that 'the classical natural law tradition is rooted in a theological perspective'; for Aquinas, 'jurisprudence was firmly rooted in the soil of Christian theology', including the existence of a 'personal God who became incarnate to save mankind and make the contents of divinely promulgated law more clearly and widely known'.[176] Natural law grounded in Christian theology also provides us with a 'revelation' of the divine which is 'personal rather than merely conceptual'.[177] The natural law 'loses its normative force if it is not considered in association with the idea of a higher law that is instituted by a personal

171 Aquinas, *Summa Theologica* I Q90 A4.
172 George Duke, 'The Common Good' in George Duke and Robert George (eds), *The Cambridge Companion to Natural Law Jurisprudence* (Cambridge University Press, 2017) 375.
173 Aquinas, *Summa Theologica* I Q92 A1.
174 See also Alasdair MacIntyre, *After Virtue* (University of Notre Dame Press, 1981) Ch 5.
175 See Anderson (n 108) 205.
176 McCall (n 7) 43.
177 Ibid 46.

Creator'; considerations of God as the essential ground of natural law are 'fundamental'.[178] The natural law also consequently provides

> a basis for God's engagement with humanity through a revealed divine law, and through the redemption made available in Christ. As such, it provides a necessary context for human reception of God's revelation, if only by providing a touchstone for our recognition of ourselves as sinful and of God's law and grace as holy and redeeming.[179]

As George acknowledges, our imperfect human rationality acknowledged by natural law theories is consonant with Christian concepts of sin and fallenness. 'We are prone to making intellectual and moral mistakes and are capable of behaving grossly unreasonably . . . we suffer weakness of will and darkness of intellect . . . we can go wrong'.[180] In this way Porter argues the natural law

> can be treated unproblematically as a Scriptural doctrine, insofar as Scripture provides both a warrant for affirming the existence of the natural law and a theological context in which it is rendered meaningful. The natural law is grounded in creation and represents one aspect of the human reflection of the divine Image; as such it provides both the benchmark for sin and a basis for the hope of restoration.[181]

'The idea of a natural law has long served as a framework within which to draw out the moral implications of centrally important theological doctrines, including the goodness of creation and the status of the human person as a free participant in God's universal providence'.[182] The natural law 'reflects both the distinctiveness of the human creature and our more basic continuity with the rest of God's creation', in the sense that we are rational creatures participating in a unified expression of God's provident wisdom.[183]

Thus, though 'religious and non-religious people can reach conclusions about moral reality' as Charles asserts, it is a misconception that the 'existence of the natural law' is 'independent of faith'.[184] Here Charles conflates epistemological and ontological claims. It is of course true that an atheist can correctly reason on moral matters (although, as I have explained, this is qualified in the sense that moral participation requires grace). But this is a separate question

178 Augusto Zimmermann, 'The Principle of Subsidiarity' in Jonathan Crowe and Constance Lee (eds), *Research Handbook on Natural Law Theory* (Edward Elgar, 2019) 392–393.

179 Porter (n 10) 329. See generally Matthew Levering, *Biblical Natural Law* (Oxford University Press, 2008).

180 George (n 4) 66.

181 Porter (n 10) 4.

182 Ibid 45.

183 Ibid 53.

184 See J Daryl Charles, *Natural Law and Religious Freedom: The Role of Moral First Things in Grounding and Protecting the First Freedom* (Routledge, 2018) 52–53.

from whether the natural law exists independently of God. The ontological claim in this chapter is that natural law is necessarily theological. Charles himself affirms this by saying that God is the 'author of nature', and by rejecting arguments that natural law is 'independent of' or 'autonomous' from Christian theology.[185] In addition, from an epistemological perspective, nature is enhanced by grace, even if we might grant that a non-Christian person is subjectively unaware of that grace operating upon them so they are actually able to grasp the natural law (though, as noted earlier, Grisez considers that a person exercising practical reason may be able to dimly perceive divine guidance as part of that process). So a theological approach to natural law is necessarily a 'properly Christian' approach to natural law, because it entails doctrines of divine knowledge, creation and human nature.[186] The fact that revelation (truth) guides reason, and nature enhances grace to apprehend the good, also means that a Christian Natural Law is associated with truth and the good.

VI. Conclusion

In this chapter I have argued that natural law is necessarily and intrinsically theological. This includes obviously theological natural law theories such as that of Aquinas, ostensibly secular contemporary natural law theories such as those of Finnis, Murphy and Crowe, and explicitly secular contemporary natural law theories such as that of Moore. In particular, these traditional and contemporary theories of natural law rely on theology, especially the existence of a transcendent divine entity who is the paradigm of moral goodness (God). In addition, since all natural law theories have a conception of the good which is most plausibly grounded in God, all natural law theories take a position on the good in this context, and therefore all natural law theories are necessarily theological. Natural law is also theological in a particularly Christian way, placing the essential natural law elements of nature, sin, grace, reason and revelation in a context which makes sense of these concepts and how they operate together. Building on these conclusions is the final step in the process of articulating a Christian Natural Law. As seen in the next chapter, the specific Christian theology of Radical Orthodoxy provides the theoretical foundation for the ontological claim that the natural law is grounded in God, and the epistemological claim that 'natural' human reason is enlightened by grace and guided by divine law to know the natural law. Analysis of the Incarnation as the focal point for the natural law reveals that a Christian Natural Law is constituted by Love, the True and the Good.

185 Ibid 75.

186 Porter (n 10) 65. See also Jean Porter, *Natural Law and Divine Law: Reclaiming the Tradition for a Christian Ethics* (Eerdmans, 1999) 164–177; Jean Porter, 'Natural Law as a Scriptural Concept: Theological Reflections on a Medieval Theme' (2002) 59(2) *Theology Today* 226. Of course, as Porter also notes, a properly Christian approach is not necessarily a uniquely Christian approach. Christianity shares some conceptual overlap with other kinds of theism.

4 Radical Orthodoxy and the Reconciliation of Christian Natural Law

I. Introduction

Chapter 2 established the context for Christian Natural Law, outlining what is meant by natural law in the Christian tradition and surveying a variety of denominational approaches to natural law. Across the Christian tradition of natural law, there is a unifying theological theme of grace enabling nature and revelation illuminating reason. Chapter 3 established the contours of Christian Natural Law in conversation with contemporary theories of natural law, arguing that any account of natural law necessarily has theological presumptions and theological content. In particular, the exercise of natural reason requires enhancement by grace and guidance through revelation.

This chapter establishes the content of Christian Natural Law. It argues that exploring the symbiotic operation of grace, nature, revelation and reason in natural law reveals three foundational theological principles which hold across Christian tradition: Love, the True and the Good. The Christian theological approach of Radical Orthodoxy reconciles these Christian principles regarding natural law as applied to religious freedom because it brings all these ideas under the rubric of a Christian theology with a focus on the Incarnation. The Incarnation is the ultimate revelation of God, an act of divine grace which enables comprehension of the divine through divinely guided and illuminated nature; this also simultaneously reconciles the Protestant and Catholic traditions of natural law. Moreover, the person who has more charity (Love) will see God the more perfectly (True), which will increase one's desire to see God, enhancing participation in the beatific vision (Good). The Incarnation is the theological foundation for natural law and thus entails Love, the True and the Good.

Section II of the chapter overviews the relationship between Radical Orthodoxy and natural law, pointing out its theological substance with the Incarnation as the central event. Section III draws on the analysis of Radical Orthodoxy, focusing on Milbank and Aquinas, to explore the symbiotic operation of grace, nature, reason and revelation in the natural law. In particular, grace enhances a sinful and flawed human nature to apprehend the natural law; yet, the effective operation of grace presupposes and requires the

DOI: 10.4324/9781032620015-5

existence of uniquely human natural capacities. Similarly, revelation guides and illuminates finite human reason impaired by sin; yet, revelation requires reason and is in accordance with reason. This symbiosis culminates in the Incarnation, a divinely gracious and paradoxical act of God revealing Himself in Christ. Section IV considers how the Incarnation establishes and entails three foundational theological principles for Christian Natural Law: Love, True and the Good. As God graciously reveals His perfect Self, so humans can have perfect knowledge of God, and thus humans can perfectly participate in the Beatific Vision, which is perfect happiness. Section V concludes Part I of the book by pointing to Part II of the book, which will explore how these three principles of Christian Natural Law provide a theological foundation for religious freedom.

II. Radical Orthodoxy and Natural Law

To review, in Christianity, natural law is seen as the law implanted in nature by God which rational creatures can perceive through reason. It is not identical to the divine law revealed in Scripture, though aspects of the divine law may also be precepts of natural law, and the divine law guides understanding of the natural law.[1] Through the exercise of reason, the natural law is the rational creature's participation in the eternal law. The eternal law is the divine intellect, the highest reason contained in the mind of God which brings order to the universe. It is the source, origin and measure of human reason and natural law, and contains the rational end of all things.[2]

The preceding chapters have identified a particular common theological theme across the Christian tradition of natural law: grace enables nature, and revelation illuminates reason.[3] As Charles argues, despite differences in emphasis, the 'crucial question is whether human reasoning and human apprehension of basic moral truth are universal, present and operative within human beings by nature'.[4] Across denominational lines, 'the historical Christian tradition, without equivocation, answers affirmatively'.[5] 'Moreover, the mainstream of that tradition holds to the conviction that although moral depravity is actual and pervasive in terms of its scope' (as the Protestants hold), 'it is limited in degree; that is, it neither eradicates our ability to choose the good . . . nor releases us from the sense of moral obligation . . . (the common good)'

1 Norman Doe, 'Natural Law in an Interfaith Context: The Abrahamic Religions' in Norman Doe (ed), *Christianity and Natural Law* (Cambridge University Press, 2017) 202.

2 Bryan McCall, *The Architecture of Law: Rebuilding Law in the Classical Tradition* (University of Notre Dame Press, 2018) 50–51.

3 See also Russell Sandberg, 'Towards a Jurisprudence of Christian Law' in Norman Doe (ed), *Christianity and Natural Law* (Cambridge University Press, 2017) 221.

4 J Daryl Charles, *Natural Law and Religious Freedom: The Role of Moral First Things in Grounding and Protecting the First Freedom* (Routledge, 2018) 66.

5 Ibid 66. See also Doe (n 1) 199–200.

(as the Catholics hold).[6] The presumption that a common morality based on a common 'human nature' is 'somehow autonomous from divine revelation and grace' is 'mistaken'.[7] Thus, the ability of humans to reason is limited in accordance with a nature affected by sin, yet is also enhanced by common grace and guided by divine revelation.

Deploying Radical Orthodoxy to further explore the operation of grace and revelation in this context reveals three foundational theological principles which hold across Christian tradition – Love, the True and the Good – and together these principles constitute what I term a 'Christian Natural Law', and provide a theological foundation for religious freedom. As I shall explore further in Part II of this book, religious freedom is part of the basic good of religion and contributes to the common good, it aims towards the true which is the revelation of God, and it culminates in the locus of the True and the Good – God Himself – who is revealed in the love of Christ expressed through the Incarnation. Charles observes:

> The orders of creation, of which natural law is a part, are part of biblical theology. They do not exist independent of – or separate from – salvation made known through Christ. Both the "creational" and the "salvific" belong to the divine economy . . . and are confessed by [all] Christians creedally.[8]

Radical Orthodoxy reconciles these theological principles comprising Christian Natural Law because it brings them under the rubric of a Christian theology with a focus on the Incarnation. Radical Orthodoxy is a 'confessional', post-secular, public theology which is 'Orthodox' in the sense that it conforms with the historic Christian creeds and 'Radical' in the sense that it critiques secular modernity by returning to the root of Christianity: the Incarnation of Christ.[9] Radical Orthodoxy critiques secular modernity through grounding theology in an incarnational account of revelation, which eliminates the modern distinction between reason and faith. The secular is not neutral and secular reason does not have its own autonomy; rather, theology and faith are the foundation for the proper exercise of reason.[10] John Milbank, a British philosophical theologian, is the most significant influence behind Radical Orthodoxy.[11]

6 Charles (n 4) 66. See also Karen Taliaferro, *The Possibility of Religious Freedom: Early Natural Law and the Abrahamic Faiths* (Cambridge University Press, 2019) 112–115.

7 Charles (n 4) 72.

8 Ibid 66.

9 See generally Alex Deagon, *From Violence to Peace: Theology, Law and Community* (Hart Publishing, 2017) 17–20, where I provide a more detailed overview.

10 James KA Smith, *Introducing Radical Orthodoxy: Mapping a Post-Secular Theology* (Baker, 2004) 35–42, 70–75.

11 See eg John Milbank, *Theology and Social Theory: Beyond Secular Reason* (Blackwell, 2nd ed, 2006); John Milbank, *Beyond Secular Order: The Representation of Being and the Representation*

Milbank contends that faith is actually a presupposition of reason. For if reason is viewed as independent of or autonomous from faith, and reason has no absolute foundations based in faith, then argument between different positions is precluded and pragmatically absurd. Any arguments which seek to go beyond tautology have to 'assume areas of given agreement', and to 'win an argument means to show the contradiction of alternative positions' – outside a 'horizon of shared faith' (or 'common feeling') no arguments would get off the ground.[12] Milbank further argues that any sharp separation of reason and faith is 'dangerous', because it implies that 'faith at its core is non-rational and beyond the reach of argument', while simultaneously implying that 'reason cannot impact on issues of substantive preference'.[13] Milbank consequently proclaims the 'grandeur of reason in its unlimited reach . . . A true metaphysical confidence in reason . . . only enjoys this confidence because it has a *faith* in the infinity of reason beyond our grasp . . . the grandeur of reason is therefore also the nobility of faith'.[14]

Indeed, the separation of faith and reason is a secular modern construct, not a Christian one.[15] As Taliaferro notes, 'it was not until the Enlightenment era that faith and reason were considered inherently opposed, and this strict division has never been established as a real one'.[16] Throughout the history of the Christian faith, its proponents have always seen themselves as simultaneously faithful and reasonable, and have seen their faith and reason as fundamentally intertwined. This is the case across the full array of Christian religious and philosophical traditions, including such luminaries of the church as Saint Augustine, Saint Anselm, Saint Thomas Aquinas, and John Calvin.[17] So in reality, reason and faith are always intertwined in a beneficial way. Reason has to make certain assumptions and trust in the reasonableness of reality. Faith has to continuously think through the coherence of its own intuitions

of the People (Blackwell, 2013). Though Milbank comes from a largely Anglo-Catholic perspective and attempts to distance himself from Reformed theology, J Todd Billings notes important areas of commonality between Milbank's theology of the gift and Calvin's theology of grace. Specifically, both Milbank and Calvin affirm that grace perfects and enhances human nature rather than destroying it, and God's grace is necessary for full human participation in the good. The synergy suggests drawing on the resources of Radical Orthodoxy is fruitful for reconciling Christian Natural Law, as I do in this chapter. One major area of difference is Milbank's lack of specific engagement with Scripture, and I remedy this deficiency by frequent and detailed engagement with Scripture, especially in Chapter 6 of this book. See J Todd Billings, 'John Milbank's Theology of the "Gift" and Calvin's Theology of Grace: A Critical Comparison' (2005) 21(1) *Modern Theology* 87.

12 John Milbank, 'Hume vs Kant: Faith, Reason and Feeling' (2011) 27(2) *Modern Theology* 276, 278.

13 Ibid 277.

14 John Milbank, 'The Grandeur of Reason and the Perversity of Rationalism: Radical Orthodoxy's First Decade' in John Milbank and Simon Oliver (eds), *The Radical Orthodoxy Reader* (Routledge, 2009) 392.

15 Deagon (n 9) 33–34.

16 Taliaferro (n 6) 123.

17 See eg Paul Helm, *Faith and Reason* (Oxford University Press, 1999).

in a process that often modifies these intuitions. Thus, 'critical faith becomes a more reflective mode of feeling', and 'reason has always to some degree to feel its way forward'.[18]

Feeling or affect is critical. At the core of political society, including legal machinations, is 'substantive feeling'; no mere formal reason could motivate humans to action. It follows then that feeling is a 'middle term' between reason and faith, or mediates between reason and faith.[19] To 'define reason quite apart from faith is to place it also quite apart from feeling'; 'by contrast . . . discursiveness is always inextricably bound up with emotions and is never merely austere'.[20] There is an element of feeling, desire and love which consists in faith united with reason, in contrast to a uniform and purely abstract rational reason. The Bible, especially the New Testament, 'resists this advance to pure abstraction by reinvoking the poetic' in a way which seeks a 'positive relationship to the properly vague abstraction of nondogmatic reason' (for example, the wisdom literature and New Testament engagement with Greek philosophy). The proper balance is proclaimed paradoxically in the idea that reason itself (*logos*) becomes Incarnate through Christ; reason thus is more 'realistically rational' as disclosing a 'rational though mysterious universe'.[21] So in the Christian framework, reason is uniquely accessed through faith, and faith involves both the intellect and the affections.

On natural law specifically, Milbank agrees that the natural law of Thomas Aquinas is 'intrinsically theological and transcendent', in contrast with the secular modern law in its being 'positivistic and immanent'.[22] Indeed, Milbank's framework for understanding reality, and consequently for interpreting Aquinas, is that accounts of human life, law and nature must be integrally theological, and this entails the rejection of any recognition of the secular or a 'pure nature' – that is, a nature apart from God's creation and the enlightenment of God's grace.[23] Following the model of Aquinas, 'appeal was made to a natural law of equity rooted in an eternal, divine law', and this to an extent 'provides an escape' from violent coercion by an overwhelming political force.[24] Milbank thus concludes that a way out of the conundrum of coercion 'is through authentic Pauline theology', which 'provides the theological framework for

18 Milbank, *Hume vs Kant* (n 12) 277.
19 Ibid 283.
20 Ibid 284.
21 John Milbank, 'The Double Glory, or Paradox Versus Dialectics: On Not Quite Agreeing with Slavoj Žižek' in Creston Davis (ed), *The Monstrosity of Christ: Paradox or Dialectic?* (MIT Press, 2009) 217–218.
22 John Milbank, 'Paul Against Biopolitics' in J Milbank et al (eds), *Paul's New Moment: Continental Philosophy and the Future of Christian Theology* (Brazos Press, 2010) 24.
23 Cf B Mulcahy, *Aquinas's Notion of Pure Nature and the Christian Integralism of Henri de Lubac: Not Everything Is Grace* (Peter Lang, 2011) 79, 96. As I explain further in Section III, grace and nature are symbiotic for the purposes of natural law. Nature cannot exist and properly function without grace, yet grace presupposes and requires nature. As with all the Christian paradoxes, this is resolved through the Incarnation.
24 Milbank (n 22) 33, 36.

Thomist natural law'.[25] More recently, Milbank has also argued that attempts to ignore the theological foundations of natural law 'inevitably denature it'; so-called secular accounts of natural law are actually 'rival alternative theologies', as I have already discussed in the previous chapter.[26] Hence, natural law is founded upon faith united with reason, the rational creature's participation in the divine intellect enabled by grace.

III. The Symbiotic Operation of Grace, Nature, Reason and Revelation

As can be seen, Milbank fundamentally grounds these arguments in Aquinas.[27] For Aquinas, reason and faith only represent 'different degrees of intensity' of 'participation and divine illumination'.[28] Reason itself requires faith since it 'presupposes the operation of faith', while faith still 'demands discursive argumentation' and is 'higher than reason' only because it 'enjoys a deeper participation in the divine reason', which is 'pure intellect'.[29] In other words, faith and reason are on the same plane and strengthen each other insofar as they take part in the divine intellect – though faith is closer to the divine mind than reason is. So 'good reason' is an 'attentive reception', via the 'mediation of the senses and discursive operations', of the 'divine light of the logos', through faith.[30] The light of revelation 'strengthens our grasp of natural principles'.[31] As Milbank notes, to 'reason truly one must be already illumined by God'.[32] Thus, Aquinas offers no support to those who claim there can be a metaphysical approach to God independent of theology. Rather, revelation supplements natural reason and enables the theoretical ascent to Truth.[33]

The illumination of reason by faith and revelation is also a kind of divine grace which enhances our natural faculties, and Aquinas makes it clear that the distinction between nature and grace is fundamental. As articulated in more detail later, it is grace, rather than nature, which allows in us attainment of the Beatific Vision.[34] More immediately, 'the distinction between nature and

25 Ibid 33.

26 John Milbank, 'A Revisionist Account of Natural Law and Natural Right' (2018) *Church Life Journal*: https://churchlifejournal.nd.edu/articles/a-revisionist-account-of-natural-law-and-natural-right/. See also John Milbank, 'Natural Law: Natural Law and Natural Right Revisited' in Nicholas Aroney and Ian Leigh (eds), *Christianity and Constitutionalism* (Cambridge University Press, 2023).

27 See generally Deagon (n 9) 35–38, 58–61, 167, 171–173, which I variously draw from for the rest of this chapter.

28 John Milbank and Catherine Pickstock, *Truth in Aquinas* (Routledge, 2001) xiii–xiv.

29 Ibid.

30 John Milbank, *The Future of Love: Essays in Political Theology* (Cascade Books, 2009) 323–324.

31 Milbank and Pickstock (n 28) xiii–xiv.

32 John Milbank, 'Knowledge: The Theological Critique of Philosophy in Hamann and Jacobi' in J Milbank et al (eds), *Radical Orthodoxy: A New Theology* (Routledge, 1999) 24.

33 Milbank and Pickstock (n 28) xiii–xiv.

34 Jean Porter, *Nature as Reason: A Thomistic Theory of the Natural Law* (Eerdmans, 2005) 384–385.

grace is likewise fundamental to the Thomistic theory of natural law'.[35] For as Aquinas clearly states:

> To see the essence of God belongs to the created intellect by grace, and not by nature . . . it is impossible for any created intellect to see the essence of God by its own natural power . . . to know self-subsistent being is natural to the divine intellect alone . . . for no creature is its own being but rather has participated being. Therefore the created intellect cannot see the essence of God unless God by his grace unites Himself to the created intellect, as an object made intelligible to it.[36]

Our human intellect and our human ability to discover truth through reason is based purely in God's grace, his gift of participation in the divine being. We cannot see God by our own 'natural' power because to see God is exactly to participate in his being, which is a matter of grace rather than nature. So the grace of God makes Him intelligible to our human intellect so that we can participate in His being. This participation amplifies our already existing (natural) rational powers to properly comprehend the things of God and His creation:

> Our intellect . . . because it is elevated above matter in its own nature, can be raised above its own nature to a higher level by grace . . . now this increase of the intellectual powers is called the illumination of the intellect . . . by this light the blessed are made "deiform" – that is, like to God . . . hence the light of glory cannot be natural to a creature unless the creature has a divine nature, which is impossible. But by this light the rational creature is made deiform.[37]

The nature of this participation is that of an impression or an imprint, a fundamental altering of our natural state to render it aligned with divine nature.[38] As Aquinas says, 'the light of natural reason, whereby we discern what is good and what is evil, which is the function of the natural law, is nothing else than an imprint on us of the divine light'.[39] Thus, by grace, which is the light of participation in God's nature, our intellect is transformed, illuminated to become 'deiform', or like God. By grace we as rational creatures participate in the very divine nature of God, and are able to apprehend the good mediated through the divine intellect. Finnis agrees, stating that our 'power of understanding' is 'our participation in God's practical reason', and 'by this power, we grasp the basic forms of good (and thus the basic principles of the natural law)' – natural reason is 'simply the impress in us of the divine light'.[40]

35 Ibid 385.
36 Thomas Aquinas, *Summa Theologica* I Q12 Art 4.
37 Ibid I Q12 Art 5.
38 McCall (n 2) 83.
39 Aquinas, *Summa* I Q91 Art 2.
40 John Finnis, *Natural Law and Natural Rights* (Oxford University Press, 2nd ed, 2011) 402.

Applying these ideas to the symbiotic operation of nature, grace, revelation and reason in the context of the natural law, the fundamental principle is the distinction between nature and grace is 'theologically indispensable'.[41] Our natural end or purpose is connected to our supernatural end, which is the knowledge of God, and complete knowledge of God can only be enabled by supernatural grace.[42] Aquinas' view of natural law as the participation of the rational creature in God's providence, including God's gracious provision of human nature and the revelation of God's will, implies that divine law is 'at once . . . natural law, insofar as [it] reflect[s] fundamental' and correct 'deliverances of moral reasoning'.[43] That is, the norms of natural law are determined by practical reason, which is in turn informed by the end to which it is directed. And the end toward which human reason is directed is grounded in God's will and wisdom, or divine revelation.[44] As such, even a person exercising their natural reason without acknowledging God 'is participating, albeit unconsciously, in the eternal law'.[45]

Similarly, Taliaferro points out that revelation does not simply obviate natural law, nor is natural law superior to God's revelation. Rather, natural law properly understood in its theological context works with natural reason under the guidance of the divine law, in accordance with philosophical teleology.[46] Specifically, the revelation of Christianity builds on natural reason, fulfilling it and enlarging it. Natural reason is itself a grace, a gift of God which grace further enhances with revelation.[47] Importantly, natural law is not a substitute for grace and is not salvific. Grace is required to reconcile us to God and to make us know and do moral good. Common grace enables us to know and do good imperfectly, even outside of knowing and trusting God. For Christians too, natural law is necessary to remind Christians of what they ought to do. Fundamentally, following Aquinas, natural law is our participation in God's eternal law, and therefore entails recognition of God as the divine lawgiver.[48]

Human sinfulness impairs but does not totally vitiate our ability to perceive the natural law. More specifically, Levering notes that 'while all human beings know the natural law at least to some degree, explanations of the character and content of the natural law are greatly assisted by faith, and thus also by biblical revelation'.[49] Natural law is operative in all human beings who possess reason by virtue of the 'divine imprint bestowed in creation', though it is

41 Porter (n 34) 52.
42 McCall (n 2) 133–134.
43 Porter (n 34) 265–267.
44 Ibid 49–50.
45 McCall (n 2) 170.
46 Taliaferro (n 6) 62, 81, 103.
47 Ibid 112–114.
48 Doe (n 1) 200–201.
49 Matthew Levering, *Biblical Natural Law: A Theocentric and Teleological Approach* (Oxford University Press, 2008) 4.

impaired by sin.[50] Due to failures of human reason because of sin, a 'theologically neutered' approach to natural law will result in 'erroneous conclusions'; constructing natural law 'without recourse to divine revelation is analogous to building an edifice without consulting an architect'.[51] There are 'epistemological problems inherent in unaided natural law jurisprudence'.[52] Human reason therefore depends on divine wisdom, and divine revelation is the only effective means for perfect knowledge of moral truth.[53] As Aquinas summarises:

> Human reason cannot have a full participation of the dictate of the Divine Reason, but according to its own mode, and imperfectly. Consequently, as on the part of the speculative reason, by a natural participation of the Divine Wisdom, there is in us the knowledge of certain general principles, but not proper knowledge of each single truth, such as that contained in the Divine Wisdom.[54]

Sin and the Fall have had noetic effects on reason. They have caused a 'wounding of human nature' passed to every person, and further individual sin by each person has further diminished the faculty of reason.[55] This is the most significant cause of human limitation and conflict over the content of natural law. People 'have been participating in the eternal law with a great handicap caused by the effect of sin. There is a shadow obscuring the light cast from the eternal law on the mind', which means humans need guidance and direction in understanding the natural law.[56] People are not creatures of perfect reason. Our reason is affected by our illicit passions, which creates an obstacle to participation in the eternal law – both in the sense of understanding the precepts of natural law, and in the sense of applying those precepts through particular determinations.[57] So human rationality has been 'distorted by human weakness and original sin, and for that reason our attempts to formulate the natural law stand in need of correction and completion'.[58] McCall notes that Aquinas argues

> it is impossible for people to attain perfect natural goodness, embodied in the natural end of the natural law, as a result of this wounding of nature after the Fall . . . Man would appear to have an intractable problem: he is obligated to [obey] the natural law and ignorance of it is not

50 Ibid 14.
51 McCall (n 2) 44–45.
52 Ibid 46–47.
53 Ibid 172.
54 Aquinas, *Summa* I Q92 Art 1.
55 McCall (n 2) 116. For example, in 1 Timothy 4:2, Paul refers to a 'seared conscience', implying that repeated sin further damages the conscience and affects its ability to perceive the good.
56 McCall (n 2) 117.
57 Ibid 181–183.
58 Porter (n 34) 267.

an excuse; yet, he seems hopelessly incapable of overcoming ignorance of general and detailed principles of natural law.[59]

God, in His grace, has provided a means of overcoming ignorance of the natural law. The method of correction and completion is through God's revelation in Scripture, or the divine law.[60] As Aquinas puts it, 'it was necessary for man to be redirected to the works of virtue and turned away from vice, for which reasons the law of the scriptures was necessary'.[61] Due to sin, there is a 'need for the revelation of the divine law to support and sustain a natural law doctrine adequate to the divine Good that draws and fulfils the human creature'; this 'illuminative aid of divine revelation' is an act of grace.[62] Natural law loses much 'of its effective power when dissociated from the matrix of grace and revelation'.[63] McCall agrees that the divine law is necessary to correct errors in natural reason.[64] Sin has impaired reason and humans need guidance and illumination to apprehend and practice the natural law. This guidance is provided through the divine law, or the law of the Scriptures contained in the Old and New Testaments. The divine law encompasses all the natural law, and indeed is a more perfect participation in the eternal law since it is the perfect revelation of God's will, unsullied by flawed human reason.[65]

As Romans 2:14–15 shows, the existence of natural law is also confirmed by revelation. However, natural reason provides a limited and incomplete understanding of God and the natural law; revelation through Scripture is necessary for a full and complete theological picture.[66] Thus, 'the natural law cannot be rightly understood apart from Scripture, which itself establishes a central place for natural law in Christian ethical reflection'.[67] It is true that of the 'substantive moral implications' of the natural law, 'some' are 'generally available to human reason', but 'many others only become apparent from the perspective of revelation'.[68] So how is it that 'knowledge of the natural law' need not 'depend on revelation', yet revelation is necessary to understand the natural law?[69] As the preceding analysis has suggested, comprehensive and cor-

59 McCall (n 2) 183.
60 See Russell Hittinger, *The First Grace: Rediscovering the Natural Law in a Post-Christian World* (ISI, 2003) 24–32.
61 Aquinas, Prologue, *De Duobus Praeceptis Caritatis*, cited in McCall (n 2) 192 (author's translation).
62 Levering (n 49) 16.
63 Ibid 16.
64 McCall (n 2) 176–177.
65 Ibid 193–195. See generally ibid 195–210.
66 Porter (n 34) 327–328.
67 Ibid 332, see also 346. For example, as Porter (392) points out, understanding what it means to love one's neighbour requires reflection on distinctively theological claims contained in Scripture. Furthermore, the operation of grace perfects the theological virtues such as love, allowing them to reach their proper fulfilment (Porter 389).
68 Ibid 326.
69 Ibid 327.

rect knowledge of the natural law requires divine illumination. Pure reason through nature can apprehend limited and partial truth, but the full and perfect truth requires revelation and grace.

Theologically then, a 'rationalistic interpretation of the natural law turns out to be grounded in Scripture, and correlatively, the divine law revealed in Scripture is said to be congruent with natural reason'.[70] This is not contradictory, but rather recognises the symbiotic interplay of nature, grace, revelation and reason. Nature and reason enable limited and flawed apprehension of the natural law, but are enhanced and clarified by revelation and grace. Doe summarises: our use of reason to perceive natural law

> is not infallible but subject to the vicissitudes of human nature, the circumstances of time and place, and the capacity of humans not to act as God intended. For this reason and for the benefit of humans to enjoy the right relationship with God which He intended, God graciously willed revelation.[71]

As already noted, revelation comprises the divine law contained in Scripture to improve human understanding of the good. Though reason is flawed, the divine law does not destroy it or make it redundant. Reason can and should be drawn upon to interpret the divine law contained in Scripture for evaluation and formulation of moral principles. 'Reason and revelation, then, are modes by which God communicated the divine law for the flourishing of humankind . . . the light of revelation clarifies what human reason imperfectly apprehends as the will of God'.[72] The relationship is symbiotic. Reason is the servant of revelation; revelation guides reason and reason should not be relied on without revelation. Yet moral norms formulated through the divine law should also be in accordance with reason.[73]

Similarly, the relationship between nature and grace is also symbiotic. In Aquinas, 'grace perfects nature', revelation guides reason, and nature is not less reasonable than grace.[74] Aquinas explicitly says 'grace presupposes nature'.[75] That is, the operation of grace presupposes uniquely human natural capacities for rationality, love and goodness. As Porter quips, 'it is not even thinkable that God could bestow charity or the Beatific Vision on a cat'.[76] The natural law, then, can be identified in its most fundamental sense with the *Imago Dei*, as illustrated in Romans 2:14–15 where Paul states the Gentiles know the

70 Ibid 16.
71 Doe (n 1) 203.
72 Ibid 203.
73 Ibid. For a detailed articulation of this dialectic in Aquinas, see William Brewbaker, 'The Bible as a Law Book? Thomas Aquinas on the Juridical Uses of Scripture' (2010) 12 *Rutgers Journal of Law and Religion* 76.
74 Porter (n 34) 389.
75 Aquinas, *Summa* I Q99 Art 2.
76 Porter (n 34) 393.

moral law by nature.[77] Yet nature also needs grace. The divine law 'elevates natural ability to a higher plane'; it is a form of divine grace which reveals principles necessary to attain 'supernatural beatitude'.[78]

Revelation consequently is 'just a higher measure of illumination', which is 'conjoined' intrinsically and inextricably with a 'created event which symbolically discloses that transcendent reality', and to which 'all created events to a lesser degree point'.[79] This 'created event' is the Incarnation, crucifixion and resurrection of Jesus Christ, the God-man. There can be no separation of reason and revelation, for 'true reason anticipates revelation' in the sense that a reason illumined by faith will always point toward revelation – the arrival of true reason in the event of Christ the Word.[80] As reason aims towards the True, it is enhanced and guided by revelation, which is just the Incarnation of Christ. Aquinas' theory of natural law 'is paradoxical because it straddles these divisions' between reason and revelation, nature and grace, 'affirming both that the natural law reflects universal aspects of human existence' that can be apprehended in some way by all, 'and that it can only be fully understood in theological terms'.[81] This is because the centre of theology is the Incarnational Event, and in Christ Himself is 'both paradox and its resolution' – born and eternal, flesh and spirit, divine and human; 'paradox was both expected and resolvable because of the person of Christ'.[82]

John Milbank frames this phenomenon as 'incarnational paradox'. He deconstructs the word 'paradox' etymologically and describes it as an 'overwhelming' or 'double glory (*para-doxa*)' which is a 'coincidence of opposites' somehow mysteriously persisted with that 'saturates our everyday reality'; it can be described as the 'analogical' and the 'constitutively relational'.[83] Such a coincidence of opposites occurs in the Incarnation, the event of Christ where man and God are united, and where infinite meets finite and temporal meets eternal. For Christ is the transcendent and the immanent, the one in whom divinity and humanity is united forever, who is the only mediator between God and man, and who dies in order to live.[84] Milbank contends that this is the moment of true theology, and so all philosophy and reason must be framed in terms of this event.[85] In this way, the grounding of natural law in its full theological context plays a providential role. It provides a basis for 'God's engagement with humanity through a revealed divine law and through

77 Ibid.
78 McCall (n 2) 196.
79 Milbank (n 32) 24.
80 Ibid.
81 Porter (n 34) 324.
82 Taliaferro (n 6) 125.
83 John Milbank, 'The Double Glory, or Paradox Versus Dialectics: On Not Quite Agreeing with Slavoj Žižek' in Creston Davis (ed), *The Monstrosity of Christ: Paradox or Dialectic?* (MIT Press, 2009) 163.
84 John 8:58; 1 Timothy 2:5.
85 John Milbank, *Theology and Social Theory: Beyond Secular Reason* (Blackwell, 1990) xxv.

the redemption made available in Christ' and 'a necessary context for human reception of God's revelation . . . by providing a touchstone for our recognition of ourselves as sinful and of God's law and grace as holy and redeeming'.[86]

IV. The Three Principles of Christian Natural Law: Love, the True and the Good

It follows that a 'Christian Natural Law' must be understood through an Incarnational account. Our natural knowledge of reality, expressed as 'truth', is predicated on the fact that this reality is created by God and our understanding of it is on the basis of participating in what 'is': the divine Being.[87] The True is ultimately revealed through the Incarnation of Christ, the display of the divine Being. This Incarnational account of truth also allows a movement from natural or immanent knowledge towards engaging in the quest of comprehending and replicating the divine nature of love. True knowledge does not merely seek purpose and fulfilment in discovering the nature of physical reality, but ultimately reaches for the 'beatific vision', the nature of divine reality.[88] Truth is not just the pursuit of knowledge (in the pure or abstract sense), but reveals the Good and Love through seeing God. As Aquinas argues:

> The faculty of seeing God . . . does not belong to the created intellect naturally, but is given to it by the light of glory, which establishes the intellect in a kind of deiformity . . . Hence the intellect which participates in more of the light of glory will see God the more perfectly. And he will have a fuller participation of the light of glory who has more charity, because where there is the greater charity, there is the more desire, and desire in a certain way makes the one desiring apt and prepared to see the thing desired. Hence he who possesses the more charity will see God the more perfectly, and will be the more beatified [happy/blessed].[89]

In other words, charity or love is available only through revelation, the grace of God revealing His glorious self. The person who has more charity (Love) will see God the more perfectly (True) and will increase one's desire to see God, enhancing participation in the beatific vision (Good). Thus, according to Milbank, for Aquinas, fulfilling the natural law means ultimately 'to contemplate the truth . . . which . . . means . . . to seek unity with God in the beatific vision'.[90]

Levering also argues that for Aquinas, natural law as the participation in God's eternal law 'characterize[s] the graced fulfilment of natural law in

86 Porter (n 34) 328–329.
87 See Milbank and Pickstock (n 28) 19–20.
88 Ibid 37.
89 Aquinas, *Summa* I Q12 Art 6.
90 John Milbank, 'The History of Natural Law' (2018) *Church Life Journal*: https://churchlifejournal.nd.edu/articles/the-history-of-natural-law/

supernatural charity witnessed to in divine revelation. The synthesis of nature and grace exists in the eternal law'.[91] That is, divine grace is perfectly united with nature in the eternal law, the divine mind, which is the perfect fulfilment of supernatural charity (love). Grace and nature produce love in accordance with divine revelation. Grace

> both heals and perfects the natural capacities of human nature . . . this understanding of human nature . . . grounds natural law in the Trinitarian creative act . . . when turned inward towards the creature rather than outward towards the divine source and goal, natural law is deformed.[92]

Natural law, then, from a theological perspective, is fundamentally about reconciliation with God.[93] Aquinas' location of the natural law 'within the more general context of the eternal law' underscores the natural law as 'the rational creature's way of attaining the final end . . . union with God'.[94] This final end and perfection of the rational creature's natural inclinations is also an account of 'happiness', implying that happiness is necessarily found in union with God.[95]

Porter provides further support for the view that the end of natural law is contemplation of the Beatific Vision, which is perfect happiness and perfect good only available by grace. Porter argues that for Aquinas, happiness 'is the attainment of the Vision of God [Beatific Vision], which he regards as providing the fullest possible satisfaction of the human creature's capacities for knowledge and love', and is attained through divine grace.[96] As Aquinas explains, 'Man's perfect happiness . . . consists in the vision of the Divine Essence. Now the vision of God's Essence surpasses the nature' of man, and 'consequently' man cannot 'attain final happiness by his natural powers'.[97] God is the ultimate good, and final and perfect happiness consists in the direct and immediate contemplation of God, the knowledge of God, which is only attainable through divine grace.[98] God's grace is continuous with his goodness, and his grace and goodness culminate in the Beatific Vision.[99]

To reiterate, for Aquinas, since the natural law is the 'rational creature's distinctive mode of participating in God's providence', this 'implies the natural law is intrinsically oriented . . . toward the attainment of the agent's final

91 Levering (n 49) 3.
92 Ibid 12.
93 Ibid 13.
94 Porter (n 34) 321–322.
95 Ibid 322.
96 Ibid 379.
97 Aquinas, *Summa* I Q5 Art 5.
98 McCall (n 2) 173.
99 Porter (n 34) 388.

end'.[100] And the final end of the agent is happiness, which is beholding the beatific vision, or knowing God.[101] Happiness is the ultimate perfection of the intellectual nature, and the final end or purpose of life is communion with God. It follows therefore that the beatific vision meets the definition of happiness.[102] The only true good that can be associated with objective happiness is God, and this infinite good is obtained through perfect contemplation or knowledge of God.[103]

There is consequently a link between happiness, the Good and the Beautiful. The greatest happiness is experienced through the greatest Good, which is beholding and participating in the beatific vision. This also entails a link to the basic good of aesthetic experience mentioned by John Finnis. Finnis, unfortunately, provides scant exposition of the good of aesthetic experience. The entirety of his treatment in the 1980 version of *Natural Law and Natural Rights* is limited to a short paragraph:

> The fourth basic component in our flourishing is aesthetic experience. Many forms of play, such as dance or song or football, are the matrix or occasion of aesthetic experience. But beauty is not an indispensable element of play. Moreover, beautiful form can be found and enjoyed in nature. Aesthetic experience, unlike play, need not involve an action of one's own; what is sought after and valued for its own sake may simply be the beautiful form 'outside' one, and the 'inner' experience of appreciating its beauty. But often enough the valued experience is found in the creation and/or active appreciation of some *work* of significant and satisfying form.[104]

Writing with collaborators in 1987, Finnis clarifies that aesthetic experience is actually a form of the good of knowledge: 'as rational, human persons can know reality and appreciate beauty and whatever intensely engages their capacities to know and to feel. Knowledge and aesthetic experience are another category of basic good'.[105] Finnis confirms this move in the 2011 second edition of *Natural Law and Natural Rights*, observing that knowledge 'includes aesthetic appreciation of reality' and 'aesthetic appreciation [is] a kind of knowledge'.[106] Regardless of whether aesthetic experience is a distinct good or not, what is relevant here is the way it connects the Good and the Beautiful in a theological context. In particular, aesthetic experience is an active knowledge

100 Ibid 175.
101 Ibid 155–158, 166.
102 Ibid 156.
103 Ibid 166.
104 John Finnis, *Natural Law and Natural Rights* (Oxford University Press, 2nd ed, 2011) 87–88, author's emphasis.
105 Germain Grisez, Joseph Boyle, and John Finnis, 'Practical Principles, Moral Truth, and Ultimate Ends' (1987) 32(1) *American Journal of Jurisprudence* 99, 107.
106 Finnis (n 104) 448.

which 'involves contemplating and responding to the aesthetic properties of the object, such as its beauty'.[107] Both Aquinas and Finnis, then, consider that aesthetic experience is an appropriate response to beauty, and this response is pleasure or happiness.[108]

This is further support for the connection between Love, the True and the Good. As a person is more charitable or loving, they will see God more perfectly. Seeing God more perfectly is true knowledge, which is also participation in the beatific vision. And participation in the beatific vision is the pinnacle of aesthetic experience, the contemplation of perfect beauty. The necessary response to perfect beauty is perfect happiness or pleasure: that is, perfect good. McCall frames the argument as a syllogism:

> If God is by definition the perfection of truth, we are obligated by nature to love (desire) God as the perfection of truth . . . Man ought to do good and avoid evil. A rational being is inclined (or suited) to acquire knowledge, the possession in the intellect of truth. Knowledge of truth is good for a rational creature. God is the complete perfection of truth. Therefore, man is obligated to desire (love) God.[109]

Furthermore, Love, True and Good are all connected explicitly through the Incarnation. The eternal law is the divine intellect or *ratio*, the divine will and wisdom, and divine Truth. It is also directed to the Good of all. It is eternal yet promulgated in creation through the Incarnation, the Word in Creation: Jesus Christ, the *logos* and the ultimate being and action of Love.[110] As I have explained elsewhere, the revelation of God through the Incarnational event should be understood in its aesthetic and affective as well as its logical and ethical dimensions.[111] It is an event which displays the beautiful and evokes the affections, especially love. In particular, as alluded to earlier, Milbank places emphasis on the imagination and the 'poetic moment', which is the 'realisation or manifestation of the Beautiful', an integral part of our 'poetic existence in Christ'.[112] This metaphysics of the person points the way to 'understanding humanity as fundamentally poetic being', which is fully participated in through the revelation of Beauty in the Trinitarian relations.[113] 'Poetic existence can then be described as a fundamental [Christian] activity and as a fundamental

107 Michael Spicher, 'The Distinct Basic Good of Aesthetic Experience and Its Political Import' (2013) 87 *American Catholic Philosophical Quarterly* 711, 712.
108 Ibid 720.
109 McCall (n 2) 150. See also Aquinas, *Summa* I Q 16 Art 5, where Aquinas states clearly that God is Truth, and the perfection of truth.
110 McCall (n 2) 55–58. See also McCall (n 2) 232 where he states that the eternal law is the source of truth.
111 See Deagon (n 9) 39–40.
112 John Milbank, *The Word Made Strange: Theology, Language, Culture* (Blackwell, 1997) 123.
113 Ibid 124.

mode of knowledge'.[114] Ultimately then, charity (love) or 'doing good', requires a 'free, gratuitous response to God's free gratuitous gift' as something beyond boundaries or precedents, something 'creative' – and this requires an engagement with the poetic and a 'discovery of true poetic bounds of possibility' – ultimately modelled by the love of the Trinity God displayed in the Incarnation of Christ.[115]

Hendrianto also affirms this argument.[116] He notes that 'there exists an interconnection between love and happiness, in which God is the ultimate object of happiness, and the attainment of happiness involves both sensitive and rational love'.[117] For Hendrianto, our love for God is both affective and rational, grounded in knowledge of God and His grace.[118] Perfect knowledge of God, or Truth, results in perfect happiness, which is the Good. As Aquinas points out, 'the intellect needs to reach the very Essence of the First Cause [God] to reach the perfect happiness', and the 'highest object' of the intellect is the 'Divine Good'.[119] Furthermore, one of the purposes of revelation, the divine law, is to direct humans towards their proper supernatural purpose, which is obtaining happiness through loving God and loving one's neighbour.[120] Aquinas therefore equates perfect happiness to the Good, and the Good is knowledge of God, which is Truth. And the knowledge of Truth, which is the Good, is both made possible by and produces divine Love.

Crowe summarises that it is 'plausible' to view the good as unified in the sense that 'the only basic good is love, understood as radical and unconditional openness to flourishing in both oneself and others', with the other basic goods representing its various aspects.[121] This further demonstrates the unity of love and the good. McCall also points out that the good is intrinsically related to being. The common good is 'objectively oriented' to the Good; to be good means to 'partake of the attribute of goodness', which is a transcendental relation 'to the same universal' good, 'indeed to God'.[122] In this sense the basic goods and the common good are ultimately apprehended and realised through participation in the divine: God as the ultimate Good or *summum bonum*.

Accepting that natural law has its ontological origin in and revelation by the mind of God will therefore result in greater and more accurate knowledge and

114 Ibid 129.
115 Ibid 134.
116 Stefanus Hendrianto, 'Aquinas on Law, Love and Happiness' in Zachary Calo, Joshua Neoh and Keith Thompson (eds), *Christianity, Ethics and the Law: The Concept of Love in Christian Legal Thought* (Routledge, 2023) 130.
117 Ibid 130.
118 Ibid 133–134.
119 Thomas Aquinas, *Summa Theologica* vol II, Q3 Arts 5, 8.
120 Hendrianto (n 116) 139–140.
121 Jonathan Crowe, *Natural Law and the Nature of Law* (Cambridge University Press, 2019) 56.
122 McCall (n 2) 31, 300.

practice of the good. Where secular versions of natural law aim to explain via patterns, Christianity explains the world via a 'person'; 'the revelation of the three divine persons within God makes philosophy, and hence law, personal rather than merely conceptual'.[123] The Beatific Vision is the full knowledge of God in His personal and Trinitarian reality, including the Incarnation, and 'because God is supremely intelligible and good, and the source of every other kind of intelligibility and goodness, the Vision represents the fullest possible satisfaction' of the intellect and affections, perfect knowledge (Truth) and perfect happiness (Good).[124] And this knowledge is 'unequivocally' beyond our natural knowledge, and cannot be attained unless 'God bestows new principles of knowledge and love in the created intellect'.[125] That is, the perfect knowledge of the Beatific Vision is only by 'grace'.[126] Similarly,

> the love of God stemming from the direct knowledge of God comprising the Vision is spontaneous and all-encompassing. Just as God is the supremely intelligible reality which satisfies the created intellect, so God is the supremely loveable desideratum which fulfils every desire . . . God is supremely loveable because supremely intelligible.[127]

Since this vision 'only comes by grace', natural law is linked with divine law, 'which gives a deeper degree of participation in the eternal law of God . . . to imagine that one could fulfil the natural law without the aid of grace would be to fall into the heresy of the Pelagians'.[128] We can discern the natural law through the exercise of reason, but reason 'can only be perfected by the counsel which is the gift of the Holy Spirit'.[129] Indeed, for Aquinas, in the final analysis 'the proper exercise of the natural law is dependent on the Incarnation' because the Incarnation of the *Logos*, 'who is also *Nomos* himself', is the ultimate act of grace.[130] And this gracious act of love by God (*Agape*) enables the revelation of God, perfect Truth (*Aletheia*), which produces the perfect Good (*Bona*) of perfect happiness.

V. Conclusion

As such, the Incarnation is the ultimate revelation of God, an act of divine grace, which enables comprehension of the divine (consistent with the Protestants) through divinely guided and illuminated nature (consistent with the

123 Ibid 46.
124 Porter (n 34) 381.
125 Ibid.
126 Ibid 383.
127 Ibid 382–383.
128 John Milbank, 'The History of Natural Law' (2018) *Church Life Journal*: https://churchlifejournal.nd.edu/articles/the-history-of-natural-law/
129 Ibid.
130 Ibid.

Catholics). The Incarnational approach to grace and nature characteristic of Radical Orthodoxy therefore reconciles the Protestant and Catholic traditions of natural law. Moreover, the Incarnation is the theological foundation for natural law and entails Love, the True and the Good. The Incarnation is Truth, the revelation of God in Christ. Yet the Incarnation as an act of grace also displays Love, Christ selflessly sacrificing Himself on the cross for the forgiveness of sins. And this act of grace which reveals the Truth of Christ divinely enables human participation in the divine relationship, the Beatific Vision, which is the ultimate Good. Therefore, through the gracious revelation of Christ who is the Truth, humans are able to comprehend and participate in the divine economy, which is Love and the Good. In the following chapters, each of these principles of the Good, the True and Love will be examined in turn to see how they provide a robust Christian Natural Law foundation for religious freedom.

Part II

Christian Natural Law as a Foundation for Religious Freedom

5 *Bona*

Basic Goods and the Common Good

I. Introduction

Part I of this book articulates a Christian Natural Law by describing the ways in which various Christian traditions have positioned themselves with respect to the natural law, analysing contemporary natural law theories to suggest that all natural law is intrinsically theological in a Christian sense, and arguing that a theological natural law culminates in the Incarnation of Christ and is therefore properly Christian. Through this process I have identified the common themes of Love, Truth and the Good which hold across the various Christian traditions of natural law, and which also makes sense of the relationship between nature, grace, reason and revelation: grace enhances nature and revelation guides reason. These symbiotically combine to enable apprehension of Love and the Good through Truth. In Part II of this book I explain how Christian Natural Law provides a robust ontological foundation for religious freedom grounded in Love, Truth and the Good. In subsequent chapters I focus on divine revelation as Truth and the grace of Love as aspects of a Christian Natural Law foundation for religious freedom. This chapter focuses on apprehension of the Good as one aspect of the Christian Natural Law foundation for religious freedom, and in particular how religious freedom is itself a good.

This chapter argues that the Good, which is composed of the basic goods and the common good, provides a foundation for religious freedom by encouraging people to pursue the basic good of religion which contributes to a flourishing human community. For Aquinas, the ultimate human end is participation in the beatific vision, intellectual union with God. The good of religion entails pursuing this end, and entails freedom to facilitate the efforts of persons and communities to establish a harmonious relationship with the transcendent source of meaning and value known as God. Religious freedom also enhances the common good, which is one of the principles of the basic good of practical reasonableness, by respecting the intrinsic dignity and human rights of the person and providing the stability and peace of a just political order.

Section II of the chapter briefly clarifies the idea of religious freedom before Section III demonstrates that religious freedom is an essential component

DOI: 10.4324/9781032620015-7

of pursuing the basic good of religion. Religious freedom allows people to consider the deep questions of life such as origins, meaning, value and destiny. Reflecting on our place in the universe, and our relationship with the transcendent, helps us discover truth about ourselves and others, and act consistently with conscientious judgement. Section IV subsequently argues that religious freedom is good because it enhances what legal philosophers call the common good. Religious freedom is the fundamental freedom; denial of religious freedom entails the denial of associated rights of conscience, speech and assembly. Furthermore, studies have shown that religious freedom pacifies social conflict and has a positive effect on pluralism, democracy and diversity. Conversely, the denial of religious freedom actually undermines social peace. Section V explains that since the purpose of just laws is to protect the common good, and the common good is protected and enhanced by religious freedom or the pursuit of true religion, it follows that the existence of a just political order requires the legal protection of religious freedom. Since religious freedom is also the pursuit of true religion, this points to another connected aspect of the Christian Natural Law foundation for religious freedom: the True, which will be considered in the next chapter. Section VI concludes.

II. Clarifying Religious Freedom

John Witte Jr. explains that religious freedom is a 'foundational part' of the development of human rights, 'and today it is regarded as a cornerstone in the edifice of human rights'.[1]

Fundamentally, religious freedom is about the freedom of individuals and groups to decide the nature of their religious beliefs and act upon them without incurring legal penalties. Religious freedom is sometimes viewed as something which is purely individual. It is just about beliefs and practice and has no public dimension. But viewing religion as individual in this sense ironically undermines the good of religion for individuals. Religious freedom extends beyond private belief and acts of worship to public and associational contexts such as proselytisation, social and business interactions, employment, cultural and charitable activities, education and so on.[2] For many religious people these external manifestations of religion are just as central and important to them as private belief, prayer and worship.[3] Witte clarifies that

> freedom of religion embraces a number of fundamental principles of individual religious liberty – freedom of conscience, exercise, speech,

1 John Witte Jr, *The Blessings of Liberty: Human Rights and Religious Freedom in the Western Legal Tradition* (Cambridge University Press, 2021) 6.

2 This section of the chapter draws on Alex Deagon, 'Is Religious Liberty Loving in Principle?' in Michael Quinlan and Keith Thompson (eds), *Inclusion, Exclusion and Religious Freedom in Contemporary Australia* (Connor Court, 2021) 21–24.

3 Nicholas Aroney, 'Freedom of Religion as an Associational Right' (2014) 33(1) *University of Queensland Law Journal* 153, 161 at FN 46.

> association, worship, diet, dress, and evangelism; freedom from religious discrimination, coercion, and unequal treatment; freedom of religious and moral education; and freedom of religious travel, pilgrimage, and association with coreligionists abroad.[4]

However, it also involves freedom of groups in public contexts, including

> freedom of religious groups to organize their own polity and leadership; to hold and use corporate property; to define their own creed, cult, confessional community, and code of conduct; to establish institutions of worship, education, charity, and outreach; and to set standards of admission, participation, and discipline for their members and leaders.[5]

This idea is recognised in influential human rights instruments such as the *International Covenant on Civil and Political Rights*. For example, Article 18 states:

1. Everyone shall have the right to freedom of thought, conscience and religion. This right shall include freedom to have or to adopt a religion or belief of his choice, and freedom, either individually or in community with others and in public or private, to manifest his religion or belief in worship, observance, practice and teaching.
2. No one shall be subject to coercion which would impair his freedom to have or to adopt a religion or belief of his choice.
3. Freedom to manifest one's religion or beliefs may be subject only to such limitations as are prescribed by law and are necessary to protect public safety, order, health or morals or the fundamental rights and freedoms of others.
4. The States Parties to the present Covenant undertake to have respect for the liberty of parents and, when applicable, legal guardians to ensure the religious and moral education of their children in conformity with their own convictions.

This indicates the actions associated with the principle of religious freedom are rights exercised by individuals and groups, individually and in community with others, and publicly or privately. It includes freedom of belief and to change beliefs, but also extends to manifestation. Note in particular art. 18(4), which obliges states to have respect for the liberty of parents to educate their children in conformity with religious convictions. One significant method of achieving this obligation is facilitating the ability of faith-based schools to educate in accordance with their faith-based ethos, as parents may wish to choose this. Religious freedom in principle, and with particular regard to associated

4 Witte (n 1) 6.
5 Ibid.

actions, is subject only to legal limitation which is *necessary* (not merely reasonable) to protect public safety, order, health, morals or fundamental rights and freedoms of others. This is a high threshold which requires substantive proof before any legal limitation is appropriate.[6]

From these principles, at least eight actions associated with the principle of religious freedom can be deduced, which are in addition to, overlap and complement the actions articulated above by Witte:

1 Freedom of belief, including freedom to choose or change belief.
2 Freedom of worship.
3 Freedom to establish places of worship.
4 Freedom to interpret holy text without government interference.
5 Freedom to read holy text in public.
6 Freedom to preach and proselytise (engage in teaching and propagation of the religion with intent to produce more followers).
7 Freedom to establish associations which provide education, healthcare, charity and other contributions to society in accordance with religious belief and practice.
8 Freedom from being required to affirm particular beliefs as a condition for holding a job in the public sector, stand for elections, study in university, or work in professions such as law (for example, the freedom of religion provision in Section 116 of the Australian Constitution protects any person seeking to hold a public office under the Commonwealth from being subject to a religious test).[7]

As such, religious freedom is not merely freedom of worship or the pursuit of individual good. It includes the ability of religious individuals to contribute to social good in accordance with their beliefs, and the ability to form associations which contribute to social good in accordance with religious belief.[8] Sections III and IV explain how religious freedom contributes to these individual and social aspects of the Good.

III. Religious Freedom and the Basic Goods

The first principle of the natural law is to pursue Good and avoid evil. The Good comprises the basic goods and the common good, which together protect religious freedom. As established in Part I of the book, these aspects of the

6 See Alex Deagon, 'Maintaining Religious Freedom for Religious Schools: Options for Legal Protection After the Ruddock Review' (2019) 247(1) *St Mark's Review: A Journal of Christian Thought and Opinion* 40, 49–50.

7 Section 116 of the Australian Constitution states: 'The Commonwealth shall not make any law for establishing any religion, or for imposing any religious observance, or for prohibiting the free exercise of any religion, and no religious test shall be required as a qualification for any office or public trust under the Commonwealth'.

8 J Daryl Charles, *Natural Law and Religious Freedom: The Role of Moral First Things in Grounding and Protecting the First Freedom* (Routledge, 2018) 7.

Good may be superficially secular but are actually theological. Tollefsen notes that, following Aquinas, 'the good of religion holds the highest place among goods . . . understanding that good . . . as having God as its object . . . God, or the apprehension of God, is a good such as to satisfy all desires; this would justify the claim that this good is the highest'.[9] For Aquinas, the ultimate human end is 'beautitude, perfect fulfilment, to be found only in the beatific vision, a form of intellectual union with the Divine Creator'.[10] The good of religion has to do with pursuing this end, and entails freedom to facilitate the efforts of persons and communities to establish a harmonious relationship with a transcendent source of meaning and value, which is usually called God. 'Anyone can see that persons' participation in this good depends . . . essentially upon the freedom with which they choose to act for that good'; the good of religion therefore entails a religious freedom which goes beyond, yet is enmeshed with, temporal existence.[11]

The good of religion also produces a political solidarity between citizens by motivating virtuous conduct and opening the political to the transcendent.[12] As Chavura, Gascoigne and Tregenza identify, our public 'doctrine' of human rights, human dignity and moral equality 'is established on deep layers of Christian sediment'.[13] These ideas are 'not only in large part the product of the Christian moral revolution that helped make the West, but are philosophically incoherent without the kind of metaphysical grounding provided by . . . Christian natural law theory'.[14] Porter argues that a 'practical implication' of a Thomistic or Christian Natural Law is natural or human rights, which entails three aspects:

> The human person properly enjoys freedom of action in some sphere of life; this freedom can properly be asserted, and should be safeguarded, even over against competing claims; and finally, this claim has legal force, and if no mechanisms for defending it exist, they should be created.[15]

Consequently there are limits on legal obedience that can be enacted by the state, which are in effect immunities from interference with the pursuit of

9 Christopher Tollefsen, 'Natural Law, Basic Goods and Practical Reason' in George Duke and Robert George (eds), *The Cambridge Companion to Natural Law Jurisprudence* (Cambridge University Press, 2017) 144.

10 Ibid 156.

11 Gerard Bradley, 'Natural Law Theory and Constitutionalism' in George Duke and Robert George (eds), *The Cambridge Companion to Natural Law Jurisprudence* (Cambridge University Press, 2017) 399–400.

12 See Alex Deagon, 'The Name of God in a Constitution: Meaning, Democracy, and Political Solidarity' (2019) 8(3) *Oxford Journal of Law and Religion* 473, 473, 486.

13 Stephen Chavura, John Gascoigne, and Ian Tregenza, *Reason, Religion and the Australian Polity: A Secular State?* (Routledge, 2019) 208–209.

14 Ibid 255–256.

15 Jean Porter, *Nature as Reason: A Thomistic Theory of the Natural Law* (Eerdmans, 2005) 355–356.

basic human goods.[16] For example, there is an immunity from interference with persons pursuing the basic good of religion, which entails a right to enjoy freedom of action in the religious sphere requiring legal protection. That is precisely what religious freedom is. Thus, the 'norms of natural law can provide the basis for a common understanding of human rights – an understanding that can be shared even in the absence of religious agreement'.[17] The basic good of religion, embedded in a Christian Natural Law, in this way provides a theological foundation for a commonly understood and accepted right to religious freedom.

Using the schema of the basic goods provided by Finnis, the relevant basic goods which provide a natural law argument for religious freedom are 'religion' as already mentioned, and 'practical reasonableness' which will be discussed further later. It is worth noting that Crowe does not view religion or spirituality as its own basic good, but rather sees spiritual reflection as aspects of the goods of 'understanding' (people understanding themselves and their environment and constructing meaningful identities around spirituality) and 'meaning' (a person's pursuit of meaning by shaping one's self-identity through religion, for example).[18] However, since there is broad agreement within the natural law tradition that religion or spirituality is one of the basic forms of good (as Crowe acknowledges), and I am adopting Finnis' schema which accepts this, I will assume for my purposes that religion is one of the basic goods.[19] The substantive principles in Crowe's version remain similar to the other mainstream articulations so it does not make much analytical difference.

With respect to the good of religion, according to Finnis, religion brings an 'order' to be 'brought into one's character and activity through inner integrity and outer authenticity' through reflecting on 'the lasting order of the whole cosmos' and the 'origin of that order'.[20] An intelligent human freedom which masters one's character acknowledges the need to subordinate that character to a being which is uniquely 'free, intelligent and sovereign'.[21] Though some may reject the existence or relevance of a traditional Christian God, it is not reasonable to deny that it is

> peculiarly important to have thought reasonably and (where possible) correctly about these questions of the origin of the cosmic order and of

16 Ibid 356–357.

17 Robert George, 'Natural Law, God and Human Dignity' in George Duke and Robert George (eds), *The Cambridge Companion to Natural Law Jurisprudence* (Cambridge University Press, 2017) 68.

18 Jonathan Crowe, *Natural Law and the Nature of Law* (Cambridge University Press, 2019) 51–55.

19 See eg Jonathan Crowe, 'Intelligibility, Practical Reason and the Common Good' in Jonathan Crowe and Constance Lee (eds), *Research Handbook on Natural Law Theory* (Edward Elgar, 2019) 296–297. As discussed in Chapter 3, we are able to rely on Finnis' framework once it is explicitly supported by a robust metaphysical foundation. This is what Christian Natural Law provides.

20 John Finnis, *Natural Law and Natural Rights* (Oxford University Press, 2nd ed, 2011) 89.

21 Ibid.

> human freedom and reason . . . and . . . that importance in large part consists in this: that if there is a transcendent origin of the universal order-of-things and of human freedom and reason, then one's life and actions are in fundamental disorder if they are not brought, as best as one can, into some sort of harmony with whatever can be known or surmised about that transcendent other and its lasting order.[22]

Charles characterises this as human beings having an 'ultimate duty' to 'follow truth wherever it may lead', recognising that they are subject to a transcendent authority.[23] This is because, as Finnis contends, 'God is an unrestricted, absolute value' and 'harmony with God (religion) is a basic human value'.[24] Finnis concludes:

> The ground for treating religious conscience as especially important is that it is really of great importance that people should seek and form a responsible judgment about an issue of unsurpassed importance: the truth about the origin, significance and destiny of the entire universe and of human beings as the only beings within our experience who are capable of engaging with reality in this uniquely profound way.[25]

With respect to practical reasonableness, which is thinking reasonably about how to pursue the basic goods in one's life, there are nine requirements.[26] Two are directly relevant to the question of religious freedom: the requirements of the common good (considered in detail in Section IV), and 'following one's conscience'.[27] The exercise of conscience is essential to make practical moral judgements, though it is possible that one's conscience can be mistaken. The 'dignity of even the mistaken conscience' 'flows from the fact that practical reasonableness is not simply a mechanism for producing correct judgements, but an aspect of personal full-being, to be respected . . . whatever the consequences'.[28] George neatly summarises how both these goods of religion and practical reasonableness support religious freedom:

> The natural law argument for religious liberty is founded on the obligation of each person to pursue the truth about religious matters and live in conformity with his conscientious judgements. This obligation is, in turn, rooted in the proposition that religion – considered as conscientious truth-seeking regarding the ultimate sources of meaning and

22 Ibid 89–90.
23 Charles (n 8) 105–106.
24 Finnis (n 20) 410.
25 John Finnis, 'Equality and Religious Liberty: Oppressing Conscientious Diversity in England' in Timothy Shah, Thomas Farr, and Jack Friedman (eds), *Religious Freedom and Gay Rights: Emerging Conflicts in the United States and Europe* (Oxford University Press, 2016) 26–28.
26 Finnis (n 20) 100–126.
27 Ibid 125.
28 Ibid 125–126.

> value – is a crucial dimension of human well-being and fulfilment. It is among the basic human goods that provide rational motivation for our choosing. The right to religious liberty follows from the dignity of man as a conscientious truth-seeker.[29]

Thus, religious freedom is an important and necessary implication of the goods of religion and practical reasonableness. For people to truly grapple with their place in the universe and their relationship with the transcendent, they must be free to think, speak, act and gather in ways which enhance this process. Practical reasonableness allows persons to make reasonable moral judgements according to conscience about their religious beliefs and any corresponding external obligations to manifest their beliefs. Even if their conscience is mistaken, their dignity as a human requires their judgements to be respected. In fact, the good of religion is just religious freedom. Any aspect of religion as a good is a function of the free practice of religion. For example, personal well-being, communal gathering, and social peace are all the result of the practice of religion, not mere religious belief. I explain this further in Section IV. For religion to be realised as a good it must be practiced freely, which implies generous legal protection of religious freedom.

IV. Religious Freedom and the Common Good

The other relevant requirement of the basic good of practical reasonableness is to consider that which will enhance the common good. Duke, adopting a broad definition of the common good for a political community according to Aquinas, states that it is a unity of order which is derived from and applicable to 'the universal good of God'.[30] From a theological perspective the common good entails the development of what Joel Harrison calls 'a cooperative order'. In this 'cooperative order', 'all persons are given their appropriate positions', an ordered harmony in the community of the city where all citizens contribute and fulfil their role.[31] The coordination of different communities and individuals within those communities is attentive to the dignity of persons and their place within a created order, enabling the pursuit of shared goods in different ways. These relationships are perfected in a life of charity – selfless affection which is recognised by mutual dependence and responsibility, and demonstrated through offering ourselves as gifts of service.[32] Such a harmonious human community which satisfies our existential desires is ultimately

29 George (n 17) 68–69. See also Robert Vischer, *Conscience and the Common Good* (Cambridge University Press, 2010).

30 George Duke, 'The Common Good' in George Duke and Robert George (eds), *The Cambridge Companion to Natural Law Jurisprudence* (Cambridge University Press, 2017) 374.

31 Joel Harrison, 'Dworkin's Religion and the End of Religious Liberty' in Rex Ahdar (ed), *Research Handbook on Law and Religion* (Edward Elgar, 2018) 96; Augustine, *Concerning the City of God Against the Pagans* (Penguin, 2008) 876.

32 Harrison (n 31) 94–98.

grounded in the highest Good, the object of our desires and satisfaction of our anxieties: God Himself. In relating to God in this way, we also deepen our horizontal relationships: 'Love the Lord your God, and love your neighbour as yourself'.[33] Augustine argues that to love a person for the sake of God invests them with a 'transcendental significance' as loved by God.[34] A harmonious social and political order is predicated upon common agreement on the objects of love. Where the love of the earthly city is disordered, focusing on self, ambition and conflict, the love of the heavenly city focuses on God, and therefore reconciliation with the other. 'Orienting oneself to God commits one to a deeper relationality with others'.[35] These 'networks of charity' extend throughout social, economic and political contexts, manifesting in the freedom of the church, economic and political associations, trade unions, educational bodies and families.[36] For Augustine they are grounded in a love of God and neighbour and displayed in right and virtuous living – a life of charity.[37]

More broadly, then, the common good of a political community is a 'unity of order that is distinguishable from a mere aggregate of individual goods', a 'structured unity' derived from the ordering of individuals towards their common goal.[38] The common good entails the 'justice and peace of a well-ordered polity'.[39] Justice is a 'certain form of equality or a proper relation among persons', and peace is 'the proper ordering of citizens and the absence among them of strife and discord'.[40] Duke thus defines the 'natural law common good' as 'a state of affairs in which each individual within a political community and the political community as a whole are flourishing'.[41] This means the natural law conception must be sufficiently common (properly shared aims) and sufficiently good (normatively desirable reasons for action). It is not consequentialist and does not involve the weighing or computation of benefits, for this ignores the incommensurability of goods (that they are not reducible to some higher good) and the exercise of practical reasonableness in choosing how to uphold the goods.[42] The common good is common because it is good for all persons.[43]

Murphy categorises conceptions of the common good as 'instrumental', 'aggregative' or 'distinctive'.[44] The instrumental conception sees the common

33 Ibid 97. See Luke 10:25–37.
34 Harrison (n 31) 94.
35 Ibid 95–96.
36 Ibid 97.
37 Ibid 97–98.
38 Duke (n 30) 374.
39 Ibid.
40 Ibid.
41 Ibid 376.
42 Ibid 377–378.
43 Bradley (n 11) 399.
44 See eg Mark Murphy, 'The Common Good' (2005) 59 *Review of Metaphysics* 133, Mark Murphy, *Natural Law in Jurisprudence and Politics* (Cambridge University Press, 2006). Murphy supports the 'aggregative' conception.

good not as a basic good itself, but as a set of conditions which are instrumental to the realisation of the basic goods, including the communal good of human cooperation which serves the fulfilment of the basic goods.[45] The aggregative conception sees the common good as the state of affairs in which all individuals in a political community are fully flourishing, or seeking the basic goods. The distinctive conception sees the common good as a distinct kind of good that is literally the good of the community as a whole, apart from the individual goods of its members, pursued in a community which also pursues the various goods of its members. 'A just and peaceful state of affairs is integral to the well-being' of each member of the community.[46]

Duke, I think correctly, argues that these three accounts are actually 'reconcilable aspects of the natural law common good'.[47] The instrumental aspect addresses the question of whether the common good is a basic good. The aggregative and distinctive conceptions focus on the goods of individuals in the community and the good of the community respectively, and these are simultaneously instrumental to enabling flourishing individuals within a community. Crowe agrees.[48] Perceiving the common good as entailing these three aspects is a 'more fruitful analysis'; 'there is no inconsistency – and much explanatory and normative power – in a theory of the common good that regards each view as capturing something important about the notion'.[49] For Crowe, the instrumental account provides rights and duties which create the space for the pursuit of the basic goods, the aggregative account provides reasons to support others in their pursuit of the basic goods, and the distinctive account enhances social connectedness 'through valuing other people's projects and commitments alongside' our own, which is a pursuit of intrinsic value directly contributing to the basic good of friendship.[50]

Crowe thus argues that the common good cannot be reduced to merely instrumental or aggregative conceptions because 'they cannot account for the role the common good plays in bringing the basic goods about'.[51] In particular, also incorporating the distinctive conception 'captures the idea that there is inherent value in participating in the goods in common with others'

45 Finnis supports the 'instrumental' conception. See John Finnis, *Natural Law and Natural Rights* (Oxford University Press, 2nd ed, 2011) 155–156; John Finnis, 'The Authority of Law in the Predicament of Contemporary Social Theory' (1984) 1 *Notre Dame Journal of Legal Ethics and Public Policy* 115; John Finnis, 'Public Good: The Specifically Political Common Good in Aquinas' in Robert George (ed), *Natural Law and Moral Inquiry* (Georgetown University Press, 1998).

46 Duke (n 30) 378–382.

47 Ibid 376–377, 382–383.

48 Jonathan Crowe, *Natural Law and the Nature of Law* (Cambridge University Press, 2019) 88–90.

49 Ibid 90.

50 Ibid.

51 Jonathan Crowe, 'Intelligibility, Practical Reason and the Common Good' in Jonathan Crowe and Constance Lee (eds), *Research Handbook on Natural Law Theory* (Edward Elgar, 2019) 303.

which cannot be reduced to a set of material conditions or an aggregate of individual goods.[52] 'The common good entails a role for the community in providing positive assistance to those whose participation in the basic goods would otherwise be impeded'.[53] This means the common good is 'thick' (it assumes a specific account of human goods rather than a mere set of rights and duties) and 'wide' (it encompasses the whole of humanity rather than just local communities).[54]

McCall also agrees that instrumental, aggregative and distinctive conceptions of the common good are all essential aspects of the common good rather than competing conceptions, though he does not use the terminology of those accounts. Rather, he argues that though the common good is the composite of individual goods, it is more than the collection of private goods. It is also a distinctive good which is common to all. The common good is the good of an individual and the good of others in combination. It is not utilitarian. The idea of the common good is opposed to a 'collectivist agenda that obliterates individual goods'; rather, the common good is a universal good and a unity of the good which simultaneously inheres in individuals.[55] The common good is 'the unity of order proper to the group' which also takes into account the good common to every member of that group.[56] The common good of a political community also includes 'peace, prosperity and training in virtue' necessary for individuals to realise the basic goods individually and as a community.[57]

Returning to religious freedom specifically, Charles clarifies that the common good is found in 'promoting the dignity of the human person' through facilitating the conditions by which individuals can most effectively flourish separately and together.[58] This has three components. First, 'respect for the person as such' in terms of upholding their fundamental and inalienable rights (including freedom of religion); second, the 'social wellbeing and development' of the group through ensuring each person in the group has what is needed to lead a fulfilling life (such as sustenance, shelter, family, culture, education and so on); and third, 'peace' through the 'stability and security of a just order'.[59] Focusing on the first component, Charles agrees that 'religious freedom is a fundamental good – in fact, the most basic of human goods – which gives meaning to all others'; this is because the denial of religious freedom precedes the denial of all other freedoms such as speech and assembly, and such denial usually results in state and/or vigilante violence.[60] Religious

52 Crowe (n 48) 89.
53 Ibid 116.
54 Ibid 88. See also ibid 95–98.
55 Bryan McCall, *The Architecture of Law: Rebuilding Law in the Classical Tradition* (University of Notre Dame Press, 2018) 32, see also 31–33.
56 Ibid 34.
57 Ibid 37, see also 299–300.
58 Charles (n 8) 214.
59 Ibid 214–215, 259.
60 Ibid 17.

freedom is the 'first freedom – it is the guarantor of all other human freedoms and inalienable rights'.[61] Religion exists as a reminder that the state is not the ultimate authority, and religious communities, exercising their autonomy, establish a wide range of mediating associations which serve the community. Hence, 'religion exists . . . to foster the common good', and freedom of religion is necessary for this process because it guarantees individual and group freedoms within the community.[62]

Witte also explains that the protection of religion and religious freedom 'has proved critical for the protection of many other individual and associational rights', also satisfying the other components of the common good.[63] Religious institutions supplement or replace the state in helping to implement and protect communities and their human rights. 'Many social scientists and human rights scholars today have thus come to see that providing strong protections of rights and liberties for religious individuals and religious institutions enhances, rather than diminishes, human rights for all'.[64] Witte concludes religious freedom is

> the first freedom from which other rights and freedoms evolve. Several recent comprehensive studies of the state of religious freedom in the world today have shown that proper protection of religious freedom in a country is strongly associated with other freedoms, including civil and political liberty, press freedom, and economic freedom, as well as with multiple measures of well-being . . . [W]herever religious freedom is high, there tend to be fewer incidents of armed conflict, better health outcomes, higher levels of earned income, prolonged democracy, and better educational opportunities.[65]

Religious freedom is therefore a fundamental freedom which gives meaning to all others because the denial of religious freedom precedes the denial of all other freedoms such as speech and assembly. If one cannot believe freely, then one cannot speak freely. And if one cannot speak freely, then one cannot gather freely around a common belief.

So religious freedom contributes to the common good because it helps create a peaceful and just order which sets the conditions for individuals to pursue the basic goods such as religion through the right of religious freedom

61 Ibid 105.
62 Ibid.
63 Witte (n 1) 7–8.
64 Ibid.
65 Ibid. See also Robert Woodberry, 'Protestant Missionaries and the Centrality of Conversion Attempts for the Spread of Education, Printing, Colonial Reform, and Political Democracy' in Timothy Shah and Allen Hertzke (eds), *Christianity and Freedom: Volume I Historical Perspectives* (Cambridge University Press, 2016), where Woodberry provides arguments and authorities to show that religious liberty is associated with better social, political and economic outcomes.

and associated rights (the instrumental aspect), which in turn helps individuals flourish and lead a fulfilling life (the aggregative aspect) and enhances communal good as a whole (the distinctive aspect).[66] Religious freedom also contributes directly to the stability and security of a just and peaceful political order in numerous ways.[67] Finke and Mataic show that facilitating religious freedom is important for the common good by empirically demonstrating how repression of religion is associated with violence and social conflict. 'Although government restrictions on religion are often justified in an effort to reduce tensions and conflict, research suggests that the opposite occurs; government restrictions are associated with higher levels of tension and conflict' and, in a vicious cycle, 'social restrictions lead to higher levels of government restrictions, which in turn lead to persecution that is more violent. Following the heightened violent persecution, religious groups respond with heightened social restrictions'.[68] One of the 'strongest predictors' for social restrictions are 'government favouritism for a single religion', which entails government discrimination against religion.[69]

Similarly, Carlson-Thies argues that an 'extensive freedom for religious institutions to be distinctive – to depart from generally accepted practices and standards – is necessary to achieving the common good'.[70] Providing freedom for religious groups to govern themselves enables the creation of diverse facilities and services which develop in accordance with different moral and religious convictions. These diverse convictions do not imply disrespect or harm towards groups that do not believe or act in accordance with such convictions, but rather contribute towards a rich tapestry of understandings which seek to promote the common good using different methods.[71] Diverse institutions provide a safe haven for diverse individuals with varying self-understandings and convictions, as opposed to policies which flatten or eliminate religious diversity.[72]

66 For a further extended discussion of the different aspects of the common good also see Gary Chartier and Jere L Fox, 'Natural Law, the Common Good and the State' in Jonathan Crowe and Constance Lee (eds), *Research Handbook on Natural Law Theory* (Edward Elgar, 2019) 349–357.

67 See Alex Deagon, *A Principled Framework for the Autonomy of Religious Communities: Reconciling Freedom and Discrimination* (Hart Publishing, 2023) Introduction and Chs 2, 5 and 6, which the material in the rest of this section variously draws upon.

68 Roger Finke and Dane R Mataic, 'Promises, Practices and Consequences of Religious Freedom: A Global Overview' (2019) 15(3) *University of St Thomas Law Journal* 587, 601.

69 Ibid 595–600.

70 Stanley Carlson-Thies, 'The Common Good Requires Robust Institutional Religious Freedom' (2019) 15(3) *University of St Thomas Law Journal* 529, 529.

71 Ibid 532–533.

72 Ibid 533. See also Richard W Garnett, 'Religious Freedom and the Nondiscrimination Norm' in Austin Sarat (ed), *Legal Responses to Religious Practices in the United States: Accommodation and Its Limits* (Cambridge University Press, 2012) 194, 194–227; Nathan A Berkeley, 'Religious Freedom and LGBT Rights: Trading Zero Sum Approaches for Careful Distinctions and Genuine Pluralism' (2015) 50 *Gonzalez Law Review* 1, 1–28.

Shah also contends that 'institutional religious freedom' is an 'essential service to the common good'.[73] Protecting religious institutions is important because they are 'independent centres of value formation and inculcation that is beneficial to society' and therefore 'perform a valuable social function'.[74] For example, Berg has argued that religious freedom does not simply benefit its adherents, but 'also preserves space for religion and religious communities to benefit the broader society (including by benefiting individuals)'.[75] The economic, social and cultural impact of faith-based organisations significantly enhances the common good.[76] Violations of religious freedom rights would cause many such organisations to either fold or reduce their services, which would undermine the common good.[77]

A statement in this respect by the US Conference of Catholic Bishops' Ad Hoc Committee for Religious Liberty is compelling:

> It is about whether [religious believers] can make our contribution to the common good of all . . . Can we do the good works our faith calls us to do, without having to compromise that very same faith? Without religious liberty properly understood, all . . . suffer, deprived of the essential contribution in education, health care, feeding the hungry, civil rights, and social services that religious [people] make every day, both here at home and overseas. What is at stake is whether [we] will continue to have a free, creative, and robust civil society . . . Religious believers . . . include neighbours helping each other, community associations, fraternal service clubs, sports leagues, and youth groups. All these . . . make their contribution to our common life . . . Restrictions on religious liberty are an attack on civil society.[78]

73 Timothy Shah, 'Institutional Religious Freedom in Full' (2020) 10(2) *Journal of Christian Legal Thought* 29, 29.

74 B Jessie Hill, 'Reconsidering Hostile Takeover of Religious Organisations' (2020) 97 *Washington University Law Review* 1833, 1855–1856. See also Richard W Garnett, 'Assimilation, Toleration, and the State's Interest in the Development of Religious Doctrine' (2003) 51 *University of California Los Angeles Law Review* 1645.

75 See generally Thomas Berg, 'Religious Freedom and the Common Good: A Summary of Arguments and Issues' (2019) 15(3) *University of St Thomas Law Journal* 517, 518. Berg expands on these arguments in detail in Thomas Berg, *Religious Liberty in a Polarized Age* (Eerdmans, 2023).

76 Berg (n 75) 520–521.

77 See eg Stephen V Monsma, *Pluralism and Freedom: Faith-Based Organizations in a Democratic Society* (Rowman and Littlefield, 2011) 15–44; Stephen V Monsma and Stanley W Carlson-Thies, *Free to Serve: Protecting the Religious Freedom of Faith-Based Organizations* (Brazos Press, 2015); Thomas Berg, 'Freedom to Serve: Religious Organizational Freedom, LGBT Rights, and the Common Good' in William N Eskridge Jr and Robin Fretwell Wilson (eds), *Religious Freedom, LGBT Rights, and the Prospects for Common Ground* (Cambridge University Press, 2018).

78 Cited in Charles (n 8) 259.

Furthermore, many studies have shown religious freedom to be 'positively related to a number of public goods' such as development, security, business and health.[79] Religious institutions 'play an important philanthropic role' by 'increasing literacy, reducing poverty, promoting development, providing access to potable water, running counselling centers, leading peace and reconciliation processes, among innumerable other contributions'.[80] 'Religious freedom is believed to not only be an integral part of the "bundled commodity" of human freedoms, it is also closely related to the general betterment of people's lives'.[81] Therefore, since undermining religious freedom undermines all other rights and social goods, it would logically follow that undermining religious freedom undermines a peaceful and just society. Indeed, that is precisely what the research shows. There is a positive correlation between religious freedom and pluralism, democracy, diversity and social peace. Wuthnow also explains why religious freedom is good for democracy specifically. Religious freedom animates political conversations grounded in robust moral convictions, providing diverse perspectives which open up conversations about what is required for the common good.[82] Conversely, studies show restrictions on religious freedom actually increase social tensions and fracture, undermining democratic processes and the pursuit of the common good.

Kao and Burke provide extensive empirical evidence to further support these claims, drawing from the comprehensive study of global religious freedom by Brian Grim and Roger Finke.[83] Cultural hostility towards religion can drive a government towards restricting peaceful religious practice and even excluding certain beliefs from the public square. Grim and Finke 'debunk the myth that religious diversity or religiousity are the drivers of social conflict'; rather, 'the more a government restricts religion, the more social hostilities tend to increase'.[84] Such restriction and hostility has an exacerbating effect, leading to the further decline of religious freedom, starting with social marginalisation and progressing to economic and legal penalties, and finally vigilante or state-sanctioned violence.[85] Kao and Burke outline the findings which demonstrate a positive correlation between religious freedom and pluralism, and

79 Nikay Saiya, Stuti Manchanda, and Rahmat Wadidi, 'Did Religious Freedom Exacerbate COVID-19? A Global Analysis' (2023) 62(4) *Journal of Religion and Health* 2799–2819.

80 Ibid 13.

81 Ibid 3.

82 See Robert Wuthnow, *Why Religion Is Good for American Democracy* (Princeton University Press, 2021).

83 See Emilie Kao and Monica Burke, '*Masterpiece Cakeshop* and Authentic Pluralism in a Post-*Obergefell* World' (2020) 24(1) *Texas Review of Law and Politics* 97; Brian Grim and Roger Finke, *The Price of Freedom Denied: Religious Persecution and Conflict in the Twenty-First Century* (Cambridge University Press, 2010).

84 Kao and Burke (n 83) 99. See also Charles (n 8) 16, 109–110.

85 Kao and Burke (n 83) 99.

the consequent creation of conditions which facilitate peaceful coexistence and social flourishing:

> Strong religious freedom creates the conditions for authentic religious pluralism to flourish. First, religious freedom affirms the idea that individuals and institutions that hold different beliefs have equal rights under the law to live according to those beliefs in thought, speech, and action in both the public sphere and in private. It creates a level playing field for the competition of ideas . . . Freedom has a pacifying effect on social conflict . . . frictions dissipate, creating a virtuous cycle.[86]

Moreover, the virtues of secular liberal democracy such as freedom and equality (which produce religious freedom) in turn have their foundation in Christian ideas.[87] Various studies have found that Christianity and religious freedom are the foundation for constitutional democracy. One example is a famous article by Robert Woodberry which shows that missionary activity laid the foundation for the thriving liberal democratic societies we are part of today.[88] Indeed, Christianity has been the major influence on the formation of liberal constitutional democracies with religious freedom.[89] Christianity is therefore 'a deep and enduring source of human rights and liberties in the Western legal tradition', including religious freedom.[90] Respect for the dignity of the individual, human rights, a commitment to equality, and concern for the poor are largely foreign to ancient religions, and reflect the uniquely Christian claims that humans were created in the image of God and that God sacrificed himself for the good of humans through Christ.[91] Samuel Moyn's careful and attentive exposition shows how Christianity underpins modern

86 Ibid 98–100.

87 See eg Perez Zagorin, *How the Idea of Religious Toleration Came to the West* (Princeton University Press, 2003); Bruce Ward, *Redeeming the Enlightenment: Christianity and Liberal Virtues* (Eerdmans, 2010); John Witte Jr and Frank Alexander (eds), *Christianity and Human Rights* (Cambridge University Press, 2010); John Milbank and Adrian Pabst, *The Politics of Virtue: Post-Liberalism and the Human Future* (Rowman and Littlefield, 2016).

88 Robert Woodberry, 'The Missionary Roots of Liberal Democracy' (2012) 106(2) *American Political Science Review* 244. See also Kody Cooper and Justin Dyer, *The Classical and Christian Origins of American Politics: Political Theology, Natural Law, and the American Founding* (Cambridge University Press, 2022).

89 See eg Francis Oakley, *The Watershed of Modern Politics: Law, Virtue, Kingship, and Consent* (Yale University Press, 2015); Nicholas Aroney and Ian Leigh (eds), *Christianity and Constitutionalism* (Oxford University Press, 2023); John Witte Jr, *The Blessings of Liberty: Human Rights and Religious Freedom in the Western Legal Tradition* (Cambridge University Press, 2021). Other scholars who have traced Christian influences in the Western legal tradition include Quentin Skinner, *The Foundations of Modern Political Thought I and II* (Cambridge University Press, 1978); Harold Berman, *Law and Revolution: The Formation of the Western Legal Tradition* (Harvard University Press, 1983); Remi Brague, *Eccentric Culture: A Theory of Western Civilization* (St Augustine's Press, 2009).

90 Witte (n 1) 14. See eg Chs 1–3.

91 Steven Smith, *Pagans and Christians in the City* (Eerdmans, 2018) 206–207.

human rights discourse – not only through vague appeals to Christian conceptions of dignity which overlook inimical Christian conduct over the centuries, but more compellingly through the concrete anxieties of World War II atrocities which led to human rights being a project more of the Christian right than of secular liberals.[92] And consequently it is religious freedom in the Christian tradition which

> remains the cornerstone for protection of many other rights . . . because religion provides the ethical grounding necessary to a human rights regime; because it underpins notions of human dignity, community, and human nature and need; and because of the place of religious institutions alongside the state in realizing rights, especially in transitional societies.[93]

Thus, the idea of religious freedom has an intrinsic connection with a Christian framework grounded in natural law. Religious freedom relies on respecting the dignity of the individual and their capacity to believe and reason, and creating the conditions where a person can believe, gather and act freely. These correspond to the idea of the common good as respecting the rights of individuals and creating a peaceful and just order in which persons can flourish as individuals and as a community, including through the practice of religion. As Garnett concludes, religious freedom 'is a crucial aspect of the common good, one in which – like clean air and safe roads – everyone has a stake'.[94] Since religious freedom contributes to a thick and wide conception of the common good grounded in a Christian Natural Law, the true nature of religious freedom as substantively good and universally common is revealed. This provides persuasive appeal for the idea of religious freedom even to those who may not subscribe to the specific metaphysical premises of Christian Natural Law.

V. The Good of True Religion

This returns us to the issue of where religious freedom fits with the common good in the schema of Christian Natural Law. According to Aquinas, the 'common good sought by human law' is 'peace within the community and attainment of individual habits of virtue of its members'; this is the 'natural and supernatural common good of man'.[95] The natural and supernatural common good includes 'religion' and 'salvation'.[96] 'Therefore, in order that man might

92 Samuel Moyn, *Christian Human Rights* (University of Pennsylvania Press, 2015).
93 Ian Leigh, 'Religious Liberty and Human Rights: Their Origin, Their Development in the Anglo-American Legal Tradition, and Why They Are Still Needed' (2023) 38(1) *Journal of Law and Religion* 118, 119.
94 Richard W Garnett, 'Religious Freedom and the Churches: Contemporary Challenges in the United States Today' (2020) 33 *Studies in Christian Ethics* 194, 200.
95 McCall (n 55) 314.
96 Ibid.

have peace and virtue, it was necessary for laws to be framed'.[97] As such, law 'is not an end in itself': 'all law must be an ordinance of reason directed to the common good, and every level of the legal architecture is ultimately ordered to the highest common good, the end of the eternal law, God himself'.[98] The political common good is a component of the 'higher common good of the natural and divine laws and ultimately the eternal law', which means a law must be proximately directed to the political common good and ultimately directed to the 'common good of all men as fixed by the eternal law' in order to be just.[99] The form of just human laws must provide that any burdens created are laid equally in proportion with a view to the common good. This means 'pursuing the common good does not exclude pursuing something advantageous to an individual member as long as the contemplated action benefits the common good and also the private good of the individual'.[100] Similarly, it is inconsistent with the common good and unjust for a law to disproportionately burden any individuals and communities who are part of the political community. This may mean appropriate limitation of individual goods with regard to the common good.[101]

Crowe concludes that the common good is 'plausibly best realised' when we provide space (norms of non-interference) for people to pursue the basic goods and positive duties to facilitate people's pursuit of the basic goods.[102] In a religious freedom context, this implies non-interference with people pursuing the good of religion, and legal protection to facilitate people's pursuit of the good of religion. Appropriate and proportionate limitation of other individual goods for this purpose are just because, as demonstrated in the previous section, religion and religious freedom is an essential aspect of the common good. Concordantly, limitation of religious freedom which disproportionately burdens individuals and communities, ostensibly for the pursuit of some individual good, is unjust because it detracts from the common good.

Therefore, the common good allows the reconciliation of two contradictory features of political authority: its ultimate purpose is to serve the good of individuals, and 'it can require the subordination of individual goods to the good of the community'.[103] This also means there is a generic moral obligation to obey the law to create a stable and just system for pursuing the basic goods, which is part of the common good. However, if there are 'grossly unjust laws' which entail 'obvious or exceptional cases of injustice', then obligation to obey the law may be defeated.[104] That is, if there is a law which directly impedes a basic good, such as a law disproportionately restricting religious freedom

97 Aquinas, *Summa Theologica* I, Q95 Art 1.
98 McCall (n 55) 340.
99 Ibid 340.
100 Ibid 342.
101 Ibid 342–343.
102 Crowe (n 48) 242.
103 Duke (n 30) 389.
104 Ibid 390–391.

(which impedes the good of religion), then that law may not possess authority because it unjustly damages the common good. According to Christian Natural Law then, religious freedom consequently may entail disobedience to an unjust law which damages the good of religion and therefore the common good. However, as we shall see in a moment, a more coherent approach which upholds a stable and peaceful political order, just laws, the common good and the basic goods is to provide legal accommodation to protect religious freedom (for example, by providing positive legal rights for religious freedom).

Religious freedom in this sense also 'protects religion' by 'encouraging the pursuit of religion within multiple groups and sites of authority', which 'secures the free creation of communities of solidarity, fraternity, and charity'.[105] Religious freedom not only protects against coercing faith, but facilitates the quest for 'true religion' through providing freedom to individuals and communities which seek transcendent truth for the good of both the individual (as suggested in Section III) and the broader community (as suggested in Section IV), or the common good.[106] As Harrison summarises:

> The pursuit of 'true religion' then – that is, a quest to orient oneself rightly in relation to God – is also an orientation for the entire community. It is neither simply an extra-temporal good – an end outside of history – nor a single good for individual choosing. Rather, it shapes our institutions, our actions, and our communal economic and political life. As integral to the common good, true religion shapes the bringing about of recognisable social goods – hospitals, schools, institutions of care, cooperative work endeavours, and sites of worship. Civil authority is tasked with pursuing the common good, a vision of right relationship in which virtuous living is encouraged.[107]

In addition, religion only becomes a virtue when it cares for truth and takes into account the common good.[108] This is consistent with the purpose of just laws, and the common good itself, being to train in virtue. So it is also just and necessary for laws to protect religious freedom as a pursuit of true religion, because such laws facilitate the pursuit of religion as a virtue, which is part of the common good. Since religious freedom is the 'desirable' quest for the pursuit of true religion which shapes our good life, Harrison suggests that religious claims should be generously accommodated.[109] Taliaferro agrees, observing that 'the use of natural law theory in actual jurisprudence on religious freedom might result in an increased use of the legal standard of

105 Joel Harrison, *Post-Liberal Religious Liberty: Forming Communities of Charity* (Cambridge University Press, 2020) 21–22.
106 Ibid 142–143.
107 Ibid 158.
108 Charles (n 8) 131.
109 Harrison (n 105) 23–24.

"reasonable accommodation"' because it 'employs constructive dialogue and negotiation'.[110]

Religious freedom, or the freedom to believe and act in accordance with one's convictions, therefore has 'eminently social implications' and is 'a necessary prerequisite for and the result of human flourishing'.[111] It is grounded in a 'transcendent source of morality', a Christian Natural Law.[112] Intrusion into that liberty may only be justified where the interference is 'based on some objective good' which yields good for individuals and the community.[113] Thus, religious freedom enhances the common good by respecting the dignity of persons with freedoms, facilitating the creation of communities which enhance 'cooperative order' among citizens, and by contributing to social peace.[114] As discussed in Section IV, the idea of cooperative order is intrinsically linked to the virtue of charity or love, the creation of a mutually responsible and dependent care for each other, oriented towards the love of God. The law of love, the principle to love your neighbour as yourself, also reflects the substantive nature of the common good as concerned for the good of the individual in community with others. This points to the third aspect of a Christian Natural Law: Love, which we will explore in the final chapter. Understanding religious freedom as the pursuit of 'true religion' also points to the second aspect of a Christian Natural Law which undergirds religious freedom: the True. This will be explored in the next chapter.

VI. Conclusion

This chapter has considered how the Good provides an essential aspect of a Christian Natural Law foundation for religious freedom. It argues that the Good is anchored in God as the paradigm of good and comprises the basic goods and the common good. The basic goods of religion and practical reasonableness combine to provide that it is good for humans to reflect on their relationship with the divine, seek to order their lives in harmony with the divine and exercise their conscientious judgement in doing so. The law ought to respect and consequently protect the ability of humans to practically reason

110 Karen Taliaferro, *The Possibility of Religious Freedom: Early Natural Law and the Abrahamic Faiths* (Cambridge University Press, 2019) 139. See also Deagon, *Reconciling Freedom and Discrimination* (n 67), where I draw on theological perspectives to articulate a principled framework for reconciling religious freedom and equality. Reasonable accommodation is a central aspect of this framework.

111 Charles (n 8) 251.

112 Ibid 251–253.

113 Ibid 251.

114 See also Joel Harrison, 'Dworkin's Religion and the End of Religious Liberty' in Rex Ahdar (ed), *Research Handbook on Law and Religion* (Edward Elgar, 2018) 94–98; Alex Deagon, 'Reconceptualising Law: "Pagan" Violence and Augustinian Peace' (2020) 33(3) *Journal for the Academic Study of Religion* 286, 298–300.

and seek true religion.[115] Practical reasonableness also requires consideration of the common good, which can be defined as a just and peaceful political order which respects the dignity of humans and their inalienable rights (including religious freedom) and therefore enables humans to flourish individually and as a community. Religious freedom enhances the common good because it demonstrably upholds a stable and peaceful political community, supports human dignity and rights, and facilitates the flourishing of individuals in community. Since the common good entails a peaceful and just political order along with the development of virtue through the pursuit of true religion, a peaceful and just political order which has the common good as its purpose should provide appropriate and proportionate legal protection for religious freedom. This is one pillar of the Christian Natural Law foundation for the idea of religious freedom, and its reliance on the common good means it has universal appeal. The next chapter considers the True as an essential aspect of a Christian Natural Law foundation for religious freedom, which is the pursuit of true religion.

115 For a similar detailed analysis arguing that religious freedom is a good which is worthy of status as an individual and fundamental human right, see Daniel Philpott, 'Why Religious Freedom Is a Human Right' (2023) 68(3) *American Journal of Jurisprudence* 177–194.

6 *Aletheia*

Divine Revelation

I. Introduction

The previous chapter explained how the Good provides an essential aspect of the Christian Natural Law foundation for religious freedom. Religious freedom is a good because it enables us to pursue the ultimate Good, God Himself, and enhances human flourishing through this process. Hence, the good of religious freedom is anchored in the potential for the knowledge of God, or 'true religion'. The True, then, is also an indispensable aspect of the Christian Natural Law foundation for religious freedom.

This chapter argues that the True is a necessary component of a Christian Natural Law foundation for religious freedom in two interconnected senses. First, religious freedom aims for the pursuit of truth. Second, the truth religious freedom pursues is theological – in the biblical text, 'truth' is translated as *aletheia*, which means the revelation of God through Christ. Divine revelation in Scripture provides a theological foundation for religious freedom both textually and conceptually. As I emphasised in Chapter 1 of this book, this is not to say that secular arguments for religious freedom do not exist. There are many.[1] However, as I explained in Chapter 1, in my view these arguments fail to grapple with the transcendent dimension of religious freedom. Articulating the different theological arguments for religious freedom in the context of the True directly engages with this neglected transcendent dimension and underscores the necessity of theology for a Christian Natural Law foundation of religious freedom.

Section II of this chapter sets out the two senses of the True. Religious freedom pursues truth, and this truth is the revelation of God. Both these sources are a unity through general and special revelation. In this way, general revelation reveals truth through natural law, and special revelation reveals truth through Scripture, and both are intrinsically theological. Section III outlines textual arguments for religious freedom which are contained in Scripture,

1 See citations in Chapter 1. See also David Little, 'Human Rights, Public Reason, and the International Protection of the Freedom of Religion or Belief' in John Witte Jr and M Christian Green (eds), *Religion and Human Rights: An Introduction* (Oxford University Press, 2011).

DOI: 10.4324/9781032620015-8

while Section IV outlines conceptual arguments. Of course, since the conceptual arguments are often drawn from particular texts, there is some overlap between the two. Fundamentally, the textual and conceptual arguments for religious freedom are focused on the creation of humanity in God's image (the *Imago Dei* which entails that humans are truth-seeking moral creatures with a free will to love), the law of love and the nature of faith (that faith is a genuine heart transformation and love by nature cannot and should not be compelled), and a distinction between the role of the state which is the steward of temporal good, and the role of the church and conscience as the steward of spiritual good. Section V provides specific ancient and modern illustrations of these general principles by considering particular figures and movements in history: Tertullian, Augustine, Calvin and Reformed theology, Locke, and modern Catholicism. While these diverse characters have equally diverse emphases with respect to theological justifications for religious freedom, and have upheld the lofty theological principles in their practices only to varying extents, they exhibit a common consistency in their steadfast reliance on theological Truth, revealed in Scripture and by the person of Christ, as the cornerstone of religious freedom. Section VI concludes, identifying points of relevance for discussing religious freedom with a contemporary pluralistic audience, and suggesting the centrality of Love in a Christian Natural Law foundation for religious freedom. Love is the subject of the final chapter of this book.

II. Religious Freedom and Truth

As Charles observes, religious freedom is 'an ability to order one's own choices in accordance with truth. At bottom, religious freedom is the condition for the pursuit of truth'.[2] Taliaferro also recognises that the natural law basis for religious freedom also 'points to a higher truth that is beyond man and even beyond nature, viz., the Christian God, creator of both nature and man'.[3] As such, religious freedom is concerned with the quest for 'true religion', which is the quest to orient oneself rightly with God.[4] So the True is an aspect of a Christian Natural Law foundation for religious freedom in two interconnected senses. First, religious freedom aims for the pursuit of truth. Second, the truth religious freedom pursues is theological – in the biblical text, 'truth' is translated as *aletheia*, which means the revelation of God through Christ.[5]

2 J Daryl Charles, *Natural Law and Religious Freedom: The Role of Moral First Things in Grounding and Protecting the First Freedom* (Routledge, 2018) 16, 21.

3 Karen Taliaferro, *The Possibility of Religious Freedom: Early Natural Law and the Abrahamic Faiths* (Cambridge University Press, 2019) 122.

4 Joel Harrison, *Post-Liberal Religious Liberty: Forming Communities of Charity* (Cambridge University Press, 2020) 142–143.

5 See Alex Deagon, *From Violence to Peace: Theology, Law and Community* (Hart Publishing, 2017) 121–122, 134–137.

That religious freedom pursues theological truth is suggested through the doctrine of the unity of truth. Truth revealed in Scripture cannot contradict truth discovered by natural reason. This is expressed through the metaphor of God's double gift of truth as revealed through the book of Scripture (special revelation) and the book of nature (general revelation). Since the same good and truthful God is the author of both books, they cannot disagree with each other, assuming both books are properly understood.[6] In our context, this implies natural law should accord with Scripture generally, and particularly with respect to religious freedom.

Demonstrating an agreement between natural law and Scripture generally is part of the task in this book. In Part I of the book, I set out theological responses to natural law, show that natural law is theological, and identify the specific theological themes of the Good, the True, and Love which provide the framework for Christian Natural Law. As Levering explains, divine revelation supports a theological idea of natural law, and the precepts of revelation express what is contained in the natural law as truth.[7] Divine revelation illuminates and clarifies the natural law.[8] Zimmermann further argues that the investigation of divine revelation is a valuable and beneficial exercise because the authority of and grounding for natural law comes through its association with the eternal law, the law of God. In particular, natural law theory 'may be grounded' in Scripture itself.[9]

VanDrunen points out that Romans 1:18–32, in conjunction with Romans 2:14–15, is the part of Scripture most associated with natural law. Romans 1 explains that God has revealed His eternal power and divine nature through creation, and this leaves people without excuse. Natural revelation puts people under a moral obligation to their Creator.[10] The idea that law could be related to something other than the law of the state was expressed by Paul in Romans 2:14–15:

> For when nations, who do not have the law, by nature do what the law requires, they are a law to themselves, even though they do not have the law. They show that the work of the law is written on their hearts, while their conscience also bears witness, and their conflicting thoughts accuse or even excuse them.

6 Ibid 45–46.

7 Matthew Levering, *Biblical Natural Law: A Theocentric and Teleological Approach* (Oxford University Press, 2008) 1–2.

8 Ibid 16.

9 Augusto Zimmermann, 'The Principle of Subsidiarity' in Jonathan Crowe and Constance Lee (eds), *Research Handbook on Natural Law Theory* (Edward Elgar, 2019) 392–393.

10 David VanDrunen, 'A Natural Law Right to Religious Freedom: A Reformed Perspective' (2012) 5(2) *International Journal of Religious Freedom* 135, 137–138. For a summary of VanDrunen's approach to natural law, see Mary Anne Plaatjies van Huffel, 'Natural Law in the Reformed Tradition' in Norman Doe (ed), *Christianity and Natural Law* (Cambridge University Press, 2017) 131–132.

Here Paul is distinguishing between those nations which have a written moral law, and those who do not. But even those who do not have a written moral law know by nature or conscience what the moral law requires, and act in a corresponding way. People can know and practice the moral law 'by nature'. This text has traditionally been understood to affirm that the Gentiles had access to God's law apart from special revelation. This law written on the heart and attested to by conscience was identified with the natural law, and the Decalogue was understood as restating this natural law and summarising it as love of God and neighbour.[11]

Scripture therefore affirms that natural law is available to all, even those who do not have the divine law. This is the beginning of moral reasoning. However, it is not the end. Since the natural law is participation in the eternal law, knowing natural law will and should eventually lead to the author of natural law, God Himself. And the particular determinations of human law informed by natural law require guidance through what God has specifically revealed in the divine law, or Scripture. Divine assistance is necessary for both our natural and supernatural ends.[12] The basic norms of nonmaleficence in the Decalogue were regarded by Aquinas as summary statements of natural law, 'and as such they were seen as . . . imperatives of divine law'.[13] Similarly, McCall points out that the natural law can be summed up by the biblical Golden Rule, that you ought to do for others what you want done for yourself.[14] The natural law is therefore authored by God, affirmed and clarified in Scripture, and known through the exercise of divinely endowed reason.[15] Scripture is the divine law, the most perfect participation in the eternal law as the revelation of it, and so our natural law reasoning, which is limited and imperfect participation in the eternal law, must be harmonised with the divine law.[16]

The natural law can also be 'seen as a distinctively human expression of creation's reflection of the Creator'; the world as creation reflects some of God's goodness and intelligibility.[17] Paul's remarks in Romans 2:14–15 also suggest that the natural law provides a redemptive context through grace and revelation.[18] That is, natural law is part of the created apparatus leading to true religion: the knowledge of God. Indeed, 'truth' in the New Testament is most commonly a translation of *aletheia*. *Aletheia* is derived from *alethes*, which has

11 Jennifer Herdt, 'Christianity and Natural Law and Natural Rights' in John Witte Jr and Rafael Domingo (eds), *Oxford Handbook of Christianity and Law* (Oxford University Press, 2024) 582–583.
12 Bryan McCall, *The Architecture of Law: Rebuilding Law in the Classical Tradition* (University of Notre Dame Press, 2018) 429–432.
13 Jean Porter, *Nature as Reason: A Thomistic Theory of the Natural Law* (Eerdmans, 2005) 220.
14 McCall (n 12) 119.
15 Ibid 172, 195.
16 Ibid 198–201. For a detailed account for how this may occur in particular determinations of human law, see ibid 212–223.
17 Porter (n 13) 329. See eg Psalm 19: 'the heavens declare the glory of God' and following.
18 Porter (n 13) 329.

its root in the combination of *a*, the first letter of the Greek alphabet and a particle used as a prefix to express a negation, with *lanthano*, a prolonged form of a primitive verb which means to be hidden, concealed, or secret. Thus, the root form of *aletheia* expresses a meaning equivalent to the notion of negating a secret, revealing a thing that has been concealed, or exposing something hidden. *Truth is revelation*. A major way that *aletheia* is used in the New Testament is to express the truth of Christianity, or that which is *revealed* by God about himself and humanity through the Scriptures.[19] What is more, Christ identifies Himself as God and as *aletheia*, the Truth.[20]

Hence, there is also agreement between natural law and Scripture with respect to religious freedom specifically. Since divine revelation has the function of illuminating and clarifying the natural law, and natural law is theoretically accessible to all persons through divinely endowed reason and conscience, additional reliance on the divine law for the principles of religious freedom strengthens the existing natural law arguments grounded in the Good which were provided in the previous chapter.[21] In particular, Witte identifies that the articulation of human rights and religious freedom in the Western tradition begins with the biblical account of humans created in the image of God.[22] 'The genesis of natural rights and liberties rests on unchanging, eternal sources' because they are grounded in the Image of God created within humans by God, and in Jesus Christ as the Truth.[23]

Religious freedom was sometimes marginalised by natural law theorists on the mistaken basis that liberty in belief presupposed religious relativism or indifference.[24] The error in this approach is exposed through the explicit link just drawn between revelation, truth and religious freedom. Since the principles of religious freedom are located in revelation (as this chapter will show), which is God's truth, they are grounded in an objective truth of unsurpassed importance. The next two parts of the chapter set out these theological

19 See eg John 17:17; John 8:31–32. See the general discussion in Deagon (n 5) 121–122.

20 John 1:1–6; John 14:6. See Deagon (n 5) 134–137.

21 Levering (n 7) 19–20. See Norman Doe, 'Natural Law in an Interfaith Context: The Abrahamic Religions' in Norman Doe (ed), *Christianity and Natural Law* (Cambridge University Press, 2017) 200–202 for a summary of Levering's argument. See also David VanDrunen, *Divine Covenants and Moral Order: A Biblical Theology of Natural Law* (Eerdmans, 2014), where VanDrunen sets out a substantive account of natural law in Scripture informed by Reformed covenant theology, and contrasts this with Levering's account which is more limited in the scope of its biblical exegesis. Consistent with Part I of this book, VanDrunen argues that natural law is intrinsically theological in the sense that it operates through the developing covenant relationships between God and humanity. Natural law is therefore operative both salvifically in the sense of providing awareness of God's moral standards, and ethically in the sense of providing standards of the good for application in human social contexts.

22 John Witte Jr, *The Blessings of Liberty: Human Rights and Religious Freedom in the Western Legal Tradition* (Cambridge University Press, 2021) 290.

23 Zimmermann (n 9) 393.

24 Robert George, 'Natural Law, God and Human Dignity' in George Duke and Robert George (eds), *The Cambridge Companion to Natural Law Jurisprudence* (Cambridge University Press, 2017) 68.

foundations for religious freedom. First, the idea of religious freedom can be derived from the text of Scripture itself. Second, the idea of religious freedom has been historically developed through conceptual analysis of biblical ideas and structures.

III. Textual Arguments

The Bible is the primary text for Christian reflection on human rights. It is not a textbook, but it does have pertinent passages on both spiritual and political freedom that have inspired Christian teaching on the origin, nature and purposes of human rights, including religious freedom.[25] Mathis observes that 'no explicit biblical mandate for the notion of religious liberty exists, yet biblical ethics and principles support the idea, which permeates both the Old and New Testaments'.[26] Freedom of religion is a faithful way to live out God's love and grace in the world.[27] This section sets out various passages of Scripture that support or promote religious freedom, with brief explanations. Broader concepts and principles derived from these passages are considered in more depth in the following part, although there will obviously be some overlap.

In the Protestant context, Confessions summarising biblical teaching include sections on religious liberty which cite specific passages. For example, freedom of religion is an important strand of Baptist theology. The Baptist Faith and Message 2000 states that 'God alone is Lord of the conscience', which means that people should have 'free and unhindered access to God', and the state and the church should be separated. Baptists have long argued that the role of the magistrate is only to handle civil transgressions, and leave God-given conscience free from compulsion. The state has no jurisdiction over the conscience or religious questions; these are between God and individuals. This is also reflected in the conduct of Jesus in the Gospels, where he always call people to voluntarily follow him and never coerces.[28] Chapter 20 of the Westminster Confession of Faith, on Christian Liberty and Liberty of Conscience, similarly sets out arguments that God is Lord of the Conscience and freedom of conscience is an essential requirement of genuine faith.[29] Most fundamentally, the Bible affirms that 'God created man in his own image'

25 Witte (n 22) 17, 20–21. See also Paul Copan, 'The Biblical Worldview Context for Religious Liberty' in Angus Menuge (ed), *Religious Liberty and the Law: Theistic and Non-Theistic Perspectives* (Routledge, 2018).

26 Rebecca Mathis, 'The Roots of Religious Liberty in Scripture' (2012) 55(4) *Sewanee Theological Review* 389, 389. For a detailed account of religious liberty from a biblical-theological perspective which engages with many of the themes in the rest of this chapter, see Andrew Walker, *Liberty for All: Defending Everyone's Religious Freedom in a Pluralistic Age* (Brazos Press, 2021).

27 Mathis (n 26) 390.

28 Paul Goodliff, 'Natural Law in the Baptist Tradition' in Norman Doe (ed), *Christianity and Natural Law* (Cambridge University Press, 2017) 148–151. See Romans 13, James 4.

29 Passages cited in support of these principles include Genesis 1:27; 2:7; Matthew 6:6–7, 24; 16:26; 22:21; John 8:36; Acts 4:19–20; Romans 6:1–2; 13:1–7; Galatians 5:1,13; Philippians

(Genesis 1:27), and humans are therefore endowed with inherent dignity. This dignity entails agency to love and trust in God.

Scripture also provides statements regarding the separation of church and state. In Matthew 22:21 ('therefore render to Caesar the things that are Caesar's, and to God the things that are God's'), Jesus distinguishes between the limited authority of the state and the complete authority of God. Though believers owe some deference to the state, where there is tension between the requirements of the state and the requirements of God, the duty to God prevails.[30] Wilken characterises this as Christianity acknowledging two sovereignties, one temporal and the other spiritual, one the power of the monarch or the state, and one the power of priests and the church. This later became known as the doctrine of the two swords or the two kingdoms, with separate jurisdictions, though ultimately the spiritual realm has greater authority than the earthly realm.[31] Earthly rulers have no power over souls, and true faith cannot be forced.[32]

The separation of church and state has deep biblical roots, even going back to the ancient Israelite practice where the King could not serve as priest or enter the sanctuary to perform priestly duties.[33] The Old Testament account of Shadrach, Meshach and Abed-Nego in the Persian Court (Daniel 4:28–29), where they refuse to bow down and worship King Nebuchadnezzar in violation of the command to worship God alone, also suggests that a king has no competence to govern the conscience.[34] When Jesus says not to fear those who kill the body but cannot kill the soul (Matthew 10:28), he is also underscoring that the state does not command the conscience. Only God has sovereignty over the conscience; faith is a gift of God and it cannot be coerced.[35]

The New Testament distinguishes between the spiritual and the temporal in other ways, emphasising repeatedly that Christians are citizens of the eternal world. Christians are called to remain separate from the world and not be conformed to its secular ways (2 Corinthians 6:17–18; Romans 12:2). Christians have their true commonwealth in heaven (Philippians 3:20–21). The Apostle Paul speaks of a wall of separation instituted by the law of God (Ephesians 2:16). As Witte explains:

> These passages and others have inspired Christians over the centuries to develop dualistic theories of religion and politics, church and state– two

3:20; 1 Timothy 2:1–2; James 4:12; 1 Peter 2:12–17; 3:11–17; 4:12–19. Most of these will be considered in more detail later.

30 Mathis (n 26) 394–399. See also Charles (n 2) 160–161. I consider this in more detail later.

31 Robert Wilken, *Liberty in the Things of God: The Christian Origins of Religious Freedom* (Yale University Press, 2019) 33–36.

32 Ibid 56–57.

33 Charles (n 2) 119 FN 105. See Deuteronomy 17; 1 Samuel 13; Matthew 22:15–22; Mark 12:13–17; Acts 5:27–33; Romans 13:17; 1 Peter 2:13–17.

34 Wilken (n 31) 111.

35 Ibid 115.

> ways, two cities, two powers, two swords, two kingdoms, two realms, and two institutions of religion and politics, of spiritual and temporal life. Today such images are captured in constitutional injunctions to separate church and state, and to protect the rights and autonomy of churches and their leadership.[36]

There are further references to dual jurisdictions in the New Testament. For example, in Acts 4:19–20 ('whether it is right in God's sight to listen to you rather than to God, you must judge; for we cannot keep from speaking about what we have seen and heard'), we see that God alone exercises authority over conscience, and loyalty to God trumps all other considerations.[37] The consciences of Peter and John 'dictate obedience to divine commandment over human instruction'.[38] Similarly, the Apostle Peter's argument that he 'must obey God rather than men' in Acts 5:29 recognises an ultimate authority higher than the state or human law.[39] These passages suggest acknowledgement of and deference to God's authority rather than the civil or state authority in the event of conflict. It follows that since secular liberal states cannot take a religious position (ie they are incompetent to declare that certain religious beliefs are definitely true or false), they must be open to the possibility that particular religions are true and citizens are indeed subject to a higher authority than the state. Hence, states ought to provide religious freedom for citizens to believe and practice in accordance with that higher authority.

In addition, the call to love your neighbour, expressed in the Old Testament (Leviticus 19:18) and affirmed in the New Testament (Matthew 22:37–40), entails 'extension of religious freedom to all' as a 'powerful act of godly love'.[40] The law of love is brought into conversation with the role of the state in Romans 13:1–10, extracted here in full:

> Let every person be subject to the governing authorities. For there is no authority except from God, and those that exist have been instituted by God. Therefore whoever resists the authorities resists what God has appointed, and those who resist will incur judgment. For rulers are not a terror to good conduct, but to bad. Would you have no fear of the one who is in authority? Then do what is good, and you will receive his approval, for he is God's servant for your good. But if you do wrong, be afraid, for he does not bear the sword in vain. For he is the servant of

36 Witte (n 22) 22–23. See also the general discussions in John Witte Jr, 'Facts and Fictions About the History of Separation of Church and State' (2006) 48 *Journal of Church and State* 15; Gerhard Robbers, 'Christianity and the Law of Church-State Relations' in John Witte Jr and Rafael Domingo (eds), *The Oxford Handbook of Christianity and Law* (Oxford University Press, 2024).

37 Mathis (n 26) 394–399. See also Charles (n 2) 160–161.

38 Mathis (n 26) 393.

39 Taliaferro (n 3) 124.

40 Mathis (n 26) 401–402.

> God, an avenger who carries out God's wrath on the wrongdoer. Therefore one must be in subjection, not only to avoid God's wrath but also for the sake of conscience. For because of this you also pay taxes, for the authorities are ministers of God, attending to this very thing. Pay to all what is owed to them: taxes to whom taxes are owed, revenue to whom revenue is owed, respect to whom respect is owed, honor to whom honor is owed. Owe no one anything, except to love each other, for the one who loves another has fulfilled the law. For the commandments, "You shall not commit adultery, You shall not murder, You shall not steal, You shall not covet," and any other commandment, are summed up in this word: "You shall love your neighbor as yourself." Love does no wrong to a neighbor; therefore love is the fulfilling of the law.

As I have explained in detail elsewhere, this passage suggests the civil authorities should generally be obeyed as a function of the law of love. However, where the civil authorities attempt to impose unjust laws, it would be contrary to the law of love to obey them.[41] In the context of laws which prohibit religious freedom, it is entirely appropriate to resist such laws for at least two reasons. First, the passage mandates obedience to the law of the state as a function of conscience. But if the law of the state is undermining the exercise of conscience, then that logically undercuts the authority of the law. It would be incoherent to obey a law undermining conscience for the sake of conscience. Second, religious freedom is an outworking of the law of love.[42] Using similar logic, it would be incoherent to obey a law undermining the law of love as a function of the law of love. More properly though, any just political order ought to have laws protecting religious freedom for the sake of conscience and the law of love.

These ideas are illustrated in the life of the Apostle Paul as recounted in the New Testament. In particular, Paul's conduct in Acts is a scriptural model of religious freedom. Paul was bold in his proclamation of the gospel of Christ while faced with state and vigilante violence. He asserted his legal rights as a Roman citizen to preach and not be arrested and bound without cause, and a right to appeal directly to Caesar.[43] Charles also observes that we have in the Apostle Paul a biblical model of using the natural law in the practice of religious freedom. In the Areopagus address (Acts 17:16–34), Paul appeals to the nature of the cosmos and human nature in making known the one true God, and God's ultimate revelation in Christ.[44] This is divine law which can be used as a guide for religious freedom. More significantly, Scripture commands that Christians are to follow Paul and use him as a model, just as he follows

41 See Alex Deagon, 'Rendering to Caesar and God: St Paul, the Natural Law Tradition, and the Authority of Law' (2014) 13(3) *Law, Culture and the Humanities* 469.

42 See Alex Deagon, 'Is Religious Liberty Loving in Principle?' in Michael Quinlan and Keith Thompson (eds), *Inclusion, Exclusion and Religious Freedom in Contemporary Australia* (Connor Court, 2021).

43 See Acts 22:22–29; Acts 25:1–12.

44 Charles (n 2) 55–56.

Christ.[45] It follows that believers in the world can and should support and assert legal rights for the protection of religious freedom. Paul also directly commands Christians that freedom is not for self-indulgence, but for service in accordance with the law of love.[46] Religious freedom is an expression of love which flows from knowing God and proclaiming Him in humility, faith and truth.[47]

Finally, the Parable of the Wheat and the Tares (or the Parable of the Weeds) ought to be noted. Since it has been said that this parable is 'the proof passage for religious liberty',[48] it is extracted in full here:

> [Jesus] put another parable before them, saying, 'The kingdom of heaven may be compared to a man who sowed good seed in his field, but while his men were sleeping, his enemy came and sowed weeds among the wheat and went away. So when the plants came up and bore grain, then the weeds appeared also. And the servants of the master of the house came and said to him, "Master, did you not sow good seed in your field? How then does it have weeds?" He said to them, "An enemy has done this." So the servants said to him, "Then do you want us to go and gather them?" But he said, "No, lest in gathering the weeds you root up the wheat along with them. Let both grow together until the harvest, and at harvest time I will tell the reapers, 'Gather the weeds first and bind them in bundles to be burned, but gather the wheat into my barn.'"' . . . And [Jesus'] disciples came to him, saying, 'Explain to us the parable of the weeds of the field.' He answered, 'The one who sows the good seed is the Son of Man. The field is the world, and the good seed is the sons of the kingdom. The weeds are the sons of the evil one, and the enemy who sowed them is the devil. The harvest is the end of the age, and the reapers are angels. Just as the weeds are gathered and burned with fire, so will it be at the end of the age. The Son of Man will send his angels, and they will gather out of his kingdom all causes of sin and all law-breakers, and throw them into the fiery furnace. In that place there will be weeping and gnashing of teeth. Then the righteous will shine like the sun in the kingdom of their Father. He who has ears, let him hear.'[49]

The idea is that since we cannot infallibly discern who will believe and who will not believe, non-Christians, the tares/weeds, should be allowed to grow in the midst of the wheat/seed, the faithful Christians.[50] This logically entails freedom for both groups to peacefully coexist.

45 1 Corinthians 11:1.
46 Galatians 5:13–14.
47 1 Timothy 2:1–4. See also 1 Peter 3:11–17 and 1 Peter 2:12–17, where the Apostle Peter provides similar sentiments.
48 Rex Ahdar and Ian Leigh, *Religious Freedom in the Liberal State* (Oxford University Press, 2nd ed, 2011) 40–41.
49 Matthew 13:24–30, 36–43.
50 Wilken (n 31) 56.

IV. Conceptual Arguments

Broadening this analysis to explain in more detail the historical and conceptual development of religious freedom on the basis of the aforementioned texts, the principle of religious liberty has a distinctly Christian pedigree, following from key theological doctrines such as intrinsic human dignity through God's creation of humans in his image, and Christ's assumption of human nature through the Incarnation.[51] As Steven Smith argues, 'religious freedom has primarily been the product of Christian . . . sources and influences'; these ideas include human dignity as being made in the Image of God (Genesis 1:26–1:28), the distinction between the civil and spiritual realms (Matthew 22:21), and the 'necessarily uncoerced nature of saving faith' (Isaiah 29:13).[52]

Wilken points out that 'religious freedom rests on a simple truth: religious faith is an inward disposition of the mind and heart and for that reason cannot be coerced by external force'.[53] The Christian history of religious freedom is concerned with three themes: 'religious belief is an inner conviction accountable to God alone and resistant to compulsion', that 'conscience is a form of spiritual knowledge that carries an obligation to act', and 'that human society is governed by two powers', in the sense that Christ distinguishes between Caesar and God in Matthew 22.[54] Christian thinkers consequently formed the view that religious freedom is a 'natural right that belongs to all human beings'.[55]

With respect to the creation of humans in the image of God, this means humans are uniquely 'truth-seeking moral creatures with the capacity to reason and to choose to love and worship God', and as such, religious propagation is a matter of persuasion so that all people may proclaim their beliefs and individuals can freely come to authentic faith (Acts 17:27).[56] Every human deserves utmost respect due to their dignity of bearing God's image. This entails reason, will, and conscience, and the ability and freedom to make choices, including in

51 See especially Wilken (n 31); Timothy Shah and Allen Hertzke (eds), *Christianity and Freedom Volume I: Historical Perspectives* (Cambridge University Press, 2016) and the chapters contained in there, which overlap and engage with many points in this chapter. For a nascent account of this argument with further references see Alex Deagon, 'Reconciling John Milbank and Religious Freedom: "Liberalism" Through Love' (2019) 34(2) *Journal of Law and Religion* 183; Alex Deagon, 'Is Religious Liberty Loving in Principle' in Michael Quinlan and Keith Thompson (eds), *Inclusion, Exclusion and Religious Freedom in Contemporary Australia* (Connor Court, 2021).

52 Steven Smith, 'Christianity and the Law of Religious Freedom' in John Witte Jr and Rafael Domingo (eds), *The Oxford Handbook of Christianity and Law* (Oxford University Press, 2024) 606–609.

53 Wilken (n 31) 1.

54 Ibid 4.

55 Ibid 5.

56 Li-Ann Thio, 'Christianity and Religious Freedom in the Asian Context' in John Witte Jr and Rafael Domingo (eds), *The Oxford Handbook of Christianity and Law* (Oxford University Press, 2024) 619.

religion.[57] The human person is uniquely capable of rational knowledge and self-direction. This also implies that decisions as to what to believe and how to practice that belief ought to be respected.

At the same time, the Image of God is explicitly linked to the natural law through the connection of conscience as the source and meaning of natural law. Hence, Porter concludes, conceiving the human in the Image of God also gives a central place to 'the exercise of intellectual capacities and rational autonomy' to find 'perfection and happiness' which, as we saw in Chapter 4, culminates in the knowledge of God.[58] And the way people obtain the knowledge of God is through faith – their will, reason, desires and conscience operating in harmony – which is just religious freedom. Moreover, this exercise of natural capacities is 'more or less isomorphic with the fundamental tenets' of divine law or revelation.[59] In this sense, Christian Natural Law which draws from both general and special revelation provides a robust conceptual framework for religious freedom.

Irving-Stonebraker also gives a corroborative historical and conceptual account of religious freedom.[60] Generally, as I have noted in Chapter 2 and in this chapter, the theological foundation for religious freedom lay in the distinction between the sacred and the secular, and in the various forms of that doctrine such as the two kingdoms. Through natural law, the idea of conscience was generalised for all people of all religions and none, not just Christians.[61] Similarly, the claims of Scripture that intersectional identities (class, ethnicity, gender) had no bearing on each human being's distinctive value as created in the image of God was 'completely anomalous in the ancient world', and this idea that 'all human beings are of equal worth' and 'inherently precious' is the 'core of human rights', including religious freedom.[62] Scripture also places a high regard on conscience and the voluntary nature of faith. Jesus' instruction to his disciples is to make more disciples through teaching, not coercion (Matthew 28:19–20). Faith is a persuasion of the mind and conscience, which is part of being made in the image of God and therefore applies

57 Witte (n 22) 18. Similarly, see Nicholas Wolterstorff, *Understanding Liberal Democracy: Essays in Political Philosophy* (Oxford University Press, 2012) 193–200 where Wolterstorff argues that Christian theology grounds human rights in the sense that since we bear the *Imago Dei* and consequently God's image as loving, rational, willing, and creative beings, and God has chosen relationship with us through Christ who assumed our very nature, we have an intrinsic dignity which requires that we ought to treat each other with honour. These obligations for honourable treatment manifest as various rights which inhere in all humans by virtue of their humanity as God's friends. See also the discussion in Pamela Slotte, 'Christianity and Human Dignity' in John Witte Jr and Rafael Domingo (eds), *The Oxford Handbook of Christianity and Law* (Oxford University Press, 2024).

58 Porter (n 13) 230.

59 Ibid.

60 Sarah Irving-Stonebraker, 'The Forgotten History of Religious Liberty: Richard Johnson Lecture, 2020' (2021) 45(4) *Journal of Religious History* 644–658.

61 Ibid 5–9.

62 Ibid 2–3.

to all humans. 'This was the basis upon which Christians began to argue that conscience ought to be protected'.[63] Irving-Stonebraker summarises:

> Freedom of conscience became the archetypal natural right because conscience is at the ontological core of the human person. The biblical vision of the human being, which was the historical basis for natural rights claims, was that humanity was created in God's image and endowed with a rational conscience. Protecting that conscience subsequently became the basis for protecting other rights.[64]

Shah traces the development of arguments for universal religious freedom in some of the early patristic writers, including Justin Martyr, Athenagoras, Tertullian and Lactantius. He notes Tertullian in particular advocated for religious freedom (and first coined the term 'religious liberty') in an unprecedented, universal way, claiming it is a fundamental human right or privilege of nature that a person should be able to worship according to their convictions without being compelled.[65] Wilken agrees, and emphasises that the ultimate source for Tertullian was the Bible. Tertullian's approach reflects the biblical view of the dignity and worth of a human being as the *Imago Dei*, clearly articulated in Genesis 1:26–27. This most fundamentally means that humans are free, free to render ourselves to God and not to Caesar as Jesus commands us to do (Matthew 22:21).[66]

Roger Williams is another exponent of religious liberty as a natural right grounded in Scripture. Twiss has argued that for Williams, freedom of conscience is a 'subjective natural right created by God'.[67] Williams argued for freedom to practice religion on the basis of the inherent and equal value of all human beings created in the image of God, with the ability and duty to

63 Ibid 3. See generally Helen Alvare and Jeffrey Hammond (eds), *Christianity and the Law of Conscience* (Cambridge University Press, 2021).

64 Irving-Stonebraker (n 60) 6–7.

65 See Timothy Shah, 'The Roots of Religious Freedom in Early Christian Thought' in Timothy Shah and Allen Hertzke (eds), *Christianity and Freedom Volume I: Historical Perspectives* (Cambridge University Press, 2016). See also Wilken (n 31) 11–18; Taliaferro (n 3) 105–108, 115–120. I will consider Tertullian in more detail in the next section.

66 See Robert Wilken, 'The Christian Roots of Religious Freedom' in Timothy Shah and Allen Hertzke (eds), *Christianity and Freedom Volume I: Historical Perspectives* (Cambridge University Press, 2016) 65. Many of the points in Wilken's chapter are expanded in his subsequent book (Wilken [n 31]). See also Wilken (n 31) 11–18; Taliaferro (n 3) 105–108, 115–120. See also generally Steven D Smith, 'Christianity and the Law of Religious Freedom' in John Witte Jr and Rafael Domingo (eds), *The Oxford Handbook of Christianity and Law* (Oxford University Press, 2024).

67 Sumner Twiss, 'Roger Williams and Freedom of Conscience and Religion as a Natural Right' in Sumner Twiss, Marion Simion, and Rodney Peterson (eds), *Religion and Public Policy: Human Rights, Conflict, Ethics* (Cambridge University Press, 2015). See also Cory Higdon, 'Roger Williams, Natural Law, and Religious Liberty' (2021) 63(1) *Journal of Church and State* 85.

pursue truth.[68] Williams held a strong view that the church should be separate from the state and the liberty of all persons should be respected, grounded in Scriptures such as the Parable of the Wheat and Tares, Jesus rebuking his disciples who wished to call down fire on the Samaritans, Jesus saying that one should render to God what is God's, and Paul's statement that the weapons of spiritual warfare are not physical. The office of the magistrate is to preserve the civil realm in peace and order, while the church's role is to focus on worship and the consciences of people.[69] As will be discussed in further detail in the next section, these kinds of arguments drew on John Calvin and anticipated John Locke.[70]

I have also argued elsewhere that conceptually, Christians have always understood that the beliefs grounding their ethics are matters of faith, or persuasion.[71] In particular, as Christ is revealed to the mind, the mind is persuaded. As the mind is transformed by faith, it participates in the glory of Christ by imitating Christ and then loves one's neighbour as a reflection of Christ, which is the law of love articulated by the Apostle Paul in the New Testament.[72] This law of love, modelled on and enabled by the Incarnation and crucifixion of Christ, consequently encourages love for one's neighbour in terms of humility and sacrifice. Importantly, this is not forced or coerced, but rather freely volunteered as an imitation of Christ in trust that the action will be reciprocated.[73] Charles agrees, observing that 'Truth does not impose itself by force or violence but rather by the force of its own truth'.[74] Religious belief 'cannot be compelled because it is compelled already . . . by our own best grasp of the truth . . . religion is not so much chosen as it is accepted, as a truth one has discovered or learned'.[75]

On the principle of religious freedom more specifically, the 'law of love' approach seeks to create a harmonious and inclusive space where a person can freely express, debate and choose faith perspectives without being subject to state, community or individual violence. There should not be arbitrary legal or political constraints on the expression of perspectives. Love, in fact, requires going beyond the boundaries of law or moral duty. In particular, we need to

68 Irving-Stonebraker (n 60) 9–10.

69 Wilken (n 31) 147–149.

70 Ibid 154. See also David Little, 'Constitutional Protection of the Freedom of Conscience in Colonial America' in Timothy Shah and Allen Hertzke (eds), *Christianity and Freedom Volume I: Historical Perspectives* (Cambridge University Press, 2016) 239–246, where Little overviews the 'Rhode Island Experiment' of disestablishment and freedom of conscience presided over by Williams. Little notes in particular the arguments by Williams that conscience is internal and can only be moved by reason and conviction, not by coercion through external force. Religious coercion is therefore impossible, incoherent and intolerable (239–242).

71 See Alex Deagon, 'Reconciling John Milbank and Religious Freedom: "Liberalism" Through Love' (2019) 34(2) *Journal of Law and Religion* 183.

72 Romans 13:8–10.

73 Colossians 3:8–17.

74 Charles (n 2) 16.

75 Ibid 105, 160–161.

go beyond mere legal duty (for example, to just avoid hate speech, blasphemy or vilification) and selfish interest (the aggressive pursuit of our own agenda without due consideration for alternative views, or the prideful need to be seen as right), desiring to truly act with humility, love and sacrifice just like Christ did in humbling himself to death on a cross for our forgiveness.[76]

> Do nothing from selfish ambition or conceit, but in humility count others more significant than yourselves. Let each of you look not only to his own interests, but also to the interests of others. Have this mind among yourselves, which is yours in Christ Jesus, who, though he was in the form of God, did not count equality with God a thing to be grasped, but emptied himself, by taking the form of a servant, being born in the likeness of men. And being found in human form, he humbled himself by becoming obedient to the point of death, even death on a cross.
>
> (Philippians 2:3–8)

In this practical sense love of neighbour in a religious freedom context means doing or refraining from particular associated actions through properly cultivating the Christian virtues: listening and engaging rather than pre-judging, interpreting expressed views charitably and asking questions to clarify and learn rather than assuming or misrepresenting the views of others, and not engaging in malicious or contemptuous conduct. Love of neighbour avoids 'anger, wrath, malice, slander' and lying, and pursues 'kindness, humility, meekness and patience' with honesty, forbearance, compassion and forgiveness.[77] Most importantly, as noted, perspectives should be adopted by means of peaceful persuasion rather than coercion.

Finally, Ahdar and Leigh set out a detailed conceptual argument for religious freedom from a Christian perspective.[78] They summarise the argument in the form of eight overlapping principles: 'the principle of voluntariness', which is that faith is personal, dependent on freedom and non-coercion; 'the Christological injunction', that Christ was humble and did not force anyone to join him; 'the persecution injunction', that persecution in the name of Christianity denies the faith and is offensive to God; 'the fallibility principle', that God alone is sovereign and infallible, and the possibility of human error means we should be cautious in judging religious matters; 'the eschatological or providential confidence', that God's purposes and truth will ultimately prevail and the erroneous and deceitful will fall; 'the ecumenical or universal principle', that God speaks to a degree through all genuine religions and elements of the truth may be found in them, though the fullest and surest expression is Christianity; 'the principle of the unrestricted conscience', that all persons must

76 See Philippians 2:3–8.

77 Colossians 3:8–13.

78 Rex Ahdar and Ian Leigh, *Religious Freedom in the Liberal State* (Oxford University Press, 2nd ed, 2011) 24–50.

have the freedom to follow the call of conscience and pursue the truth as they perceive it; and finally, 'the dual authority principle', that the state's authority is limited to earthly and civil matters, and is subject to a higher authority which governs spiritual matters.[79]

In terms of the details, salvation is a gift from God (Romans 6:23), and no one can be coerced to receive a gift.[80] Christ did not come to destroy people, but to save them, and both Christ and the apostle Paul rejected the use of human weapons to further the kingdom of God (Luke 9:56; John 18:36; 2 Corinthians 10:3–4).[81] The Parable of the Wheat and the Tares (Matthew 13:24–43) underscores the fallibility of human judgement.[82] We do not know who are the wheat and who are the tares, and we should leave them to grow together until God judges at the last day. There is a possibility we may destroy the true believers by seeking to coerce those who do not believe. 'God's purposes will ultimately prevail', as Gamaliel unwittingly explained to the Pharisees who were persecuting the apostles (Acts 5:33–39).[83] The dual authority principle is most clearly expressed in Christ's command to render to Caesar that which is Caesar's, and to God that which is God's (Matthew 22:21).[84] And in the event of a conflict between Caesar and God in a matter of conscience, the constant refrain in Scripture is 'we ought to obey God rather than men' (Acts 5:29).[85] For these reasons, as Charles notes, the historic Christian moral tradition, or what I term a Christian Natural Law, provides a unique and robust framework to resolve the perennial problem of religious freedom, pluralism, diversity and tolerance.[86]

V. Ancient and Modern Examples

This section illustrates the general textual and conceptual arguments of the previous two sections by providing specific examples of how different perspectives drew upon these theological resources to articulate the principles of religious freedom. I consider Tertullian, Augustine, Calvin and Reformed theology, Locke, and modern Catholicism. By definition these examples are selective and not comprehensive, but I have chosen these because they arise frequently in the literature discussed in the previous sections. I also draw on these examples to articulate some further aspects and implications of my Christian Natural Law foundation for religious freedom. Despite some internal tensions between ideas and/or actions in these examples, there is consistency across the principles articulated. These provide an idea of religious freedom grounded in

79 Ibid 50.
80 Ibid 38.
81 Ibid 38–39.
82 Ibid 40–41.
83 Ibid 41.
84 Ibid 25.
85 Ibid 47.
86 Charles (n 2) 140.

the True as an objectively existing ideal manifested through Scripture and in the person of Christ, yet an idea which is also comprehensible and applicable to those who do not share Christian beliefs.

A. Tertullian

Tertullian, a third-century Christian theologian and apologist, was 'likely the first author to use the term "religious freedom", which he termed as a "human right"' grounded in nature and conscience.[87] Though Tertullian effectively invented the term, he drew on an ancient Jewish tradition that the only true worship that pleases God is genuine, of the mind and heart.[88] The full quote is contained in a critique of the Roman policy of persecuting Christians:

> It is a fundamental human right, a privilege of nature, that every man should worship according to his own convictions . . . It is not part of religion to coerce religious practice, for it is by choice and not coercion that we should be led to religion.[89]

For Tertullian and the early Christians, following God was not a matter of ethnicity or earthly power, but pursuing the truth. The argument was not a modern one of a legally enforceable right against the state, but rather that it is the proper and natural end of humans to seek truth freely according to conscience. Coercion violates this natural and proper end of humans created in God's image. 'What emerges, in short, is the idea that following God is free in that it stems from the will and conscience. It cannot and ought not, be coerced'.[90]

For Tertullian, this non-coercion argument was grounded in Scripture, where God's people are asked to choose him (Deuteronomy 30:15), and nature, that we are all created in God's image (Genesis 1:26–27). By virtue of being a creation in God's image, we are possessed with reason and divine life, including power to choose and act.[91] Yet Tertullian also innovated by grounding religious liberty in a natural right to believe without coercion, which therefore applied to all persons and all religions, not just Christianity.[92] Consequently, an important aspect of Tertullian's defense of religious freedom is its universal nature. Even though Tertullian rejected all non-Christian beliefs as false, he held that every person nevertheless has, as a privilege or capacity of nature, a human right to worship according to their own convictions. He

87 Taliaferro (n 3) 105.
88 Shah (n 65) 54–55.
89 Tertullian, 'To Scapula' in A Roberts and J Donaldson (eds), *Anti-Nicene Fathers, Volume 3, Latin Christianity: Its Founder Tertullian* (Hendrickson, 1994) 105.
90 Irving-Stonebraker (n 60) 4–5. See also Wilken (n 31) 13; Josef Lossl, 'Law and the Church Fathers' in John Witte Jr and Rafael Domingo (eds), *The Oxford Handbook of Christianity and Law* (Oxford University Press, 2024) 34–37.
91 Wilken (n 31) 14–15.
92 Shah (n 65) 55.

grounded this in a nascent kind of biblical natural law argument that all persons have a soul, created by God, and that consequently they have some basic awareness of divine truth.[93] True religion at its core is about the relationship between the individual and divinity, and a person's pursuit of authentic relationship with the divine that is part of our human nature.[94] This 'appeal to the divine spark' in all people means people should be free to come to knowledge of the truth without coercion.[95] For Tertullian, 'worship must be offered in truth, otherwise it ceases to be worship'.[96] Of course, this reflects later, more developed arguments by Thomists and Calvinists that there is a natural law, and such a natural law is a foundation for religious freedom. These arguments have been canvassed in Chapter 2 and this chapter, and are also considered later in this section.

Thus, Tertullian's seminal contribution is he managed to ground his notion of religious freedom in divine law, yet addressed it to an audience who did not share his theological presuppositions. Taliaferro argues this opens the 'possibilities of religious freedom, for his appeal admits the validity of both human and divine law and wisdom operating simultaneously in the political and legal spheres'.[97] Tertullian insisted on the truth of Scripture and it was the foundation for all his arguments. Yet he also understood and deployed human reason to support these scriptural arguments.[98] Tertullian allows us to avoid the mistake of assuming religious freedom is just another human right. As Taliaferro explains:

> Religious freedom is the only human right that recognises two distinct realms of authority, human and divine . . . to reduce it to a purely immanent human right does violence to the very nature of religion, and therefore of religious freedom . . . religious freedom is therefore distinct among the human rights because as one such right, it must answer to human law, but for it to have authority with religion and religious people it must answer to divine law.[99]

B. Augustine

Augustine of Hippo, the celebrated Bishop of the fourth century who is one of the greatest thinkers in human history, is complex on the matter of religious freedom. He considered that coercion may be justified to create a situation where Christianity could be accurately taught and practiced. This is why schismatics and heretics were often targeted with coercion and severe punishments, while pagans and Jews were only subject to rational arguments – the former

93 Taliaferro (n 3) 115–118.
94 Shah (n 65) 55.
95 Taliaferro (n 3) 115–118.
96 Ibid 120.
97 Ibid 106.
98 Ibid 107–110.
99 Ibid 123–124.

were a much more present and immediate threat to the stability of the church because the error was more subtle and insidious.[100] For example, Augustine succumbed to the temptation to coerce the Donatists to orthodox Christian belief, based on some dubious interpretations of Scripture.[101]

Augustine pointed to the use of coercion in the Parable of the Great Banquet, the use of force by Christ to effect Paul's conversion, and Jesus' clearing of the moneychangers from the temple.[102] He also could argue that even if a compelled conversion is an oxymoron (as 'we cannot be compelled to love God; that would not be love in any sense freely given'), forced conversion may result in genuine heart conversion, and/or forced conversion of a parent may result in genuine conversion of a child.[103] But, with the greatest of respect to Augustine, these are not strong arguments. Parables are not purely didactic and one should always exercise caution in drawing doctrinal principles from them which are beside the main point, Christ's conversion of Paul was the use of supernatural power which humans do not possess and cannot wield (and so this cannot be reasonably seen as a precedent), and Jesus' treatment of the moneychangers has nothing to do with conversion at all. Even if these were persuasive examples, they have been downplayed as exceptions to the rule.[104] And Augustine's possible consequentialist arguments are contrary to 'more fundamental theological principles' which rely on the 'essential dignity' of humans being created in the 'divine image', and therefore humans must have freedom to choose to love God (or not).[105]

As Ahdar and Leigh explain, though Augustine did use state apparatus to coerce, this was for him a last resort after a decade of promoting less extreme measures.[106] Without excusing Augustine's conduct, the Donatists were creating political difficulties in the local community, including physical attacks against Catholic Bishops. After more diplomatic means failed, Augustine 'reluctantly concluded that only force would constrain the Donatists', and he then tried to find biblical justification.[107] Despite Augustine's actions in this context, in his general teaching and preaching he maintained a consistent position that faith cannot be coerced by violence. He argued from Romans 10:10 that true faith requires confession, and confession must be genuine, from the heart.[108] Relying on 1 Corinthians 5:12–13, he also argued that those outside the faith should be attracted to the truth through gentleness.[109] We can reject

100 Lossl (n 90) 38. See also Ahdar and Leigh (n 78) 32–34.
101 Wilken (n 31) 31–32.
102 Ahdar and Leigh (n 78) 37.
103 John Rist, 'Augustine and Religious Freedom' in Timothy Shah and Allen Hertzke (eds), *Christianity and Freedom Volume I: Historical Perspectives* (Cambridge University Press, 2016) 112–113.
104 Ahdar and Leigh (n 78) 37.
105 Rist (n 103) 113, 118, 120.
106 Ahdar and Leigh (n 78) 26–27.
107 Wilken (n 31) 31; Rist (n 103) 112.
108 Wilken (n 31) 32.
109 David Lantigua, 'Faith, Liberty and the Defense of the Poor' in Timothy Shah and Allen Hertzke (eds), *Christianity and Freedom Volume I: Historical Perspectives* (Cambridge University Press, 2016) 194.

the inconsistencies of Augustine's actions while accepting the general principles he articulates regarding the voluntaristic nature of faith.[110]

Shah explains that paradoxically, Christianity has been a source of both political and moral disappointment and political and moral hope. Indeed, it has been a political and moral disappointment because it has been a hope. Christian guilt is especially jarring and egregious in light of Christian principles, and Christian principles have always pointed beyond Christian practice. Yet, modern thinkers have only been able to critique Christian practice because they have absorbed principles of human dignity and religious freedom that are indispensably grounded in Christianity. In that sense, Shah says provocatively, 'perhaps those of us committed to the principle of religious freedom as well as other liberal freedoms should call ourselves Christians . . . regardless of our confessional point of view'.[111] And as Smith pithily summarises, religious freedom is something 'Christianity just demonstrably required from the beginning, even if many Christians failed to recognise that fact'.[112] This theme arises again with respect to John Calvin.

C. *Calvin and Reformed Theology*

As explained in Chapter 2, Calvin, the sixteenth-century Reformer, argued that God had written the natural law in the human heart, revealed it in Scripture, and summarised it in the Decalogue. Religious freedom is a fundamental right because people are called to honour and obey God above all other commandments. The State and the Church are separate entities, and it is the role of the Church to steward spiritual affairs. Calvin argues, based on passages such as Romans 13, that the State is ordained by God and should be obeyed. However, where the State does not permit religious freedom by requiring Christians to dishonour God, the State usurps God's authority and civil disobedience is an appropriate response (and even a mandatory response according to Acts 5:29).[113] As Witte also points out, Calvin developed a distinct theology of rights and in particular a robust doctrine of liberty of conscience which formed the foundation for constitutional religious liberty rights advocated by the Calvinists.[114]

Calvin claimed that humans had original natural rights of freedom, bestowed by God.[115] Little explains that Calvin distinguished between the

110 As Rist does: see Rist (n 103). I make a similar argument in Alex Deagon, 'Reconceptualising Law: "Pagan" Violence and Augustinian Peace' (2021) 33(3) *Journal for the Academic Study of Religion* 286, 299–300.

111 Shah (n 65) 36–37.

112 Smith (n 52) 611.

113 John Witte Jr, 'Calvinist Contributions to Freedom in Early Modern Europe' in Timothy Shah and Allen Hertzke (eds), *Christianity and Freedom Volume I: Historical Perspectives* (Cambridge University Press, 2016) 211–213.

114 John Witte Jr, *Reformation of Rights: Law, Religion and Human Rights in Early Modern Calvinism* (Cambridge University Press, 2007) 2–3.

115 David Little, 'Calvin and Natural Rights' (2009) 10(3) *Political Theology* 411, 416.

inner forum, the conscience, and the outer forum, civil authority, and argued that the former was governed by spiritual authority and outside the jurisdiction of the state. And just as the state cannot compel the person in matters of conscience, so the church cannot either.[116] Human laws are not binding on the conscience, and indeed the conscience is entitled to pass judgement on human laws, entailing a natural right to freedom of conscience.[117] However, there is tension in Calvin's writings on this point. After the notorious execution of Michael Servetus for Trinitarian heresy, Calvin seemed to advocate for a closer relationship between church and state, suggesting that the magistrate has a role in enforcing sound doctrine and the position of the church.[118] Similarly, Witte notes that while the early Calvin developed a robust theory of the liberty of the Christian conscience, the later Calvin diminished the role of the individualistic conscience in favour of corporate religious liberty in cooperation with the state to maintain decency and order.[119]

Wilken similarly provides an instructive account of Calvin's writings on liberty of conscience, arguing that Calvin struggled with the blurring of secular government and inward conscience in Romans 13. To resolve this Calvin distinguished between laws governing the body, which are properly the domain of magistrates, but do not apply to matters of conscience. In religious matters, the conscience must be free. Christians are subject to civil authority, but in matters of faith they are subject only to God. Yet Calvin also believed piety and a publicly supported church is essential for a flourishing polity.[120] As Calvin increasingly involved himself in civil governance of Geneva, he began to merge the two realms in both theory and policy (through arguing that the magistrate is also the custodian of the faith), which culminated in the unfortunate execution of Servetus.[121]

Despite this tension, the theological basis for Calvin's traditional position is clear.[122] The conscience is that faculty by which humans know moral good and evil, and by which knowledge can be accused or excused.[123] VanDrunen grounds Calvin's understanding of conscience in Calvin's commentary on Romans 2:14–15, going as far as to say that for Calvin, conscience is the 'law written on the heart', and 'natural law is the apprehension of conscience'.[124] All

116 Ibid 420.

117 Ibid 424.

118 Ibid 421.

119 For a detailed account, see John Witte, 'Moderate Religious Liberty in the Theology of John Calvin' (1996) 31 *Calvin Theological Journal* 359. For another balanced discussion of this tension see Ahdar and Leigh (n 78) 27–34.

120 Wilken (n 31) 68–71.

121 Ibid 72.

122 See Constance Lee, 'The Secularisation of Conscience: A Natural Law Critique' (2024) 4 *Australian Journal of Law and Religion* 57, 71–73.

123 Romans 2:14–15; John Calvin, *Institutes of the Christian Religion*, ed John T McNeill, tr Ford Lewis Battles (Westminster Press, 1960) bk 2 ch 7 s 1.

124 David VanDrunen, 'Conscience and Natural Law in Scripture' in Helen Alvare and Jeffrey Hammond (eds), *Christianity and the Law of Conscience* (Cambridge University Press, 2021) 42.

humans have this capacity by virtue of being created in God's image (Genesis 1:26–27). Both the existence and operation of conscience is a gift of common grace.[125] Through conscience, humans can perceive God and the good in a limited way, as through a darkened mirror.[126] Therefore, conscience should be protected so humans can exercise it and, by grace and guidance in the revelation of Scripture, come to know God through Christ.[127]

VanDrunen notes that conscience is at least partly formed through the natural law.[128] This implies freedom of conscience is informed through and supported by natural law and Scripture. Giles suggests the Calvinist or Reformed doctrine of common grace provides the foundation for religious freedom, because the exercise of conscience is only possible 'due to the operation of God through the Holy Spirit'.[129] The theory of common grace intersects with religious freedom in recognising the capacity of all humans to understand and exercise agency with respect to a 'universal moral law', which is just the natural law.[130] However, VanDrunen argues that from a Reformed perspective, people only have a penultimate natural law right to religious freedom.[131] The fact that Scripture commands Christians to be concerned for the welfare of their fellow believers (John 13:34–35) and to love all their neighbours (Luke 10:25–37) may be sufficient motivation to get Christians interested in issues of religious liberty, but it is not sufficient to ground a natural right.[132] VanDrunen bases this argument in an exposition of relevant Scripture. First, he notes that Romans 1 indicates certain forms of religious freedom are untenable, though they may point to an inherent human dignity which ought to be respected. Genesis 8–9 then establishes that God has called humans to productive cultural activity which is not discriminatory on the basis of religion, nor are humans given jurisdiction over religious worship which lacks a human victim.[133]

Romans 1 demonstrates the existence of a natural law, and the immorality of idol worship suggests that humans have no ultimate natural law right to religious freedom. Rather, as the rest of Romans attests, natural law establishes human sinfulness and the need for God, and there is a requirement to reconcile with and worship the one true God which can only occur through the death and resurrection of Jesus Christ by the preaching of the

125 Calvin (n 123) bk 1 ch 15 s 2.
126 1 Corinthians 13:12 (King James Version); Calvin (n 123) bk 3 ch 2 s 20.
127 Calvin (n 123) bk 1 ch 15 s 2.
128 VanDrunen (n 124) 48.
129 Jessica Giles, 'The Interrelationship between Freedom of Thought, Conscience, and Religion and the Rule of Law' (2023) 38(3) *Journal of Law and Religion* 376, 393. See also the Scripture references by Giles contained there.
130 Ibid 394–395.
131 David VanDrunen, 'A Natural Law Right to Religious Freedom – A Reformed Perspective' (2012) 5(2) *International Journal for Religious Freedom* 135, 135.
132 Ibid 136.
133 Ibid 137.

gospel.[134] Yet the natural law under the Noahic Covenant does require treating humans with the respect they deserve as a matter of dignity and due to the great moral task of creation stewardship, including in matters of religious freedom.[135] The blessing of the Noahic Covenant, that all humans have the privilege of participating in flourishing human society regardless of religious belief and practice, indicates that there is a natural law right a person may enforce against others who seek to deprive them of this privilege due to their religious belief or practice, or against those who otherwise punish them due to their religious belief or practice.[136] This is the penultimate natural law right of religious freedom.

However, Wolterstorff points out that if we have an objective natural duty to worship God, as VanDrunen would appear to concede, then we have a subjective natural duty to worship God in accordance with entitled convictions. And if we have a subjective natural duty to worship God in accordance with our entitled convictions, we have a natural right to worship God in accordance with our entitled convictions, which is just religious freedom. And this natural right to religious freedom, by its character, would be a pre-eminent right over any other natural duties/rights and would require legal protection.[137] So though Wolterstorff and VanDrunen arrive at the same essential conclusion, Wolterstorff through this argument would characterise religious freedom as an ultimate right due to its correlative ultimate duty of worship, rather than rendering religious freedom a second-order natural law right as VanDrunen does.

The distinction VanDrunen makes between ultimate and penultimate religious freedom is nevertheless helpful when considered within the framework of Christian Natural Law. For a Christian Natural Law, Love, the True and the Good, the three fundamental pillars, are found in the pursuit and culmination of divine relationship. It is only by truly knowing the God of love in Christ that perfect Good may be experienced, and religious freedom is oriented towards this unique end. Religious freedom is supported by Christian Natural Law only to the extent that it is a journey (albeit in some cases a road long and winding) with a direction and a destination. Religious freedom is love, good and true in Christ, rather than in the mere existence of religious freedom. In this sense it can be said that religious freedom is penultimate or instrumental (oriented to God) rather than ultimate (oriented to itself), though of course the arguments in Part I of the book suggest God is the ultimate end for humanity. In any case, the intrinsic dignity bestowed upon humanity through being created in God's image and having Christ assume human nature, and humans having the capacity and opportunity for entering into relationship with God, certainly grounds a natural law right to respect religious freedom through legal protection.

134 Ibid 139–140.
135 Ibid 139–141.
136 Ibid 143, 145.
137 Wolterstorff (n 57) 349–351.

D. *John Locke*

It might seem odd to consider John Locke at this point. There is a view that John Locke provides the archetypal secular justification for religious freedom in a liberal state.[138] However, Locke was steeped in an environment of Calvinist theological thinking, and this is reflected in his writing, where Locke gives expression to Calvinist and Reformed theology, and emphasises the importance of natural moral law.[139] Wilken also points out that Locke was significantly influenced by Calvinism, and from Calvinism derived his own theories regarding the natural law. There is no evidence that Locke had actually read Calvin himself, but the Calvinist thinking was culturally entrenched at the time.[140] Indeed, Waldron argues Locke's social and political philosophy cannot be understood apart from its theological basis. In particular, Locke's view of human dignity and equality was deeply grounded in Christian doctrine, and the veracity of Scripture was a working premise in his writing. Locke was 'intensely interested in Christian doctrine', and his discussion is 'saturated with Christian assumptions'.[141] It is an 'anachronism' to 'treat Locke's argument as though it were a secular argument'.[142] Wilken similarly claims that 'Locke's ideas on religious freedom cannot be understood without reference to Christianity'.[143] Locke therefore offers a political framework 'fully compatible with orthodox Christian belief'.[144]

Locke in his *First Treatise* observes from Genesis 1:26 that all men are created equal and endowed by their Creator with rights, exercised through the intellect and will.[145] Furthermore, although insisting there is only one way to heaven, Locke emphasised individual conscience and responsibility in finding that way. Since 'man cannot be forced to be saved', religious truth cannot be imposed by the state.[146] Locke cites Psalm 51 as an example of how true religion is from the heart.[147] He does not empty faith of its transcendent dimension, and is firm in asserting that religion has substantive content: it is belief in and obedience to the Christian God.[148] Locke further argues that full and true knowledge of religion sufficient for salvation can come only through divine

138 See eg Russell Blackford, *Freedom of Religion and the Secular State* (Wiley-Blackwell, 2012).
139 Charles (n 2) 93–95.
140 Wilken (n 31) 173.
141 Jeremy Waldron, *God, Locke, and Equality: Christian Foundations in Locke's Political Thought* (Cambridge University Press, 2002) 12.
142 Ibid 15.
143 Wilken (n 31) 179.
144 Matthew Franck, 'Christianity and Freedom in the American Founding' in Timothy Shah and Allen Hertzke (eds), *Christianity and Freedom Volume I: Historical Perspectives* (Cambridge University Press, 2016) 270; Waldron (n 141) 27–28, 151; Augusto Zimmermann, *Christian Foundations of the Common Law: The United States* (Connor Court, 2018) 62, 66. For a detailed account see Wilken (n 31) 169–179.
145 John Locke, cited in Waldron (n 141) 25.
146 Zimmermann (n 144) 69.
147 Wilken (n 31) 170.
148 Ibid 175.

revelation. Revelation is above and goes further than reason, but is never contrary to reason.[149] As such, Locke was a 'deeply devoted Christian who was committed to obedience to God as mankind's Creator'; he knew that true religion could only result from persuasion and a changed mind, and coerced religion was only likely to breed hostility and hypocrisy.[150]

On natural law, Locke wrote that the natural law is an 'eternal rule to all men' which everyone can recognise and uphold, and any human law must be 'conformable to the will of nature, i.e. to the will of God'.[151] Yet Locke 'insisted that most men could not hope to understand the detailed requirements of the law of nature without the assistance of the teachings and example of Jesus'.[152] The Bible is a confirmation of natural law principles. This natural law provided a pre-political framework for fundamental natural rights which are 'God-given and inalienable', including liberty.[153] Such rights set limits to state authority, and where state authority does not recognise and protect those rights, it ceases to be a legitimate authority.[154] Freedom of speech and freedom of conscience are therefore the essence of the classical Christian toleration articulated by Locke.

Locke claimed that spiritual matters were within the sphere of conscience, 'the individual's divinely endowed capacity to recognise spiritual truth', and therefore were outside the jurisdiction of the state.[155] The state can only operate through coercion, and coercion cannot produce true and genuine belief. The protection of religious freedom from the state is therefore a function of the state's duty to protect liberty, and is necessary for the individual to realise spiritual truth and their meaningful commitment to that truth. Moon calls these 'religious reasons' for toleration.[156] Locke is 'resolute' that the 'magistrate can neither legislate nor coerce on religious matters', and his famous argument for a law of nature that no one ought to harm life, health, liberty or possessions is grounded in his claim that we are all created by God for His pleasure and His business.[157] Heyman agrees, demonstrating that Locke provided arguments for God's existence and nature and human reason to establish natural rights and duties, including to worship God and believe the truth. This forms the foundation for his *Letter Concerning Toleration*, where Locke argues that the right of religious liberty should be afforded to all in accordance with the love

149 Steven Heyman, 'Transforming Natural Religion: An Essay on Religious Liberty and the Constitution' (2023) 48 *Brigham Young University Law Review* 1447, 1458.

150 Charles (n 2) 128.

151 John Locke, *Second Treatise of Government*, Ch 11, sec 135.

152 Waldron (n 141) 12.

153 Zimmermann (n 144) 66–68, 70.

154 Ibid 68–69.

155 Richard Moon, '*R v Big M Drug Mart*: The Unavoidable Pragmatism of Religious Freedom' in Renae Barker, Paul Babie, and Neil Foster (eds), *Law and Religion in the Commonwealth: The Evolution of Case Law* (Hart, 2022) 85.

156 Ibid.

157 Charles (n 2) 93–95.

Christians ought to show all people, even non-Christians. Therefore, there should be a strict separation of church and state, in the sense that it is improper for the state to interfere with individual religious liberty through either imposing religious observance or coercing in matters of religion.[158]

Locke's primary writings on religious freedom are contained in the Letter.[159] Locke distinguishes between civil and religious societies. The civil society, or the Commonwealth, is the domain of the Magistrate, which can only exercise power to protect life, health, liberty and property. The religious society is the Church, concerned with the salvation of souls. Locke argues, based on both reason and Scripture, that the Magistrate should never coerce people in matters of religion, and should instead tolerate different perspectives to the extent those perspectives are lawful and consistent with the protection of life, health, liberty and property. Similarly, religious groups should not seek to use the power of the state to solve religious disagreement. Religious truth is to be pursued through the freedom of individual conscience.

In particular, Locke's argument was that toleration should be 'the chief characteristical mark of the True Church'.[160] This is because by its nature true religion cannot be coerced. Locke quotes Luke 22:25 to declare that the Church should not declare Lordship over persons, and Galatians 5:6 to argue that faith works 'not by force, but by love'.[161]

> The Toleration of those that differ from others in Matters of Religion, is so agreeable to the Gospel of Jesus Christ, and to the genuine Reason of Mankind, that it seems monstrous for Men to be so blind, as not to perceive the Necessity and Advantage of it.[162]

Coercion does not produce true faith and is contrary to love, and Locke draws on the biblical definition of faith as persuasion at multiple points:

> All the Life and Power of true Religion consists in the inward and full perswasion of the mind: And Faith is not Faith without believing . . . But true and saving Religion consists in the inward perswasion of the Mind; without which nothing can be acceptable to God.[163]

Conversely, the Magistrate's 'Power consists only in outward force' (Romans 13), and therefore 'the care of souls' is not committed to the Magistrate; indeed, the Magistrate has no authority by God or man 'to compel any one

158 Heyman (n 149) 1455–1457.
159 John Locke, *Letter Concerning Toleration*: https://oll.libertyfund.org/titles/goldie-a-letter-concerning-toleration-and-other-writings
160 Ibid.
161 Ibid.
162 Ibid.
163 Ibid.

to his Religion'.[164] Examples of these sorts of arguments in the Letter could be multiplied.

David explains that Locke's toleration 'entails a peaceable, tolerant morality towards religious others, whether Christian or not'.[165] It also entails 'a minimal (and Protestant) Christianity, grounded in the biblical texts'; a person is responsible for their own salvation and ought to pursue the truth, but coercion must be eschewed.[166] One of the reasons coercion must be eschewed is due to our ignorance of spiritual things. Since no one has infallible knowledge of religion, no one has the right to impose their religious views as though they are divine requirements.[167] Locke also frames toleration as a theological disposition in this context. Toleration includes 'charity, meekness, and good will in general', and 'peace and friendship in the diversity of opinions' which results from our fallible knowledge.[168] David even says 'Locke's tolerant Christianity' involves 'a series of virtues', the 'fruits of the Spirit (Galatians 5)'.[169]

However, Locke says that the magistrate ought to intervene when religion threatens the public good.[170] Hence, he argues that atheists should not be tolerated because they deny the being of a God which undergirds all the promises and bonds of civil society, and because they do not have a religion (which means by definition their religion cannot be tolerated). He also argues that Catholics should not be tolerated because they are subject to the Pope, who as a spiritual and political authority challenges the authority of the state.[171] These contentions should be rejected by a Christian Natural Law. Regarding atheists, since atheists are humans created in God's image with the capacity for goodness and reason as discussed earlier, their consciences should be tolerated. Similarly, Catholics can be subject to the Pope as a spiritual authority without undermining deference to the state as a political authority, as suggested through the textual arguments in Section III of the chapter and in the next section on Modern Catholicism. As with Augustine and Calvin, the excesses of Locke's theory of toleration can be rejected while simultaneously recognising the theological basis and framework for the aspects of his articulation of religious freedom which can be supported.[172] Locke's letter ultimately aimed to show that independent religious associations (churches) can freely practice

164 Ibid.

165 Edward David, *A Christian Approach to Corporate Religious Liberty* (Palgrave Macmillan, 2020) 188.

166 Ibid 188–189.

167 Ibid 191. This reflects the fallibility principle discussed in the previous section.

168 Locke (n 159).

169 David (n 165) 193. This strongly aligns with the work in my previous book where I develop a theological framework for reconciling religious freedom and equality which is grounded in the Christian virtues. See Alex Deagon, *A Principled Framework for the Autonomy of Religious Communities: Reconciling Freedom and Discrimination* (Hart Publishing, 2023).

170 Wilken (n 31) 173.

171 Locke (n 159).

172 We can also recognise that more broadly, Locke's conception of separating the religious and the secular is ultimately damaging to religious freedom, as Harrison argues (see Harrison [n 4]

their Christianity publicly, and is concerned with the rights of religious communities as well as the liberty of individuals.[173]

The inescapable conclusion is that the idea of religious freedom is inextricably grounded in and connected with Christian theology. This conclusion is widely shared by leading scholars. Charles states that arguments for religious freedom 'are virtually non-existent' outside of a Christian framework.[174] And Zagorin similarly notes that the idea of religious freedom is 'almost entirely due . . . to the work of Christian thinkers'.[175] Wilken summarises that 'it was early Christian teachers who first set forth ideas of the freedom of the human person in matters of religion; it was Christian thinkers who contended that conscience must be obedient only to God; and it was the dualism of political and spiritual authority in Christian history' that produced the idea of separating church and state.[176] The idea of liberty of conscience 'rests ultimately on Christian beliefs that reach back to the Scriptures and writings of the early Church Fathers'.[177] Shah and Hertzke conclude, 'Enlightenment views on human rights were erected on a bedrock of human dignity that is inconceivable without Christianity'.[178] So, as Ahdar and Leigh point out, the 'religious roots' of toleration 'cannot be denied'; the claim that religious tolerance is a heritage of the secular Enlightenment is a 'myth'.[179]

E. Modern Catholicism

This final section considers Modern Catholicism, and in particular *Dignitatus Humanae*, which provides arguments from both natural law and Scripture that articulate religious freedom as both an individual and a communal right. It illustrates the synergy of natural law and divine revelation as aspects of the True, and as mutually reinforcing theological arguments for the idea of religious freedom. In 1965, the Second Vatican Council released its declaration on religious freedom, *Dignitatus Humanae*, which is now the authoritative

---

79–81). However, that is beside the point of this section, which merely attempts to show the basis for Locke's articulation of (his concept of) religious freedom in divine revelation.

173 Wilken (n 31) 177.

174 Charles (n 2) 128.

175 Perez Zagorin, *How the Idea of Religious Toleration Came to the West* (Princeton University Press, 2003) xii–xiii.

176 Wilken (n 31) 187.

177 Wilken (n 66) 83.

178 Timothy Shah and Allen Hertzke, 'Christianity and Freedom: Ancient Roots and Historical Innovations' in Timothy Shah and Allen Hertzke (eds), *Christianity and Freedom Volume I: Historical Perspectives* (Cambridge University Press, 2016) 13. See also Harper, who argues that the idea of human rights as it was articulated in the secular enlightenment drew from a deep Christian historical and conceptual framework focused on the universal human dignity attached to the *Imago Dei*: Kyle Harper, 'Christianity and the Roots of Human Dignity in Late Antiquity' in Timothy Shah and Allen Hertzke (eds), *Christianity and Freedom Volume I: Historical Perspectives* (Cambridge University Press, 2016).

179 Ahdar and Leigh (n 78) 28–29.

statement of the Church on the matter. The declaration grounds religious freedom in the God-given dignity and nature of the human being, such that humans should be immune from coercion in matters of religion. This means religious freedom ought to be recognised as a constitutionally and domestically protected legal right in accordance with just order.[180] The declaration is an application of soft integralism. 'Under soft integralism, the Catholic natural law tradition informs state policies and actions without actively enforcing positive laws that restrict individuals in their liberal freedom, for prudential and subsidiarity reasons'.[181] Though a soft integralist state ought to reject using state apparatus to coerce religious belief and practice, it nevertheless sees religious freedom as a supernatural good which transcends immanent political order. The secular and the sacred are integrated rather than hermetically sealed. Religious freedom remains both the ultimate right and the ultimate duty for humans to seek the truth and discover God in accordance with their conscience.[182] This can be contrasted with hard integralists who accept the use of the state to coerce religion. Such an approach is antithetical to religious freedom and the declaration in *Dignitatus Humanae*.[183]

Dignitatus Humanae argues that the 'dignity of the human person' requires that 'limits should be set to the powers of government, in order that there may be no encroachment on the rightful freedom of the person and of associations'.[184] Religious freedom requires pursuit of the 'one true religion' and the duty to worship God in accordance with conscience, which means there must be 'immunity from coercion in civil society'.[185] All humans have this right of religious freedom, that they may not be forced to act in a manner contrary to their beliefs, due to the dignity of the human person known through reason and Scripture. For the exercise of religion individually and in community, by its nature, is an 'internal, voluntary and free' act which no human power can command or prohibit.[186] Religious communities are required to exist by the nature of humans and religion, and may rightfully claim freedom to govern themselves in accordance with religious principles. The right to religious freedom contributes to the common welfare and therefore it is the duty of the state and civil society to protect it and care for it as part of a just order.[187] The declaration then specifically turns to Scripture, demonstrating that the doctrine of religious freedom 'has roots in divine revelation'.[188] It cites many of the

180 Xavier Foccroulle Menard and Anna Su, 'Liberalism, Catholic Integralism, and the Question of Religious Freedom' (2022) 47 *Brigham Young University Law Review* 1171, 1195–1196.
181 Ibid 1216.
182 Ibid 1202–1204.
183 Ibid 1205–1206. That is one reason why Locke's argument for not tolerating Catholics (or at least soft integralists) is mistaken.
184 Pope Paul VI, *Dignitatus Humanae* (1965): Dignitatis humanae (vatican.va).
185 Ibid.
186 Ibid.
187 Ibid.
188 Ibid.

passages and principles already discussed in this chapter, including that Jesus called for voluntary belief and did not coerce, and explained from the Parable of the Wheat and the Tares that people of all beliefs should grow together, and observed that we are subject to two jurisdictions, Caesar (the state) and God, the higher of which is God.[189] It further cites the writings of the Apostles that have already been discussed, including the recognition of the state as a legitimate authority (Romans 13), while simultaneously recognising the limits of state authority with respect to God as the ultimate authority: 'it is necessary to obey God rather than men' (Acts 5:29).[190]

Charles, commenting on *Dignitatus Humanae*, explains that the doctrine of the *Imago Dei* implies that every human being has dignity because they have a Creator. As we are made in God's image, we mirror God in our fundamental nature, and in our will, rationality and goodness. God cannot incarnate himself in an animal because they are incapable of reflecting the divine image; rather, 'the eternal uncreated Logos' has 'become one of us'.[191] This means human moral action must and should conform to God's moral nature – what is true and right and good. This is the natural law grounded in an objective good, a higher moral law.[192] There is an 'irreducible religious character to human dignity'.[193] Religious freedom is consequently 'rooted in a commitment to the sacredness of conscience' because it is ordered to truth, and therefore 'demands an immunity from coercion in society'.[194] Religious freedom honours the individual's duty to the Creator and his moral laws, and even the atheist's duty to conscience. *Dignitatus Humanae* shows that this understanding is revealed both through Scripture (divine law) and reason (natural law). For humans, truth is to be discovered freely, through exercising moral judgement and considering what is good and right and true. There should be no manner or context of coercion which would stymie this experience.[195] Such an approach is exemplified through Christ who acknowledged the realm of the magistrate yet warned that higher obligations to God exist (Matthew 22:15–22). Christ witnessed to the True but never imposed it. He and the Apostles relied on its intrinsically persuasive nature.[196]

David similarly explains that *Dignitatus Humanae* holds that religious freedom is grounded in the objective dignity of the human person in conformity with truth, or the 'one true religion'; to fulfil this search for truth humans must enjoy immunity from coercion.[197] In this sense, religious freedom is theological

189 Ibid.
190 Ibid.
191 Charles (n 2) 157–158.
192 Ibid 158–159.
193 Ibid 159.
194 Ibid 159–160, 101.
195 Ibid 160.
196 Ibid 160–161.
197 Edward David, *A Christian Approach to Corporate Religious Liberty* (Palgrave Macmillan, 2020) 26.

in origin, grounded in the human person's created nature. Religious freedom necessarily 'pertains to truth' and divinely guided conscience; it is not a moral licence to error or implicit right to error.[198] Communal religious freedom is similarly 'grounded in the person's free response to God and a conscientious search for truth'.[199] Hence, Hill concludes, the Roman Catholic Church has a 'rich concept of religious liberty', grounded in the traditional theological teaching of human dignity; religious freedom is the foundation of a society that promotes human dignity and is fundamental to human flourishing individually and socially, and therefore the state ought to have legal protection for individual and communal religious freedom.[200]

VI. Conclusion

This chapter has argued that the True is an essential aspect of the Christian Natural Law foundation for religious freedom. Religious freedom is good precisely because it enables true religion, the knowledge of and reconciliation with God. The True is intrinsically theological, grounded in both divinely created human nature (natural law) and divinely revealed Scripture (divine law). Scripture provides resources for religious freedom both textually and conceptually. As explained in Scripture, humans were created in God's image with a will, rationality and desires to know Him. Faith is free and voluntary, an act of love which by definition ought not and cannot be coerced. It is not the role of the state to coerce religion through law, for religion is the realm of conscience and the Spirit; yet the state is ultimately subject to God, and so should protect religious freedom through law.

Drawing these themes together, natural law is available to all but requires guidance, clarification and grounding from the divine law. The fundamental principles of religious freedom in the modern liberal state (separation between church and state and the importance of conscience in deference to divine authority) have their origin and development in theological concepts which were designed to protect believers from state interference with religion, not protect the state from religion. The state ought not to coerce in matters of religion. The state lacks competence to discern religious truth and has fallible knowledge of religious truth, so the state ought to manifest love, humility and goodwill to religious believers by being open to the possibility of religious truth. Such openness to religious truth requires legal protection for religious freedom. Furthermore, since the state has limited authority over religious truth, where the state exceeds its authority by engaging in religious coercion or otherwise undermining religious freedom, it is appropriate to assert legal rights against the state, or resist the illegitimate exercise of power by the state. Religious

198 Ibid 27.

199 Ibid 35.

200 Mark Hill, 'Christianity and Human Rights Law' in John Witte Jr and Rafael Domingo (eds), *The Oxford Handbook of Christianity and Law* (Oxford University Press, 2024) 596.

freedom is not just another human right among many. From the perspective of Christian Natural Law, religious freedom is a penultimate right in the sense that it culminates only in the true and good of God, but it is simultaneously in this sense the ultimate right as transcendentally oriented to the true and good God in accordance with divinely guided conscience. Regardless, respecting the dignity of humans created in the image of God, and on the journey of reconciliation and uniting with God, requires legal protection for religious freedom.

It remains to articulate the final pillar of the Christian Natural Law foundation for religious freedom. As has been alluded to earlier and in previous chapters, the natural law can in fact be summarised by the law of love: to love your neighbour as yourself. This love requires an openness to religious truth. As faith is a chosen act of love towards God, it by definition cannot and ought not be coerced. Religious freedom, then, or legal protection of religious belief and practice, is an act of godly love towards one's neighbour. It is also an expression of the love believers have in Christ, and the love experienced by the Trinitarian union believers partake in through Christ. The central importance of love in the context of the Christian conceptual foundation for religious freedom identifies the third aspect of a Christian Natural Law basis for religious freedom: Love, which will be considered in the final chapter.

7 *Agape*

The Law of Love, or the Culmination of the True and the Good

I. Introduction

This book has developed a Christian Natural Law and deployed it to present a transcendent foundation for the idea of religious freedom. In the first part of the book, I developed a Christian Natural Law by outlining how various Christian perspectives have positioned themselves with respect to the natural law, demonstrating that natural law is intrinsically theological in a Christian sense, and identifying common themes with respect to natural law across the Christian tradition. I drew on Radical Orthodoxy to suggest that within the Christian tradition of natural law, while grace augments nature and revelation illuminates reason, nature and reason are nevertheless indispensable. It follows that there are three pillars which undergird this Christian Natural Law: Love, the True and the Good. In the second part of the book, I explain how these three pillars support a transcendent foundation for religious freedom. Religious freedom is both an individual and social good because it is oriented towards knowing God, which is our ultimate Good. Religious freedom is about the pursuit of the truth, and the True is ultimately found in the complete knowledge of God, embodied in the person of Christ and revealed through Scripture.

This chapter on Love completes the analysis and concludes the book by arguing that Love, the True and the Good are symbiotic and mutually reinforcing aspects of a theological foundation for religious freedom. In particular, the law of love to love your neighbour as yourself, as most significantly expressed in the Parable of the Good Samaritan, underpins religious freedom. Proclaiming the parable in response to the question of what 'love my neighbour' really entails, Jesus' Good Samaritan is good because he personifies the truth of the moral law. The law of love compels us to protect those who have their most basic freedoms threatened. The first principle of the natural law – to do good and avoid evil – therefore will not be satisfied unless we advocate for religious freedom.

Section II of the chapter expands on the symbiotic nature of Love, the True and the Good, and points to its exemplification through a theological analysis of the Parable of the Good Samaritan. Section III, drawing from

DOI: 10.4324/9781032620015-9

a Christological reading of the Parable, suggests framing religious freedom through an Incarnational account which recognises both the existence and solution of paradox in the person of Christ. The unity of Christ as both divine and human points to a system which uniquely recognises religious freedom as a matter of both divine and human action. Section IV concludes by offering some final thoughts on why a Christian Natural Law foundation for religious freedom is useful in a religiously diverse society.

II. The Parable of the Good Samaritan: Symbiosis of Love, True and Good

What is Love?[1] *Agape* is the Greek word most frequently used in the New Testament to designate the love Jesus commanded for God, neighbours and enemies. It is an other-regarding care, an unclaiming and self-sacrificial love, and a universal benevolence. It is 'both particular and universal. It takes as its object the particular neighbour one confronts . . . yet it emanates from a universal love that does not discriminate'.[2] This implies that all persons have irreducible worth and dignity and ought to be equally regarded.[3] Agapic love is therefore not mere sentiment, satisfying preferences, or providing for a person's material needs, but is 'centrally concerned with promoting their moral and spiritual good – helping their souls to grow in virtue'.[4] In other words, Love is centrally concerned with the Good.

As already seen in previous chapters, Love and the Good are symbiotic and mutually reinforcing. Indeed, Aquinas states that the 'first or supreme principle' of practical reasonableness, which is a moral principle that aims to actualise the good, is to 'choose and act' in accordance with the law of love, to love your neighbour as yourself.[5] Furthermore, moral first principles are also necessary truths. Human dignity can be understood as consisting in the pursuit of truth, which is also an intrinsic good.[6] As McCall puts it, 'Truth

1 For those familiar with 1990s pop, the question inevitably triggers the titular song by Haddaway. Ironically, the refrain 'baby don't hurt me, don't hurt me, no more'. is not far from the truth.

2 Robert Cochran and Zachary Calo, 'Introduction' in Robert Cochran and Zachary Calo (eds), *Agape, Justice, and Law: How Might Christian Love Shape Law* (Cambridge University Press, 2017) 2–3.

3 See generally Gene Outka, *Agape: An Ethical Analysis* (Yale University Press, 1972).

4 Jeffrie Murphy, 'Christian Love and Criminal Punishment' in Robert Cochran and Zachary Calo (eds), *Agape, Justice, and Law: How Might Christian Love Shape Law* (Cambridge University Press, 2017) 155.

5 Thomas Aquinas, *Summa Theologica*, I Q99 Art 2. See John Finnis, 'Aquinas and Natural Law Jurisprudence' in George Duke and Robert George (eds), *The Cambridge Companion to Natural Law Jurisprudence* (Cambridge University Press, 2017) 20–21.

6 J Daryl Charles, *Natural Law and Religious Freedom: The Role of Moral First Things in Grounding and Protecting the First Freedom* (Routledge, 2018) 25–26.

is the correspondence of a chosen means to a truly desirable good'.[7] 'The common good of the divine law [which is truth] is the supernatural relation of man to God', who is the ultimate Truth and Good.[8] Humans therefore have an 'ultimate duty' to 'follow truth wherever it might lead' in recognition of the divine.[9]

Following Truth is simultaneously to pursue the Good through Love. Love is a moral duty, including self-love. Porter notes considering self-love as a moral duty might seem counter-intuitive, but it is in fact part of a deeply Thomist system of relationship between Love, the True and the Good. The life of genuine happiness, the good life, consists in the practice of the virtues. True love of self requires the pursuit of the Good. Agapic love, then, must include the love of self as true self, the perfected self pursued through the practice of virtue by God's grace and in reconciliation with Him.[10] After all, Christ's commandment is not just to love your neighbour, but to 'love your neighbour as yourself'.[11] One cannot love neighbour properly without loving self properly. The latter is a necessary antecedent of the former. This means the symbiotic relationship of Love, True and Good applies to both ourselves and others.

Charles provides a helpful analysis of the conceptual relationship between Love, True and Good in the specific context of religious freedom. Love of God and love of one's neighbour are both an act of the will, which underscores the free nature of choosing the good. Religious freedom is therefore a free act of love, of choosing the good, and therefore cannot be coerced.[12] Religious freedom 'cares for truth' and takes into account the 'common good'.[13] It 'is ordered to the truth', and so is sacred and ought to be respected.[14] The natural law as the moral principle which undergirds religious freedom is concerned with upholding the common good and 'speaking the truth in love'.[15] 'Divine revelation', which is truth, comes through the natural law which means to pursue good, and 'to pursue the good is, in the words of Jesus, to "love your neighbour"'.[16] 'Charity in truth' means 'love and truth . . . cannot exist without the other. Each needs the other', and this culminates in action which pursues the 'common social good'.[17]

7 Bryan McCall, *The Architecture of Law: Rebuilding Law in the Classical Tradition* (University of Notre Dame Press, 2018) 222.
8 Ibid 340. See also ibid 340–341.
9 Charles (n 6) 105–106.
10 Jean Porter, *Nature as Reason: A Thomistic Theory of the Natural Law* (Eerdmans, 2005) 205–206.
11 See Luke 10:25–28.
12 Charles (n 6) 85.
13 Ibid 131.
14 Ibid 101.
15 Ibid 133. See Ephesians 4:15.
16 Ibid 139, 190–191. See Matthew 22:37–40.
17 Ibid 201, 204.

Only in the truth can love shine forth and be authentically lived, for truth is the light which gives meaning and value to love. To defend, articulate, embody and pursue truth is itself a form of love.[18] Love 'rejoices in the truth'.[19] Without truth, love degenerates into emotionalism and sentimentality, devoid of content. Truth, too, needs to be understood and expressed in the economy of charity, which gives it credibility and demonstrates its authenticity and persuasive power. Truth and love together reflect God who is both *agape* and *logos*, Love and Truth.[20] Since in their essence truth and love 'belong together insofar as they principally concern our relations to others, they furnish the very basis for the common good'.[21] To speak the truth in love embodies a moral honesty which acknowledges truth while also treating a fellow person with respect as a fellow image-bearer of God. 'Love and truth are not mutually exclusive', and what is good and true cohere and are intelligible.[22]

The doctrine of divine simplicity also suggests a unity of Love, True and the Good in God.[23] God's Love is the Good and the True, God's Good is his Love and Truth, and God's Truth is his Love and Goodness.[24] Love means desiring that which is 'best or highest' for another, which is the knowledge of God, the True which is humanity's ultimate Good.[25] This love is both personal and social. When Jesus states that love fulfils the law, he does so in the context of neighbour-love, and means that law provides the content and structure of love. The law of love, in other words, performs good works for the good of the neighbour in service of love to God. Loving God and loving neighbour are a unity.[26] For religious freedom, then, loving one's neighbour requires the use of law to protect that which is best for humanity, that which will enhance our moral and spiritual good and will help us to grow in virtue, which is the ability to freely pursue the knowledge of God.

The law of love, to love your neighbour as yourself, is most significantly expressed in the Parable of the Good Samaritan. The Good Samaritan has compassion and gives expression to human solidarity.[27] As Murphy also notes, the context of the Parable demands primary concern for the fate of the human soul.[28] The Parable is stated in response to the question of what must be done to inherit eternal life. This is obviously of relevance to the idea of religious freedom, since religious freedom is centrally concerned with the

18 Ibid 201.
19 See 1 Corinthians 13:6.
20 Charles (n 6) 202.
21 Ibid 214.
22 Ibid 133.
23 There is significant scholarly debate surrounding the doctrine which I do not enter here. For a recent articulation and defense, see James Dolezal, *God without Parts: Divine Simplicity and the Metaphysics of God's Absoluteness* (Wipf and Stock, 2011).
24 See also Charles (n 6) 190.
25 Ibid 191.
26 Ibid 191–192.
27 Ibid 164.
28 Murphy (n 4) 153–154.

fate of the human soul. The expression of 'neighbour-love' in the Parable can consequently underpin a commitment to protect fellow humans, beginning with religious freedom.[29] Fundamentally, the 'Good Samaritan' exemplifies the love of neighbour and is 'good' because he demonstrates the truth of the moral law.[30] The Parable in this way unites Love, the True and the Good, providing a structure which underpins 'the sacred rights of conscience, what we call religious freedom'.[31] The Parable of the Good Samaritan is set out in full here:

> And behold, a lawyer stood up to put [Jesus] to the test, saying, 'Teacher, what shall I do to inherit eternal life?' He said to him, 'What is written in the Law? How do you read it?' And he answered, 'You shall love the Lord your God with all your heart and with all your soul and with all your strength and with all your mind, and your neighbour as yourself.' And he said to him, 'You have answered correctly; do this, and you will live.' But he, desiring to justify himself, said to Jesus, 'And who is my neighbour?' Jesus replied, 'A man was going down from Jerusalem to Jericho, and he fell among robbers, who stripped him and beat him and departed, leaving him half dead. Now by chance a priest was going down that road, and when he saw him he passed by on the other side. So likewise a Levite, when he came to the place and saw him, passed by on the other side. But a Samaritan, as he journeyed, came to where he was, and when he saw him, he had compassion. He went to him and bound up his wounds, pouring on oil and wine. Then he set him on his own animal and brought him to an inn and took care of him. And the next day he took out two denarii and gave them to the innkeeper, saying, 'Take care of him, and whatever more you spend, I will repay you when I come back.' Which of these three, do you think, proved to be a neighbour to the man who fell among the robbers?' He said, 'The one who showed him mercy.' And Jesus said to him, 'You go, and do likewise.'[32]

Christ's commandment to love your neighbour as yourself extends to showing mercy to people in peril not caused by you (such as the example given in the parable, which we are called to imitate). Specifically, we need to go beyond mere legal duty and selfish interest, and desire to truly act with other-regarding and self-sacrificing care in order to promote the good, a just political order of peaceful coexistence. As John Milbank exhorts, 'to act charitably we must break through the existing representation of what is our duty towards our

29 Charles (n 6) 163.

30 Ibid 163–164.

31 Ibid. See Alex Deagon, *From Violence to Peace: Theology, Law and Community* (Hart Publishing, 2017) 186–193 for a detailed exposition of the parable which emphasises the harmonisation of difference across ethnic and cultural boundaries. The rest of this section draws from that exposition.

32 Luke 10:25–37.

neighbour and towards God', and 'break through the bounds of duty which "technically" pre-defines its prescribed performance'.[33] This involves understanding the Parable of the Good Samaritan in its theological context.[34]

Luke's account focuses on the inclusivity or universalism of the gospel of Jesus, and particularly how Jesus sought to reconcile Jews, Samaritans and Gentiles; some commentators also argue that this Parable foreshadows the later Gentile mission recorded by Luke in Acts.[35] In other words, Luke attempts to demonstrate how discriminating categories (such as Jew versus Gentile) are dissolved in Jesus, inaugurating a global harmonious community.[36] Luke's alterations compared to the other accounts make his account more relevant to his Gentile readers, who would have had little concern for the role of scribes and the commandments of the Jewish law.[37] Jews and Samaritans especially had an extremely acrimonious relationship, a deeply entrenched process of negative stereotyping stemming back even to respective accounts of origins of the Samaritans, and a theological dispute over the proper place of worship.[38] It therefore seems that Jesus was using this parable as a hyperbole to demonstrate the extent to which one should love your neighbour, regardless of different prejudices, races or legal categories:

> Normally the Samaritans were considered apostate . . . universally regarded as objects of contempt [by Jews] . . . by having a Samaritan as the one who helps a man in need, Jesus breaks down the boundaries between Jew and Samaritan, to be sure, but most of all he makes the claim that whoever responds to human need is a true child of God and an example of love for the neighbour.[39]

Hence, all human beings, anyone who needs help and who can be helped, are to be seen as neighbours, regardless of whether they are your friend, your family, your enemy, your ruler, your servant, a criminal, or a person supposedly despised and grotesquely unlovable.[40]

33 John Milbank, *The Word Made Strange: Theology, Language, Culture* (Blackwell, 1997) 134.

34 For other overviews of the Parable's context, see Charles (n 6) 163–165; Robert Cochran, 'Jesus, Agape, and Law' in Robert Cochran and Zachary Calo (eds), *Agape, Justice, and Law: How Might Christian Love Shape Law* (Cambridge University Press, 2017) 14–15, 24–25.

35 Craig Blomberg, *Jesus and the Gospels* (B&H Publishing Group, 2009) 163–164. See also eg TJ Lane, *Luke and the Gentile Mission: Gospel Anticipates Acts* (Peter Lang, 1996).

36 Robert Gundry, *A Survey of the New Testament* (Zondervan, 1970) 94–95.

37 William Baird, 'The Gospel According to Luke' in Charles Laymon (ed), *Interpreter's Concise Commentary* (Abingdon Press, 1983) 227. These additions are found in the more truncated accounts in Matthew and Mark which nevertheless are more directed to a Jewish audience.

38 H Williamson, 'Samaritans' in J Douglas (ed), *The Illustrated Bible Dictionary Part 3* (Intervarsity Press, 1980) 1378; Phillip Esler, 'Jesus and the Reduction of Intergroup Conflict: The Parable of the Good Samaritan in Light of Social Identity Theory' (2000) 8(4) *Biblical Interpretation* 325, 329–332.

39 Arland Hultgren, *The Parables of Jesus: A Commentary* (Eerdmans, 2002) 98.

40 Murphy (n 4) 154.

The term 'half dead' in the Parable is best understood to mean that he appeared alive, but in a severe condition requiring help. This renders the actions of the priest and Levite inexcusable for Jesus, since going to the aid of another is not a matter of legal category, but of the heart and compassion (and it was the Samaritan who had compassion).[41] It is also worth remembering that the question asked of Jesus, 'who is my neighbour', was asked by a lawyer. In this context, the lawyer is an 'expert in the law', someone 'trained to interpret and teach the law of Jewish tradition'.[42] Jesus does not directly answer the question of who is the neighbour, but rather re-directs the focus towards the lawyer (and us as the reader). He effectively changes the question from 'who is my neighbour' to 'who acted like a neighbour' and 'to whom can I be a neighbour', implying that we should not try to avoid the divine demand through formal legalisation, but should instead show love to all who need it without distinction.[43] According to this anthropological reading, Jesus finally emphasises we should 'go, and do likewise'; that is, we should be like the Good Samaritan, loving and showing mercy to any who are in need without seeking to restrict the scope of the command through legal definition or ethnic prejudice.[44]

As such:

> The one who asks, 'Who is my neighbour?' thinks of others in the world as classifiable commodities. One can build fences to determine who is in the circle of those to be cared for, and who is not. Then we and all others can 'take care of our own', thinking that our help should be directed to those we are related to by ties of family or friendship – things based on law, rights, bloodlines, culture or tradition. By means of this parable Jesus calls his hearers away from a legalistic or culturally conditioned mind-set to a life of authentic love. One should not seek to define who the neighbour is, but simply be a neighbour to the one in need . . . the example of the Samaritan, who does good to a person in need without any apparent regard for religion or ethnicity, illustrates how authentic love pays no attention to religious, ethnic, or cultural distinctions.[45]

So authentic compassion, a Christian love based on selfless sacrifice, transcends the boundaries and limits imposed by law, and instead tends to establish a community life of selfless sacrifice. Indeed, the lawyer's question could be seen as a 'typical' lawyer's question, a 'boundary question of an exclusionary type' – and the common answer, in accordance with the purview of the Mosaic law, was a fellow Israelite, excluding Samaritans and Gentiles and encouraging

41 Hultgren (n 39) 96.
42 Ibid 95.
43 Baird (n 37) 228; Blomberg (n 35) 338; Gundry (n 36) 163.
44 Luke 10:37.
45 Hultgren (n 39) 100.

the engagement of group differentiation and stereotypification.[46] However, 'that a representative of one of the hated outgroups is brought along that road challenges the whole structure of group differentiation which the law functioned to maintain', and the fact that it was this representative who exhibited admirable conduct further disrupts this legally imposed alienation.[47] The agapic love shown by the Samaritan

> was, moreover, a compassion with few limits, as shown in the rich and loving detail which Jesus . . . supplies . . . The force of this case drives one to conclude that compassion which transcends legally sanctioned ethnic boundaries and discriminations when faced with real human need is a superior form of human behaviour than continuing to live within their limits.[48]

Moreover, the conduct of the Good Samaritan is not intended to be an isolated incident, but a way of life permanently instantiated in human relations. Esler explains:

> Jesus is concerned with this very issue of how a process of decategorization effected through a single event of interpersonal contact can be generalized beyond those caught up in its dynamics. In part, this is achieved, as already noted, by moving the focus from "neighbour" as the passive site of the group categorisation process to "neighbour" as a person who acts properly (and compassionately) to assist someone in need (Luke 10:36). This redefinition of the issue away from the group-oriented consideration of whether someone fits, or does not fit, within a certain social category to the active need to offer help to whomever needs it, plainly promotes a vision of human agency which extends beyond the boundaries of this narrative . . . Whereas Jesus could have broken off the conversation with the lawyer's answer, the fact that he continues with this injunction suggests a concern with doing more to generalize the behaviour of the Samaritan beyond the facts of that particular story. As already noted, Jesus utilises the story of the Samaritan's compassion to generate a new principle of moral behaviour.[49]

It is this divine vision of truly and universally loving one's neighbour that indicates its source in the love of God. As already noted, your neighbour extends to your greatest enemy, and to love your neighbour means to show mercy even to your greatest enemy.[50] Here the Parable of the Good Samaritan can

46 Esler (n 38) 335, 336–337.
47 Ibid 342.
48 Ibid 343.
49 Ibid 350.
50 See eg Matthew 5:43–48.

not only be read anthropologically, but also Christologically. In this light (that we are the person in need, helpless and dead in our sins, rescued by the sacrifice of the Samaritan who represents Christ), the logic of the parable 'raises the possibility that we first need to be shown compassion by a neighbour as a condition of becoming neighbours ourselves' – and 'only the divine persons are capable of showing us this kind of compassion', particularly by Christ who became flesh and gave himself for us – 'claiming us . . . as persons sharing his communion with the Father and the Spirit'.[51]

These observations are important for understanding the source for love of neighbour and the implications for religious freedom. We can show agapic love because we have experienced it. We love our neighbour because we have first been loved by God – the modelling of sacrificial love through Christ, who showed love, mercy and forgiveness to all humanity, his former enemies, by willingly dying on the cross in their place, enables us to love one another.[52] So Jesus says to love your neighbour means to show similar love, mercy and forgiveness to all individuals, and he commands us to do this in a model after himself. To particularise, since by grace we have had an opportunity to exercise religious freedom, and can pursue Love, the True and the Good through communion with God in Christ, so as a function of agapic love we can (and ought to) extend that same freedom to all humanity. Hence, the Apostle Paul can explicitly connect love to freedom:

> For you were called to freedom, brothers. Only do not use your freedom as an opportunity for the flesh, but through love serve one another. For the whole law is fulfilled in one word: 'You shall love your neighbor as yourself.' But if you bite and devour one another, watch out that you are not consumed by one another.[53]

In Christ, the embodiment, fulfilment and culmination of Love, True and Good, we have freedom. Yet this freedom is agapic, designed to promote and multiply love through service to others. This freedom is also morally bounded, to be exercised lovingly and in accordance with the Good, not in a selfish and self-destructive way. In this sense, protecting religious freedom is the very essence of agapic love, an act of service towards others to enable them to pursue that same Love in accordance with Truth and the Good. Following this framework contributes to a just political order, a sacred community of peace.

51 Ian McFarland, 'Who Is My Neighbour? The Good Samaritan as a Source for Theological Anthropology' (2001) 17(1) *Modern Theology* 57, 62–63.

52 See Matthew 5–6.

53 Galatians 5:13–15.

III. An Incarnational Account of Religious Freedom

A Christological reading of the Parable of the Good Samaritan therefore points to a reframing of religious freedom. As Taliaferro notes, the 'parameters of religious freedom' become more defined and principled by incorporating the natural law and divine law which guides us to 'discern true' and 'good religious practice'.[54] The Parable can perform this function as part of the divine law. In particular, focusing on Christ suggests an Incarnational account of religious freedom which recognises both the existence and solution of paradox in the person of Christ. As already noted in Chapter 4, Christ is paradoxical because through His Incarnation He is truly and fully both God and man, divine and human. Yet in Christ this paradox is 'both expected and resolvable'.[55] Christ is the meeting of transcendence and immanence, and this meeting of transcendent and immanent models the meeting of transcendence and immanence for religious freedom. Such a meeting enables an account of religious freedom not merely as an immanent kind of autonomy, but as a transcendent uniting between the human and the divine.

Christ is also a specific instance of the symbiotic relationship between Love, the True and the Good. As I explain in earlier work, the Truth of God is primarily revealed through the Incarnation of Christ. The Incarnation perfectly displays the grace of God through the demonstration of Christ loving the created order by sacrificing and giving himself for the forgiveness of sins. Therefore, Christ taking on human form and volunteering to die on the cross for people is the ultimate display of the self-giving agapic love characteristic of God. Its primary concern is for other and not self, and so it manifests the ultimate Good – to love your neighbour as a function of experiencing the love of Christ. It is this revelation of God's love in Christ which is Truth.[56]

So in Christ is embodied love and truth perfectly united. He is love and truth.[57] As Christ Himself says, 'I am the Truth'.[58] He calls Himself 'The Good Shepherd'.[59] There is none good but God, and God is Love, and Jesus is God, so He is Love and the Good.[60] The law of love, then, as displayed and instituted in Christ, is also the culmination of the True and the Good in Christ. God has created humans in his image, and incarnated Himself to become one of us. An important implication of humans bearing the image of God, and God also assuming the image of humanity, is that ideal human action also necessarily conforms to what is True and what is Good.[61] In this

54 Karen Taliaferro, *The Possibility of Religious Freedom: Early Natural Law and the Abrahamic Faiths* (Cambridge University Press, 2019) 8.
55 Ibid 125.
56 Deagon (n 31) 171–173.
57 Charles (n 6) 201.
58 John 14:6.
59 John 10:11.
60 Mark 10:18; 1 John 4:8; John 10:30–33.
61 Charles (n 6) 158.

sense, the concrete virtue of loving one's neighbour through protecting religious freedom seeks its notion of what it means to have truly human character in a place beyond or above what is human (transcendence), rather than in or beneath (immanence).[62]

Thus, as noted in the previous chapter, to 'reduce [religious freedom] to a purely immanent human right does violence to the very nature of religion, and therefore of religious freedom'; religious freedom 'is the only human right that recognises two distinct realms of authority, human and divine', and therefore a transcendent foundation for religious freedom is necessary for it to have universal appeal.[63] A religious person whose freedom is limited by an obligation to human law will immediately recognise the inferior and subsidiary nature of human law. To follow God is fundamentally to submit to an ultimate authority higher than the state. Religious freedom is consequently unique among human rights because it must simultaneously answer to human law (as a human right) and divine law (as a matter of religion).[64]

The idea of competing obligations to God and Caesar which are coherent yet in tension therefore makes perfect sense in a Christian theology characterised by the paradox of the Incarnation. In Christ, there is an overarching unity of all.[65] The unity of Christ as both divine and human commends a framework which uniquely recognises religious freedom as a matter of both divine and human action, and only an idea of religious freedom grounded in the transcendent, as I have attempted to articulate in this book, can properly satisfy this framework.

IV. The Future of Christian Natural Law and Religious Freedom

The secular alternative of marginalising religion and ignoring divine revelation is not the only option. A defense of religious freedom grounded in Christian Natural Law is possible, and needed, even in religious and religiously diverse societies.[66] I noted in Chapter 1 that it was not my primary purpose to persuade those outside the Christian tradition of the plausibility or utility of Christian Natural Law as a foundation for religious freedom. But Christianity does implicitly address this concern. As Harrison notes with respect to religious establishment, Christianity is 'hospitable to difference' because the pursuit of universal goods such as education, work, charity and community in accordance with theological virtues such as love, kindness, humility and patience is possible for all communities, not just Christians.[67] Christianity also

62 Cf John Milbank, *Theology and Social Theory: Beyond Secular Reason* (Blackwell, 1992) 328.
63 Taliaferro (n 54) 124.
64 Ibid.
65 Ibid.
66 Ibid 126.
67 Joel Harrison, *Post-liberal Religious Liberty: Forming Communities of Charity* (Cambridge University Press, 2020) 203.

recognises 'parallel communities of common endeavour' which seek the good, and right relationship, 'the possibility of harmony – precipitated by some real affinities between different groups, an emphasis on the integrity of civil society as a space of solidarity, and the hope that we are pursuing some shared goals'.[68] Harrison concludes:

> If religion entails reaching out to a God who has condescended to us, a God whose life is love, then this necessarily flows into a life of solidarity, fraternity, and charity. In other words, religious liberty only reaches the heights of true liberty when it is rightly oriented to manifesting this end, reflecting what it means to be human.[69]

So, then, 'religious liberty protects the free creation of communities of solidarity, fraternity, and charity, or what we may call "right relationship"'.[70] The implication of truth and love operating together in this way is that truth can speak to people's social realities and help build a just society for their good. Social action and the common good requires truth in love. Love anchored in truth which addresses the real needs of our neighbours is necessary for the good.[71]

And as John Milbank has also said,

> Virtue is democratic because its practice is open to all, especially the supreme virtues of love, trust, hope, mercy, kindness, forgiveness and reconciliation, which we have all in the West, whether avowedly Christians or not, inherited from the teachings of the Bible.[72]

These Christian virtues of humility, sacrifice, forgiveness and trust characterise the acknowledgement and expression of different faith perspectives, producing peaceful and loving persuasion to the good and true which is inclusive because it can be practiced by all universally. The Christian perspective produces a space for religious liberty and discourse which is characterised by the 'fruit of the Spirit': 'love, joy, peace, patience, kindness, goodness, faithfulness, gentleness, self-control'; for 'against such things there is no law'.[73] The Christian virtues are beyond law and yet fulfil the law by their nature, and therefore allow persuasion without coercion, which produces true religious freedom. These principles are exemplified through the discussions in previous chapters which have revealed synergies between Christian Natural Law and the theological principled framework for religious freedom I have already articulated in

68 Ibid 205–206.
69 Ibid 239.
70 Ibid 172.
71 Charles (n 6) 203–204.
72 John Milbank and Adrian Pabst, *The Politics of Virtue: Post-Liberalism and the Human Future* (Rowman & Littlefield, 2016) 7.
73 Galatians 5:22–23.

previous work.[74] For example, synergies can be observed in Chapter 5 through Taliaferro's claim that incorporating natural law theory in religious freedom disputes might result in the application of the reasonable accommodation standard, and in Chapter 6 through David's reading of Locke's toleration as grounded in Christian virtues such as love.

For coerced belief is not true belief, and is antithetical to love which must be voluntary. The law of love indicates that just as we would not want to be coerced into belief, so the beliefs of others should not be coerced. Similarly, just as we would not want to coerce others to violate their beliefs, so others should not coerce us to violate our beliefs. Fundamentally then, Christianity requires religious liberty because love does not compel belief. Coerced religion is not true or good religion and so is impotent. Religious freedom is loving because it is informed by and aims to proclaim the truth of the sacrificial love of Christ, seeks the good of the neighbour, and affirms the dignity of the neighbour through cultivation of the Christian virtues, the highest of which is love:

> Love is patient and kind; love does not envy or boast; it is not arrogant or rude. It does not insist on its own way; it is not irritable or resentful; it does not rejoice at wrongdoing, but rejoices with the truth. Love bears all things, believes all things, hopes all things, endures all things. Love never fails.[75]

Law based on love requires citizens to act 'agapically' towards one another, protecting all, and especially the most vulnerable.[76] To extend agapic love is to seek to promote a person's good, and since a just political order is a good, supporting a just political order through 'a just system of laws justly enforced is an exercise of agapic love for one's fellow citizens'.[77] The more practical implication of this is that the principle of religious liberty, and associated actions, should be legally protected because it is loving for all people.[78] Legal protection for religious freedom is also an instance of agapic love because it entails humility in the sense of acknowledging the possibility of the existence of the transcendent, of that-beyond-law, in the law.[79]

It is correct, as Porter explains, that Christian Natural Law justifications of human rights may struggle to obtain universal moral agreement. But there

74 See Alex Deagon, *A Principled Framework for the Autonomy of Religious Communities: Reconciling Freedom and Discrimination* (Hart Publishing, 2023).

75 1 Corinthians 13:4–8.

76 Cochran and Calo (n 2) 8.

77 Nicholas Wolterstorff, 'Love, Justice, and Law' in Robert Cochran and Zachary Calo (eds), *Agape, Justice, and Law: How Might Christian Love Shape Law* (Cambridge University Press, 2017) 121.

78 As I have noted elsewhere. See Alex Deagon, 'Is Religious Liberty Loving in Principle?' in Michael Quinlan and Keith Thompson (eds), *Inclusion, Exclusion and Religious Freedom in Contemporary Australia* (Connor Court, 2021) 25–32.

79 Linda Meyer, 'Agape, Humility, and Chaotic Good' in Robert Cochran and Zachary Calo (eds), *Agape, Justice, and Law: How Might Christian Love Shape Law* (Cambridge University Press, 2017) 69.

is an emergent consensus that human rights exist and are objective, normative, and worthy of legal protection.[80] This implies the Christian Natural Law developed in Part I of the book might have a broader application as a transcendent foundation for other human rights. In principle, one could consider whether abortion, euthanasia, just war and other practices are in accordance with Love, the True and the Good. That would be fruitful future research which is beyond the scope of this book. However, it is also a fact that the Christian Natural Law comprising Love, the True and the Good was constructed in this book with religious freedom specifically in mind. Christian Natural Law is also particularly suited to be a transcendent foundation for religious freedom because religious freedom is unique in its ultimate end of knowing God, the culmination of Love, the True and the Good. In any case, Christian Natural Law at least illuminates why human rights may be widely accepted, and for the concept of religious freedom in particular, provides a transcendent foundation which respects and emphasises its unique nature as both a divine and human matter.[81]

So, as Charles poignantly and appropriately concludes, the law of love compels us in

> neighbour-love toward those who are oppressed and who stand in dire need by virtue of having their most basic freedoms [such as religious freedom] removed. Recall an important implication of the 'Good Samaritan' model. This embodiment of 'neighbour-love' will be open to cross religious, ethnic and cultural boundaries in order to help those who stand in dire need. This, then, is the moral 'first principle' of the natural law – doing good and preventing evil – and it will not be satisfied until we are advocates for the 'sacred rights of conscience'.[82]

80 Porter (n 10) 372–374.

81 Cf ibid. But for a caution against the idea of human rights in a purely secular liberal order, see John Milbank, 'Against Human Rights: Liberty in the Western Tradition' (2012) 1(1) *Oxford Journal of Law and Religion* 203–234. In earlier work I softened Milbank's critique somewhat by proposing a 'redeemed liberalism' which is fundamentally grounded in the Christian theological narrative, and in which religious freedom exists as part of a peaceful coexistence of difference: see Alex Deagon, 'Reconciling John Milbank and Religious Freedom: 'Liberalism' Through Love' (2019) 34(2) *Journal of Law and Religion* 183–209. As should hopefully be clear by now, in this book I see religious freedom existing as a necessary aspect of a just political order grounded in Love, the True and the Good (as these concepts are understood in Christian theology, together comprising Christian Natural Law), and therefore requiring legal protection. This development is consistent both with Milbank's critique (in that this idea of a just political order is not a secular liberal order) and my earlier clarification (in that a just political order is entailed in the peaceful coexistence of difference created in a Christian theological framework, which I think the second part of this book implicitly suggests). Milbank himself states that for real religious liberty a return to considering humans as made in the image of God is needed, a notion of human dignity which is concerned with the relative positioning of humans in a just political order (Milbank 233). This supports my arguments for religious freedom in the second part of this book which rely significantly on the *Imago Dei* as variously manifested in Love, the True, and the Good.

82 Charles (n 6) 260.

Index

Kolibri 360 GmbH
Ferdinand-Jühlke-Straße 7
99095 Erfurt, Deutschland
produktsicherheit@kolibri360.de